The City of New York

A History Illustrated from the Collections of
The Museum of the City of New York

Text by Jerry E. Patterson

Foreword by Louis Auchincloss

Introduction by Joseph Veach Noble

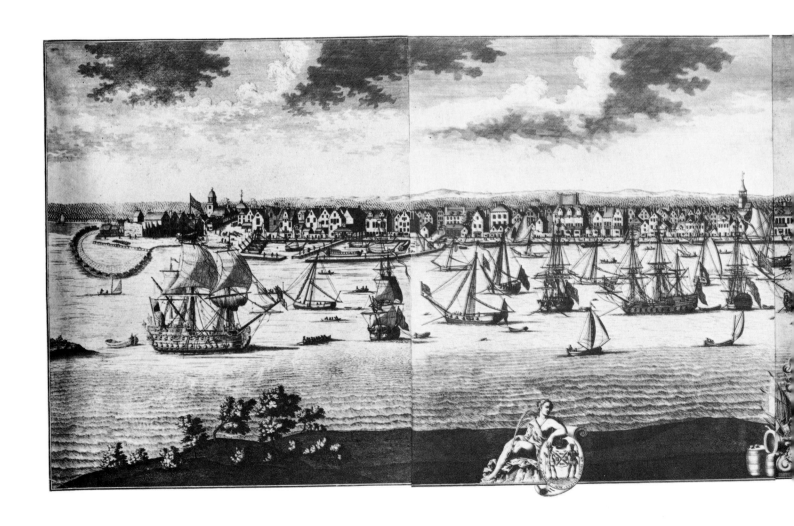

The City of New York

A History Illustrated from the Collections of
The Museum of the City of New York

Harry N. Abrams, Inc., Publishers, New York

Editor: Walton Rawls
Designer: Wei-wen Chang

Library of Congress Cataloging in Publication Data

Patterson, Jerry E.
    The City of New York

    Includes index.
    1. New York (City)—History.   I. New York (City).
Museum of the City of New York. II. Title.
F128.3.P27   974.7′1   77–15631
ISBN 0–8109–1708–4 (HC)
ISBN 0–8109–2162–6 (PB)

Library of Congress Catalogue Card Number: 77–15631

Printed and bound in Japan

CONTENTS

ACKNOWLEDGMENTS

The entire staff of The Museum of the City of New York has been most helpful, but I especially want to thank the Director, Joseph Veach Noble, and the following: Charlotte La Rue, Esther Brumberg, Steven Miller, John Noble, and Margaret Stearns.

I am grateful to Walton Rawls, Senior Editor at Harry N. Abrams, Inc., who was responsible for the editing and arrangement of the illustrations.

I appreciate the help of Arthur Vitols of Helga Studio, New York, who made most of the photographs for the book.

I am most indebted to Albert K. Baragwanath, Senior Curator of the Museum, who acted as my guide from the commencement of this book through the vast collections of the Museum and who has permitted me to draw every day on his great knowledge of the history, antiquities, and topography of our City. We have had great fun discussing the ever-controversial history of New York, and his help shows on every page of this book.

Errors are to be debited to my sole account.

For more than two hundred years writers on New York have expressed their thanks to the New York Society Library, the oldest institution of its kind in the City, and I feel quite proud also to record my gratitude to that library and its staff.

FOREWORD

The question was asked by Prince Bernhard of the Netherlands during an official visit to the Dutch Gallery of The Museum of the City of New York. After bending over to study a miniature recreation of New Amsterdam in the seventeenth century, he inquired: "Are any of these buildings still standing?" I had to reply: "None." Our visitor shrugged faintly and smiled as he passed on to the next exhibit. "You do things very thoroughly in New York," he murmured.

Although any city may be excused for allowing the crude colonial edifices of its seventeenth century to crumble and be replaced, New York must plead guilty to having allowed all but a tiny fraction of its eighteenth century buildings to suffer the same fate and, indeed, the bulk of its nineteenth century architecture as well. Any structure which antedates the First World War is a landmark. If the past is to be saved at all in our cannibal city, which eats itself every generation, it can only be in a museum.

Some such thought may have been in the minds of the small group of loyal New Yorkers who in 1923 conceived the idea of establishing The Museum of the City of New York. Their certificate of incorporation states the objective "to do all things necessary, fit or suitable to create a love for and interest in all things pertaining to the City of New York." Their inspiration was the Carnavalet, the beautiful museum devoted to the history of the City of Paris which occupies the old *hôtel* of Madame de Sévigné in the Marais. No other great American city had ever had its own museum before.

Gracie Mansion, now the official residence of the mayor, was the first home of the Museum and remained such for nine years. But soon it became evident that a much larger building would be needed. An appropriate site on Fifth Avenue between 103rd and 104th streets was offered to the trustees on condition that they raise two million dollars by June of 1928, half for the erection of the new building and half for endowment. The sum was ultimately pledged, and in 1929 the cornerstone was laid by Mayor James J. Walker. Three years later, on 11 January 1932, a date coinciding with that of Alexander Hamilton's birth, the gala opening of the present edifice was celebrated. An omen, generally regarded as auspicious, was discovered the morning after, when the man cleaning the marble floors found a single set of footprints together with matching marks which might have been made by a peg leg. There are still those who believe that the ghost of Peter Stuyvesant had given his official approval to the enterprise.

The building was designed by Joseph H. Freedlander. Five stories high, it is a modern adaptation of Georgian colonial architecture. A graceful marble portico and a red brick wall with marble trim make its facade one of the handsomest on Fifth Avenue. Through the years since its opening the great interior has been filled to overflowing with thousands of gifts. The Museum has been the primary beneficiary of the migration of New Yorkers from houses to apartments, from apartments to smaller apartments, and from these, alas, often out of the City altogether. The gifts have varied in size from the peppercorn which reputedly was used to pay the rent on Bowling Green to the giant two-ton zinc statue of Robert Fulton, and in value from a postcard of a New York view to the finest of Gilbert Stuart replicas of George Washington.

We are so conscious today of world history that we tend to lose sight of the history of our neighborhood. If one has the good fortune to live amid the architectural reminders of the past, history is always present. But in New York, where the past is constantly obliterated, children can grow up deprived of physical contact with any era earlier than that represented by the World Trade Center or the Pan Am building. Surely, one of the dimensions of life is missing in any person who resides in New York and knows nothing of the Dutch and English periods of this city or what happened here in the Revolution, the Civil War, or even in World Wars I and II. History is not only when things happen but where.

Louis Auchincloss
President of The Museum of the City of
New York

INTRODUCTION

There is magic in the creation of a museum. No sooner is it born than it exerts the magnetic force of a lodestone and begins to attract objects—any object, every object. They roll right in the door, and if you slam it shut they will burst through the transom. The trick is to be selective, to attract what is most desirable and hold on to it, while at the same time adroitly rejecting dross without alienating the donor who may also own something of real value you can liberate later.

The Museum of the City of New York has had a real advantage right from the day it was founded in 1923 in its singleness of purpose: the history and culture of New York City. It's a lot easier to be selective and to create a unified collection with that as a guidestar than to have a loose topic such as "art," or the even more ambiguous "modern art." In the latter case, what do you not collect? But, with The Museum of the City of New York you apply the acid test to each prospective object: What's its connection to New York City?

Was it made here? Was it owned and used here by a New Yorker? Does it really relate to our city? A "yes" to any of these questions and the object is a candidate for admission. If the object just happens to be in the City by a coincidence of ownership, such as a fine set of Louis XIV furniture housed on Park Avenue, or a hunk of the Great Wall of China brought back by a touring politician, or a fine Greek vase owned by an avid antiquarian, the answer is "no"; it doesn't belong.

This museum was the first in America to be created as the keeper of a single city's past. And what a past it is can be seen in our objects, our artifacts, our flotsam and jetsam beached here by the tides of history. George Washington peers out of a noble portrait by Gilbert

Stuart, and P. T. Barnum is represented by a ticket for a concert of his Swedish Nightingale Jenny Lind. A Dutch tankard of elegantly engraved silver tells us something about our city, as does Gypsy Rose Lee's chaste G-string with her name embroidered in blue silk by her own hand.

I suppose our assemblage numbers about three-quarters of a million objects. We are a definitive archive with hundreds of thousands of views of New York City. Our collection of the popular Currier & Ives prints is the country's largest representation of this famous New York firm. Certainly our collection of the work of the New York cabinetmaker Duncan Phyfe is without peer. The departments of Decorative Arts, Costumes, and Theatre and Music all have extensive and extraordinary holdings. One department even specializes in toys, with thousands of beautiful dolls, intricate doll houses, and ingenious mechanical playthings spanning the last 250 years. Elegant period rooms, colonial silverware, paintings, fire engines, and ship models fill our galleries. And to interpret all these and to relate them to the history of our city we use miniature dioramas, ultraviolet light and fluorescent paintings, magnetic tape recorders, and a new combination of multimedia technology with real historical objects.

The essential thing for a museum is to acquire, to gather together objects of current and future importance for its collection. Then comes the unglamorous but essential task of conservation, to make objects stable enough to last and be permanent for future generations. Our curators study them to extract knowledge and to be able to disseminate it to all comers. And then we exhibit the objects—the "real" things—because that's what the public comes to see at the museum.

There is a strong, mystical rapport between real objects and people, a sort of transcendental relationship which resists analysis. What is it that happens when we look at a real flintlock musket fired in the Revolutionary War? Why does the Vice-Admiralty oar, a silver mace which represented the English king at the naval court here in New York, make me stop in my tracks? Why do I get goose bumps when I see Emma Lazarus's handwritten lines, "Give me your tired, your poor, your huddled masses yearning to breathe free"?

A photograph of these things won't do it, neither will a facsimile reproduction, nor a TV show. It has to be the real thing—then it clicks. People come to see the real thing, and they believe in it, and in the museum. That's why there is no credibility gap in a museum, although it exists in almost all our other human institutions. That's why people come to the museum often as family groups. Where else do you go as a family group? In our fragmented, stratified, age-differentiated society, not many places. And in a museum the individual and the family are willing to accept new ideas because they know we try to present the truth, and in this impartial atmosphere they accept it.

Sometimes I think that our visitors intuitively search for their identity in our museum. Many urban people have lost a sense of belonging, they are so long gone from their roots. Even the alienation of the young seems in part to be a cry for help in establishing their identity. There is, of course, a continuity in our lives stretching back through our parents, our grandparents, our forebears; and The Museum of the City of New York helps us to see where we fit into the overall mosaic of our city's life.

I think our museum with its collections of real objects from our combined pasts helps us understand the world of today and see more clearly where we are going. That's why I say our museum is more than a mirror to the past.

In creating this book, what could have been a more appropriate way of showing you our collection than by using it to illustrate the unfolding saga of the history of New York City? As O. Henry is reputed to have said, "It'll be a great place if they ever finish it."

Joseph Veach Noble
Director of The Museum of the City
of New York

The City of New York

HET WEST INDISCH HUYS

1. The *Geoctroyeerde West-Indische Compagnie* (Dutch West India Company) received its charter from the States-General of the Netherlands on 3 June 1621. The company, which had a monopoly on Dutch trade with America and West Africa, was governed by a board of nineteen directors who represented the various provinces of the Netherlands. The original capital of seven million florins was raised in two years, and shares were surprisingly widely held in the Netherlands. It was estimated that more than a fifth of the inhabitants of some towns were shareholders in the GWC. The corporate headquarters in Amsterdam is shown here in a view by Jacob de Maris published in 1664. On the roof at right the building is dated 1641. Line engraving on copper, 7 1/4 × 11 1/2″. Gift of G. C. J. Boissevain. 33.225

I: MANHATTAN LANDFALL

This island is the key and principal stronghold of the country.

—REVEREND JONAS MICHAËLIUS
MANHATTAN, 1628

The Dutch West India Company was very interested in profits and hoped that its expensively established North American colony at New Amsterdam would pay large dividends. From the beginning the settlement which was to become New York City was a commercial enterprise; business is the oldest New York tradition. The West India Company expected that—like the earlier Dutch East India Company on which it was modeled—it would tap new sources of wealth for the Netherlands. The East India Company had gained unparalleled success in the spice islands of the Orient; the West India Company hoped to have similar success in producing millions of guilders from the coasts of West Africa, Brazil, and the North American continent—trading in sugar, gold, animal skins, ivory, and slaves and capturing an occasional Portuguese or Spanish treasure ship. The hope of singeing the beard of the king of Spain, the archenemy, by seizing one of his bullion-loaded vessels was ever in the hearts of all Netherlanders.

The Company's first step was to establish trading stations in Guinea and Angola on the African continent and in Brazil. Three years after its organization, the West India Company mobilized itself to move on North America. The Company chose to establish its North American station at what was already called "New Netherland," an area with vague boundaries including what is now New York, New Jersey, and particularly the Hudson River Valley.

New Netherland at that time had almost no history. In the sixteenth century a French ship commanded by Giovanni da Verrazzano had entered the waters now called New York Bay and anchored in the Narrows on 17 April 1524. The captain reported this and other discoveries along the Atlantic coast of North America to King Francis I of France, but the discovery of New York Bay did not lead to any settlement.

The later voyage of Henry Hudson, made under Dutch auspices, gave the Netherlanders their claim to the New York area. An English navigator in the service of the Dutch East India Company, Hudson sailed from Amsterdam in the spring of 1609, in the *Halve Maen (Half-Moon)*, looking for a northwest passage to the Orient. In September, 1609, he visited the island called by the Indians "Manahata" or "Manahatin" (the name was spelled many ways throughout the whole colonial period: Manatus, Manatans, Manhates, Manhattes; plural forms were especially common) and sailed up the river that now bears his name. The Northwest Passage he had originally sought was successfully navigated 360 years later by an oil tanker happily named *Manhattan.*

Between Hudson's visit to the New York region and the first settlement at Manhattan there were a number of (documented or deduced) visits by Dutch ships to "New Netherland," as the region was called from the time Hudson reported his travels. For the history of New York City, by far the most important of these visits was that of Captain Adriaen Block in 1613–14. Block, who gave his name to the large island off the coast of Rhode Island, camped during the winter of 1613–14 on the Island of Manhattan with his ship *The Tiger* at anchor in the North River. *The Tiger* burned; nevertheless, some of its remains have been recovered and are on display at The Museum of the City of New York. To replace the ship Block's men built a small yacht, presumably in part from salvage of *The Tiger.* They called it *Onrust*, which usually has been translated

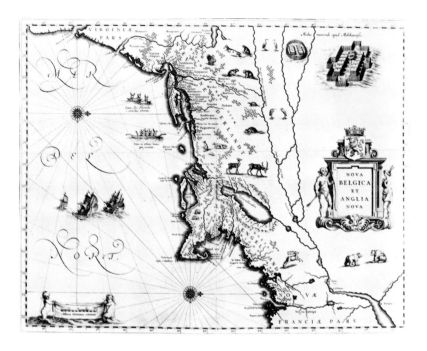

2. "Manatthans" and the settlement at "Nieu Amsterdam" are shown on this map from the world atlas published by W. J. Blaeu in Amsterdam, 1635. The Indian canoes, bears, beavers, and turkey are standard embellishments on seventeenth-century maps of the American regions. The Hudson is called the "North or Mauritius River," the Dutch having named it in honor of their Prince of Orange. What the map shows most clearly, perhaps, is that even though Europeans lived along much of the eastern coast, charted, geographical knowledge of the American continent was still imperfect. Line-engraved map, 14 1/4 × 19″. The J. Clarence Davies Collection. 29.100.2204

"restless" and looked upon as appropriate for the history of New York City—or even prophetic. Onrust is, however, also the name of an island, the last bit of dry land seen by ships leaving Holland; and, alas, this is a more likely origin of the yacht's name. In this vessel Block sailed through the East River into Long Island Sound and so on to Cape Cod, where he met a larger Dutch vessel which conveyed him home to the Netherlands. Other Dutch mariners may have landed briefly on the Island in this period on their way up the

Hudson to trade with the Indians, but none stayed permanently.

The West India Company transported the first group of settlers to New Netherland in 1624. About thirty families went on up the Hudson and established themselves at Fort Orange (now Albany). Eight men were left on Nut Island (now Governor's) in upper New York Bay. The cattle they had brought were pastured on "Manhates," where twenty promptly died from eating the Island's apparently unwholesome vegetation. The next year a large expedition in the charge of Wilhelm Verhulst (or Van Hulst), Director-General (or Governor), with Cryn Fredericksz as surveyor and engineer, arrived at Manhattan. Among the Verhulst colonists were both Dutch and French-speaking Walloons, so names in the earliest New York documents are a mix of Dutch and French—Van Dyck, De Sille, Stoffelsen, De la Montagne, Van Cortlandt, De Forest. What the settlers had in common was employment by the Dutch West India Company and a determination to barter with the Indians for furs to send back to Amsterdam. From the beginning the City was a "company town."

Fredericksz laid out a settlement grandly christened "New Amsterdam" after the European headquarters of the West India Company, but the colonists often called it "Fort Amsterdam" after the little fortification being erected. Although elaborate plans (probably too detailed) had been made by the Company for the new town and the settlers had been substantially outfitted, the colony got off to a slow start. Nevertheless, trade with the local Indians was fairly successful: in the first year 7,258 beaver skins and 857 otter and other skins were sent to Holland. Building, however, went slowly; even the vitally necessary fort did not get completed.

Things looked up when Peter Minuit, who succeeded Verhulst as Director-General, arrived in New Netherland on 4 May 1626. During the following summer Minuit made his celebrated arrangement with local Indians whereby the Island of Manhattan was purchased by the Dutch West India Company for trading goods worth sixty guilders—the famous $24 as calculated by nineteenth-century historians. Although there has been much lamentation over this deal in the past three centuries, there is no contemporary evidence that the Dutch thought they had skillfully cheated the Indians or that the Indians felt they had been robbed. Neither side regarded it as anything but an honorable and successful business arrangement. In fact, sixty guilders was good payment for a small slice of the endless wilderness which surrounded Indians and colonists alike.

The colonists, who numbered 270 men, women, and children in 1628, lived in about thirty houses on the East River near the tip of the Island—an area presently several blocks inland since the Island's southern end has been filled in and widened by man over the centuries. Pearl Street, which took its name from the numerous oyster beds nearby, was originally by the water. Six farms or "boweries" were laid out by the Company in 1628 on the present East Side below 14th Street. No. 1 was the "Great Bouwerie," later to be the home of Peter Stuyvesant.

The Hartgers view (1651) shows New Amsterdam as it must have appeared about 1626 to 1628. The Blaeu map (1635) indicates the way the best contemporary geographers positioned it on their charts.

New Amsterdam existed by and for the fur trade; the beaver certainly earned his place on the City's coat-of-arms. It has been the lasting misfortune of the beaver, his fellow rodents, and the otter that their pelts are particularly desirable for making into felt hats. In rich, cold, damp seventeenth-century Holland there was an immense demand for warm, luxurious furs which the forests of New Netherland were to supply in abundance. The Indian inhabitants, adept at catching the elusive mammals, were happy to trade their skins to the newly arrived colonists for European wares of all kinds, but particularly for good Dutch cloth. Isaack de Rasière (note his French name), secretary of the Dutch West India Company and its representative in New Amsterdam, wrote on 23 September 1626 to the Directors of the Amsterdam Chamber of the Company ("Noble, Honorable, Wise, Prudent Gentlemen," as he addressed them) reporting on town affairs and its trade—

3. This earliest known view of the Dutch settlement on Manhattan, the first view of the city that became New York, was published in *Beschrijvinghe van Virginia, Nieuw Nederlandt, etc.* by Joost Hartgers, Amsterdam, 1651. It possibly was based on the drawings of the engineer Cryn Fredericksz, who visited New Amsterdam in 1625–26. The scene was reversed in the engraving. About thirty houses are shown, probably accurately, but the fort, completed in 1628, had four bastions rather than five. The windmill at left was important in the little town's economy. Line engraving, 3 1/4 × 4 3/4". The J. Clarence Davies Collection. 29.100.792

especially in cloth with the Indians. The cloth was called "duffel" and came in various colors. Blue and "standard gray," he told the directors, were the most popular with the Indians; red could hardly be sold at all because the Indians said it hindered their hunting. Black was always in demand.

The businesslike Dutch, whose accounting methods at the time were the most advanced in the world, kept excellent records of exports, and from surviving manifests it can be seen that even at the beginning the trade in skins was very large: in 1629, 7,520 beaver skins, 370 otter, 48 mink, 36 wildcat; in 1632, 13,513 beaver, 1,661 otter; in 1635, 14,891 beaver, 1,413 otter. And these were only the exported skins; others were worn in

New Netherland or used for currency. By 1660, it was estimated that twenty-five or thirty thousand pelts were handled at Manhattan annually.

Skins and cloth were bartered, but trade was also carried on using wampum (called by the Dutch "*seawan*"). Described as strings of oblong beads made by the Indians from cockleshells found on the seashore, wampum was considered as valuable as money. There was a wampum "mine" at Montauk Point, Long Island. The Indians and Dutch both thought it important that the beads be "good, polished wampum"—unpolished beads were a sort of counterfeit. The best variety was called "Manhattan wampum." Beavers and wampum were given equivalents in currency: a beaver skin was reckoned at eight guilders; eight black and white beads of wampum equaled one stiver, a smaller Dutch coin.

Relations with the Indians continued amicable for a long time. Indians wandered peacefully along Heere Gracht (Broad Street) and were even allowed in the fort. The Dutch quickly learned enough of their language to conduct trade. In general, however, the Dutch thought the Indians a pretty poor lot: "uncivil," wrote Dominie Michaëlius, "and stupid as garden poles." Little, if any, energy was expended to convert them to Christianity although various ministers sometimes spoke of making such efforts. Absorbed in trade and indifferent to missionary activity, the Dutch failed to show the interest Spanish discoverers to the south felt in the history, religion, culture, and societal arrangements of the tribes in *their* parts of America— but then the Indians of the New York region were no Incas.

Peter Minuit built a counting house for this Indian trade. Along with the counting house the Company arranged for the settlers to have the other trappings of civilization. Before Dominie Jonas Michaëlius arrived in 1628 there was no minister on the Island, but an officer called "comforter of the sick" (a kind of deacon) conducted religious services by reading to a congregation assembled on Sunday in the loft of the horse mill. The fort, so necessary for protection against foreign invasion, Indians, and a thousand dangers that might be lurking in the dark forests on all sides, was still not completed.

The directors of the West India Company were always sending detailed instructions for it, but the settlement never seemed to be in a state of preparedness. The first fort, planned by the engineer Cryn Fredericksz, was made of sodded earthwork which naturally did not survive long in the rainy climate of Manhattan. It was of such flimsy construction anyway that the colonists' numerous pigs could continually root up the foundations. A fresh start was made in 1628, and the Company's Negro slaves—introduced into the colony from the African stations about this time—worked at its construction for the next seven years under the orders of the overseer Jacob Stoffelson, who lived at present-day 15 Pearl Street.

The church founded in 1628 by Dominie Michaëlius, the first pastor in the colony, still exists as the Collegiate Reformed Protestant Dutch Church in the City of New York, the oldest continuous Protestant communion in America. The fortieth successor of Michaëlius as minister of the church is the famous preacher and writer Dr. Norman Vincent Peale. Michaëlius is additionally important because he wrote the earliest letters from Manhattan of which the originals have survived. The letters give a rather jaundiced view of life on the Island: the poor man's wife had died on the voyage over, and he was left with several small children; he could get no assistance with his housework; his promised salary and perquisites from the Dutch West India Company—of which he was an employee like everyone else—were not forthcoming; and he found the colonists a rambunctious and rough-spoken lot. He had, however, fifty communicants, "Walloons and Dutch," at his first celebration of the Lord's Supper.

Michaëlius hated Peter Minuit, whom he considered slippery in his dealings, probably guilty of fornication, and generally wicked. Vigorous disagreement between each Director-General of New Amsterdam and each local minister was to continue throughout the Dutch period, with both sides constantly appealing to the directors of the Dutch West India Company or even over their heads to the supreme authority, the States-General of the Netherlands.

In Michaëlius's letters and various other reports to

the Company we can get an idea of Manhattan's appearance in those days. He and all the other commentators speak of the Island as full of trees and hilly, and "rocky in the middle." Grass was plentiful but—after the settlers' experience with their first herd of cattle—not considered especially healthful for livestock. A clear stream meandered along the east side of the Island where the Company's farms were situated, and all the writers praised the region's fine air. Coming from the Low Countries they did not complain of Manhattan's climate except its extremes of heat and cold, to which they were not accustomed.

Even with these advantages, New Amsterdam, indeed the whole province of New Netherland, did not prosper despite Company disbursements between 1626 and 1644 said to have reached the enormous sum of 550,000 guilders. The Company was generous in meeting its obligations, efficient in its shipments, and tolerant in its religious opinions (as will be shown), but it was slow-moving and so paternalistic that growth in the colony was effectively stifled. Manhattan especially suffered under the iron rule of the Company. No one was permitted to take up Island land on freehold: all of it was leased from the Company, usually for six years. With unclaimed and unowned lands across the rivers as far as the eye could see, some colonists naturally were disposed to desert Manhattan altogether and began to settle the Jersey shore and the nearer parts of Long Island. At the far end of Long Island the English were commencing their settlements, which could only move westward—a fruitful cause for dissension between the Dutch and English governments at home and a source of constant alarm for colonists on the scene.

To encourage immigration and settlement the Company in 1629 granted a "Charter of Freedoms and Exemptions" to all who would establish colonies in New Netherland. These colonies were the famous "patroonships," the longest surviving of which was that established by the Amsterdam jeweler Kiliaen van Rensselaer. There was never any doubt of Manhattan's destined prominence; in the charter the Company foresaw the future of New Amsterdam as the staple port for all products and the very head of the whole region.

Peter Minuit was recalled by the Company in 1632, to answer various charges brought against him (Directors-General were *always* being recalled to answer charges). The new Director-General came straight from Holland. His name, which delighted generations of comic writers including foremost Washington Irving, was Wouter van Twiller. A new minister, Everardus Bogardus, who had served the Company as "comforter of the sick" in Guinea, came over with him as the second Dutch minister. Van Twiller was Kiliaen van Rensselaer's nephew, and that relationship was his qualification for ruling the colony. His peculation was notorious; within a short time of his arrival in New Amsterdam he had possessed himself of Governor's Island and Hell Gate in the East River as personal property, added some fine boweries, and otherwise enriched himself.

Although Van Twiller was to become one of the most unpopular rulers this City has ever had, during his administration various improvements were made in New Amsterdam: a bakery, a small house for the midwife, a goat-house, and, not least, a real church, which stood on present-day 93 Pearl Street.

When the Company fussed over the colony's obvious stagnation, Van Twiller was inclined to blame New Amsterdam's lack of progress on English interlopers. "Trade," he wrote to the directors in 1636, "would go reasonably well if the English did not interfere with it by many underhand means." The English claimed to be visitors, not traders, when they came to New Netherland, "but they are well stocked with goods and do not let any skins go by if they are to be had."

Van Twiller was superseded in March, 1638, when Willem Kieft arrived in New Amsterdam. Kieft found the City in deplorable shape: "the fort totally and wholly in a ruinous condition"; the cannon dismantled; the Company boweries unoccupied and in decay; virtually every building including the church dilapidated.

On 15 April 1638, Kieft promulgated the earliest

City ordinances of which we have records. They were concerned with port regulations, days for holding court, and drinking. Lusty sailors visiting the port were already causing trouble, and an ordinance sternly forbade the citizens to harbor any sailors overnight; they were not to spend the night on shore. This was merely the first of many such ordinances throughout the colonial period directed against riotous sailors. In the eyes of the town's governance they were always a troublesome visitation. The ordinances relating to the drinking of spiritous liquors attempted to set hours of operation for the already numerous taverns of New Amsterdam; these regulations were highly unpopular and had to be frequently reiterated. Later that year an ordinance was passed to prevent employees of the Company from departing Manhattan.

The ramshackle condition of New Amsterdam finally persuaded the Company to open trade to all persons, provided merchandise was transported only in Company ships and the heavy duties were paid. In 1639, the fur trade with the Indians was thrown open to any resident of the province instead of being restricted to Company employees. Immigration was but slightly stimulated by this relaxing of the rules. Among the immigrants in 1639 were eight Englishmen, followed shortly by some English families. Soon there were so many English and they were so litigious that a special English-speaking secretary was appointed to aid the Director-General in the many English lawsuits which came before him.

Two Englishmen, George Holmes and Thomas Hall, secured from Kieft a grant of land for a tobacco plantation on Deutel (Turtle) Bay along the East River (47th to 52nd streets between the East River and Second Avenue in today's geography), a site now occupied in part by the United Nations buildings. North of this area the Company's Negro slaves were quartered on the East River around present-day 75th Street. In 1644, some of these slaves were emancipated by the Company and received grants of land. A colonist named Adriaen van der Donck received a vast grant of land stretching from the Spuyten Duyvil through present-day Riverdale on to Yonkers (derived from his honorific title

jonkheer). Hendrick de Forest was the first grantee and the first person to build on lands which were called "New Haarlem" (also spelled, like Manhattan, in many variant forms). His example was immediately followed, and in one year thirty farms were granted by the Company. Also in 1639, Jonas Bronck, sometimes described by historians as a Scandinavian, bought 500 acres in the region which would take a derivative of his name. In 1644, Kieft purchased for the Company the western end of Long Island from Coney Island to Gowanus; in 1650, Long Island was divided between the Dutch and the English.

The Dutch in New Amsterdam had three great causes for worry: the ever-increasing English settlements on Long Island; the Indians to the north and west who became restive as the Dutch colony expanded; and the Negro slaves in their midst who sometimes murdered their masters and more frequently set fire to their houses. Slave uprisings were not unknown in the Company's other possessions, and word of them reached the New Amsterdamers. The English on Long Island sometimes settled on Dutch-granted lands—Newtown (1642), Flushing (1645), Gravesend (1646)—and they were not noticeably loyal to the grantors. The first settlers of Brooklyn (1646), however, were Dutch. The frequent wars between the home countries kept suspicions warm in the New World.

Director-General Kieft's most unfortunate weakness was belligerency toward the generally docile Indians. He wanted to tax them—he called it making "a friendly contribution"—but the Company always denied that he had been given any such orders. Nevertheless, Indian resentment led to the first serious hostilities in 1643, and in 1644 "a good stiff fence" was built across the northern part of the settlement. The lane on its inner side became known as "*Waal*" or Wall Street.

One result of the Indian troubles, however, was that Kieft called a meeting of heads of families at Fort Amsterdam who selected a board of twelve men as their representatives in consulting with the Director-General —the first faint beginning of representative government in the City. Like so many of his successors, Kieft did not like the advice he received and abolished the board

NOVA AMSTELDAM

4. The extremely rare "De Wit" view was published as an inset on a map of America dated 1672. At left center near the little wooden wharf built by Governor Stuyvesant in 1648–49 are a crane for unloading boats and the gallows which apparently served mainly as a visible deterrent since it was seldom if ever used during Dutch rule. The canoes in the foreground are those found on the Blaeu map of 1635, and the Hartgers view was obviously borrowed for local color by the artist of this engraving. Line engraving on copper, 8 1/2 × 10 1/4". Gift of Mrs. William Sloane. 38.512

in 1642. Nonetheless, he and the council did establish a militia and require that every male inhabitant provide himself with "a good gun" and keep it ready for use.

When the Indians refused to be pacified Kieft had to appeal again to the citizenry, and in 1643 he selected a board which he called The Eight Men. Soldiers (including fifty Englishmen) were enlisted for an all-out campaign, but they proved too few to control the Indians. The Eight Men, going over the head of Kieft as they were only too quick to do, wrote to the directors in Amsterdam: "Our fields lie fallow and waste; our dwellings and other buildings are burnt . . . we are seated here in the midst of thousands of Indians and barbarians from whom is to be experienced neither peace nor pity. They continually rove around in parties, night and day, on the Island of Manhattans, killing our people not a thousand paces from the Fort; and things have now arrived at such a pass that no one dare move a foot to fetch a stick of fire wood without an escort." The Company was sympathetic but now nearly bankrupt and had no soldiers to send. The hostilities continued until a general peace was concluded with the

Indians at Fort Amsterdam on 30 August 1645. An ordinance then forbade the selling of liquor to Indians, one of the orginal causes of the troubles. Of course an illicit trade thrived and was for years the topic of frequent municipal thunderings. Visitors continued to report seeing fuddled Indians "running drunk along the Manhattans."

Kieft was now called back by the Company to answer for his actions but was drowned when his ship *The Princess* went down off Wales with the loss of eighty-six passengers, several tons of timber, and 14,000 beaver skins.

While Kieft was still in New Amsterdam, contemporary documents first mention Oloff Stevensen van Cortlandt, a soldier in the Dutch West India Company who arrived in March, 1638, at New Amsterdam. Active as a trader in land he founded a fortune estimated to be one of the four largest in the province at his death in 1684. He married Anneken Loockermans; two of their children married members of the Schuyler family, two married Philipses, another married a Van Rensselaer; their grandchildren married

Bayards, Jays, Van Dams, Van Hornes, Vetches, and other Schuylers and other Van Cortlandts. The Van Cortlandts have held numerous offices throughout New York history, and the Frederick van Cortlandt Mansion is one of the few colonial houses remaining in the City. The windmill on the City's arms may have been derived from that displayed on the Van Cortlandt shield.

Kieft's successor as Director-General was Petrus Stuyvesant. Although later generations called him "Peter," he signed his name "Petrus" throughout his life. Stuyvesant arrived in New Amsterdam 11 May 1647, apparently middle-aged (the date of his birth is unknown), and he was a Company man in every sense of the word. He had served the Dutch West India Company in its possessions in the West Indies (he was governor of the island of Curaçao) and had lost his right leg in a naval action there. Capable, opinionated, suspicious, hot-tempered, a stern, even harsh administrator, a rigid Calvinist, and a loyal servant of the Company, he was unpopular from the first.

It is true that the citizens of New Amsterdam were prepared to dislike *any* new director, since they had been indifferently governed for so long. Having recently experienced for the first time the heady pleasure of having a voice in municipal affairs, they were not inclined to give up the privilege even though it would almost certainly bring them into conflict with the Director-General.

Like other colonial officials of the era Stuyvesant expected to become rich in office, and he did. At New Amsterdam his salary was 250 guilders a month with a subsistence grant of 900 guilders a year. No other official in the colony received even half as much. In 1651, he bought the Company's "Great Bouwerie" and there erected a fine country home. He also built a chapel for his family, tenants, Negro slaves, and neighbors on the site of the present Church of St. Marks-in-the-Bouwerie (northwest corner of Second Avenue and 10th Street), where he is buried with his descendants to the eighth generation. His town house, "Whitehall," stood on the street which now bears its name.

New York is not a city given to hero worship, but somehow the legend of "Peg-leg Peter" has taken hold of New Yorkers, and Peter Stuyvesant is probably the nearest the City has to a folk-hero. The statue of Stuyvesant by Gertrude Vanderbilt Whitney stands in the square named for him; one of New York's most famous housing developments (situated in part on his old farm) bears his name; a school, hotel, and (currently) fifty businesses or more in the City are named for him.

Stuyvesant's first recorded ordinances were not calculated to reassure the New Amsterdamers. Only two weeks after his arrival he ordered the taverns to close at nine in the evening and prohibited their opening at all on Sunday morning—apparently a favorite tippling hour of the burghers. Cows, horses, goats, and, worst of all, hogs had been permitted by their owners to roam freely throughout the town; it saved penning them up and feeding them. Stuyvesant, always ready to proceed vigorously, ordered the hogs shot on sight, but his ordinance was no more effective than others had been, and the problem of roaming livestock remained with the City a long time. In 1657, however, New Amsterdam became the first town in colonial America to forbid the throwing of rubbish into the streets, and, generally speaking, European visitors were impressed with the Dutch cleanliness of the houses.

The movement for some popular government remained strong, and even Stuyvesant had to give in to it. He and his appointed council designated a board of nine men out of eighteen names submitted by the citizenry. Stuyvesant called their acts "responsible" as long as they corresponded with *his* views, wrote one of the men later. If they disagreed, then Stuyvesant called the nine, "clowns, usurers, rebels, and the like." Flagrant infractions of the ordinance against the sale of intoxicants on Sunday continued and aroused the board's anger; nearly a fourth of the houses in New Amsterdam were grog shops, and the more honorable trades and occupations were neglected in favor of tapping. No doubt there was some exaggeration in this view, but Dominie Johannes Backerus, who arrived in 1647, found his congregation "very much given to drink" and counted seventeen taphouses.

Dominie Backerus, although he agreed with Stuyvesant's council on the prevalent evil of sottishness in New Amsterdam, otherwise violently disagreed with the Director-General. In fact, he thundered from the pulpit on municipal problems in the best Calvinist fashion. Stuyvesant was enraged. His attempts to silence Backerus made him more unpopular than ever, and he was unable to prevent a remonstrance's being drawn up against him by eleven representatives of the citizenry and sent to the States-General in Holland, the final court of appeal. This remonstrance contained numerous recommendations for the betterment of the colony, hinted that the Company's government was both incompetent and corrupt, and said plainly that the citizens opposed the completion of Fort Amsterdam because a stronghold might enable Stuyvesant to be even more high-handed and severe on them.

The remonstrants were particularly annoyed about the state of educational affairs: "The bowl has been going round for a long time for the purpose of erecting a common school, and it has been built with words, but as yet the first stone is not laid."

The States-General, notably more liberal than their Directors-General, listened to these complaints with a receptive ear and, in 1650, recommended the formation of a municipal government. Stuyvesant's answer to the charges against him was to transfer most of the blame for the poor conditions in the City (admitted tacitly) to the shoulders of the unfortunate schout-fiscal Hendrick van Dyck. When Van Dyck got word of this, there was a tremendous quarrel, ending with Van Dyck's being removed from office charged with calling Stuyvesant, "scoundrel, murderer, tyrant, hound, baby, and other like names."

In 1653, municipal government finally came to New Amsterdam, and Stuyvesant proclaimed it, unwillingly, on February 2nd of that year. The government, still of course under the Director-General, consisted of a schout (a combination sheriff, prosecutor, and chief magistrate), two burgomasters (magistrates), and five schepens (aldermen), who together formed a court. The present City Council of New York descends directly from this body—the oldest city council in this country. Its members immediately concerned themselves with such municipal problems as the care of widows and orphans, a weighing-house and scales, and the hogs that rooted up the walls of the fort. Their relations with Stuyvesant were predictably painful.

Stuyvesant's New Amsterdam was recorded in the remarkable "Castello Plan" of 1660, of which a scale model is in The Museum of the City of New York. The "De Wit View" (c. 1672) and the "Restitutio View" (1673) also depict the City about this time.

There were 120 houses and 1,000 New Amsterdamers resident in 1656, according to a census taken that year. Earlier buildings had been constructed of wood, but Dutch brick structures roofed with red and black tile were becoming more common. We get a good idea of the typical dwelling house from a surviving contract, dated 26 April 1655, between Egbert van Borsum, ferryman on the Long Island side of the East River ferry, and two "English carpenters." The Englishmen contracted to build for Van Borsum "a dwelling house of two rooms thirty feet long and eighteen feet wide with three transom windows and a door in front, glass in the windows, and wainscoting in the principal room." This house cost 550 guilders, which was to be paid "one-third in beavers, one-third in good merchantable wampum, one-third in good silver coin," free passage on the ferry while the work continued, and small beer to be drunk on the job.

Daily life in these houses was a curious mixture of frontier and urban. The "Dutch Alcove" in The Museum of the City of New York, although of slightly later date, shows New York furniture in the Netherlandish style, which persisted well into the eighteenth century. Silver spoons, tankards, and bowls were a good way of preserving (and displaying) one's wealth and were brought from the home country by the well-to-do, but an American capability and style soon developed. Some fine New York silversmiths, however, continued the rich and dignified Dutch style.

Stuyvesant established Monday as market day in New Amsterdam and set up an annual fair. Public scales were installed in the market, but the City Council soon complained that Stuyvesant was not sending the

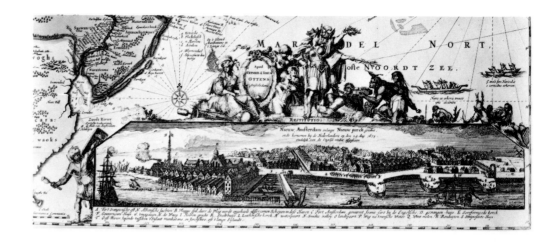

5. The "Restitutio" view of New Amsterdam takes its name from the word engraved below the elaborate cartouche which refers to the short-term (1673–74) restitution of the City to the Dutch. The soldiers on the quay and the firing of cannon at the fort represent the recapture. Many buildings, piers, and other landmarks are exaggerated in size, no doubt to add luster to the Dutch victory in the home provinces. Line engraving, 17 3/4 × 20 3/4". The J. Clarence Davies Collection. 29.100.2199

weighing fees to the City's treasury. In his letters Nicasius De Sille describes the edibles presented for sale at the market or otherwise available around the City. Oysters were plentiful and could be dredged up near the fort; Indians supplied venison, wild geese, turkeys, partridges, ducks; and beer was brewed of barley and wheat. Pigeons, now regarded only as an urban curse, served as food and were even more plentiful in the seventeenth century: "wild pigeons are as thick as the sparrows in Holland. . . . They are shot here by the thousand in our squares, streets, and gardens. They taste like partridges."

De Sille arrived in 1653 with his five motherless children and a maid. He was to serve as "first councillor for New Netherland" but was hardly off the ship before being treated rudely by Stuyvesant. He had a stormy career in New Amsterdam, but in letters to his friends at home he says, "this country suits me exceedingly well. I shall not try to leave it as long as I live." After remarking that "children and pigs multiply here rapidly," he says, "there is a lack of women; we need people to cultivate the soil and increase the population."

Into this peaceful if not particularly prosperous little town the larger world began to intrude. Holland and England went to war in 1652, and alarming rumors

were spread that the New England colonies were preparing to invade New Netherland. Orders were given for the hundredth time that Fort Amsterdam be put in defensive strength, palisades be put up along Wall Street, and a guard house be erected at present-day Wall and Pearl ("the water gate"). In the meantime English pirates under the command of Thomas Baxter, a renegade from New Amsterdam, were raiding the neighborhood of Flushing, Long Island.

Stuyvesant summoned deputies to a provincial assembly to devise means of stopping these incursions. A great *land-dag* or general assembly, consisting of ten Dutchmen and nine Englishmen who represented New Amsterdam, Brooklyn, Flushing, Midwout (Flatbush), and Gravesend, among other towns, met at the City Hall on 10 December 1654. That there were ten Dutchmen and nine Englishmen in the body is an indication of English strength in New Amsterdam even then. A remonstrance was drawn up—in English!—translated into Dutch, and presented to Stuyvesant, who refused to accept it and proceeded to declare the assembly illegal. An appeal by the burgomasters and schepens to the directors in Amsterdam met with a cold shoulder: Stuyvesant was upheld and the burgomasters and schepens were told in so many words to mind their own business—which was *not* promoting relations with the Long Island English. The council subsided and returned to quarreling directly with Stuyvesant. Like their successors in the municipal councils of New York, the first burgomasters and schepens were much concerned with their own comforts: they commissioned Jacob Steedam, an upholsterer and part-time poet, to make good cushions for their twelve chairs.

Stuyvesant's religion did not brook dissent. In 1653, he refused a petition of the Lutheran inhabitants of the City to organize a church. The directors in Amsterdam, always more tolerant than their agents, ordered him to permit "free religious exercises in their houses," but when a Lutheran minister arrived Stuyvesant had him immediately deported. No denomination other than the Dutch Reformed Church was permitted to erect a house of worship on Manhattan Island during the Dutch regime. Into the little Calvinist town, however, various alien elements were intruding. In September, 1654, the first Jews, refugees from the Dutch settlements in northern Brazil, arrived and were permitted to remain, over Stuyvesant's furious protests. He wrote to the directors about the religious situation in New Amsterdam: "For as we have here Papists, Mennonites and Lutherans among the Dutch; also many Puritans or Independents and many Atheists and various other servants of Baal among the English under this Government, who conceal themselves under the name of Christians, it would create a still greater confusion, if the obstinate and immovable Jews came to settle here."

Another religious group excited even more controversy than the Jews on arriving in New Amsterdam. The first Quakers to land compounded their dissent by being English, and women to boot. In 1657, a flagless ship from London paid a one-day visit to New Amsterdam and then rather mysteriously sailed away, leaving behind "two strong young Women" who immediately began preaching, crying out loudly in the middle of the street "that men should repent, for the Day of Judgment is at hand." This is the earliest manifestation in New York of a phenomenon still very much with us: street preaching. The inhabitants were then more alarmed than they are today; some cried "fire," and "not knowing what was the matter, ran to and fro." Stuyvesant soon put a stop to that by jailing the young women. The same year he attempted to suppress Quaker meetings in Flushing, Long Island, jailing and whipping the Friends with his customary severity.

There was a strong reaction to his measures even among his own family. As for the Quakers, on 27 December 1657 thirty-six Dutchmen and Englishmen addressed to the Director-General the famous "Flushing Remonstrance," a landmark in the history of religious toleration in America. The remonstrants mentioned to Stuyvesant the ancient rights of the Dutch to freedom of thought, "which is the outward glory of the states of Holland." Stuyvesant was unmoved by the appeal, but the remonstrants were upheld when they went over his head to the directors in Amsterdam. Although the directors were not particularly happy to have dissenters swarming into New Amsterdam, they *were* anxious for an increase in its population. Their instructions were therefore "to allow everyone to have his own belief, as long as he behaves quietly and legally, gives no offense to his neighbors and does not oppose the government," and Stuyvesant was reminded that as Amsterdam "has always practiced this maxim of moderation and consequently has often had a considerable influx of people, we do not doubt that your province would be benefited by it."

Immigrating dissenters were only one problem for Stuyvesant and the New Amsterdam citizens. English pirates continued to harass the Dutch, and rumors reached the City of secret meetings being held at Gravesend on Long Island by English subjects planning to capture New Amsterdam. A prejudice in the City against the English residents caused some of them to leave for the company of their own kind on Long Island, taking with them "their movables, furniture, beavers, and other valuables." The Anglo-Dutch War ended with a treaty, however, and the New Amsterdamers, breathing more easily, returned to their fur dealing.

Stuyvesant spent seven months in the West Indies

in 1654–55—no doubt to the relief of the citizens of New Amsterdam—establishing trade with that area. His return was demanded when an unexpected and extremely bloody Indian war broke out. In October, 1655, ten tribes totaling about 1,900 warriors attacked New Amsterdam. In three days they killed 100 Dutch, captured 150 (mostly women and children), and did damage to the unheard-of sum of 200,000 guilders in the City, the near Jersey shore, and Staten Island. Although peace was established in 1660, the Indians attacked Esopus (Kingston) in 1663 and again in 1664. With rampaging Indians to the north, increasingly mutinous English on the Island, and a new Anglo-Dutch War looming, New Amsterdam was at a critical juncture. The West India Company was now nearly bankrupt, and it was up to the citizens to raise money, repair the fort, and erect palisades around the City.

Although England and Holland were nominally at peace, on 12 March 1664 Charles II coolly granted to his brother James, Duke of York (later King James II), part of Maine, all of Long Island, Martha's Vineyard, Nantucket, and all the land west of the Connecticut River to the east side of Delaware Bay. This of course included New Netherland, to which the English had only the murkiest claim based on the voyages of the Cabots. Word of this outrageous assumption and of English plans to seize New Amsterdam reached Stuyvesant in late June, 1664, and he at once held a conference and took steps to defend the City against likely attack.

The English were not long in arriving. On 18 August the English squadron cast anchor in the bay below the Narrows, near Coney Island, virtually blockading the port, and established posts from which English vessels could sally out to raid shipping.

This English force was under the command of Colonel Richard Nicolls, who called on Stuyvesant to surrender. He refused. The English Governor Winthrop of Connecticut wrote a friendly letter to Stuyvesant enclosing another from Nicolls. Both recommended that Stuyvesant surrender Manhattan to the English force. These texts Stuyvesant refused to divulge to his burgomasters and schepens, and upon being pressed he tore the letter from Nicolls to pieces in their presence. The City was so short of supplies, however, that it could not hold out for long. Dutch and English commissioners met at Stuyvesant's bouwerie at eight in the morning of 27 August 1664 to arrange terms of surrender. The Dutch were assured by the English that they could retain their own church and their own inheritance customs; the less important civil officers and the magistrates were to remain in office until new elections. Of course all officials had to take an oath of allegiance to the English king. On 29 August the town and the fort were formally surrendered; that same day the City and province were renamed "New York" and the fortification "Fort James."

The burgomasters and schepens wrote to the directors of the West India Company at Amsterdam to inform them of these events and to blame the loss of New Amsterdam on the Company's neglect of its colony. The following month they were writing the Duke of York that they considered themselves fortunate to be under his lordship, praising Colonel Nicolls, and prophesying that under his wise governance the City would "bloom and grow like the Cedar on Lebanon."

When the remaining property of the Dutch West India Company in New York was seized by the English government, the aspirations of that great commercial enterprise on the North American continent were ended.

In 1665, a year after the surrender, the Company's most important employee, Peter Stuyvesant, memorialized the States-General of the Netherlands, defending his conduct in surrendering the province to the English. He *had* "to surrender said places through the unwillingness of the militia, the protests and menaces of the burghers, the weakness of the fort, the scarcity of provisions and munitions of war, and the small number of soldiers." He himself retired comfortably to his bouwerie. On the whole, he and his fellow New Amsterdamers were remarkably philosophical about the forced change in their allegiance. Like their innumerable descendants (real or spiritual) in New York, they could adjust to anything.

6. The earliest European artifacts in The Museum of the City of New York and the oldest relics of the Dutch occupation of Manhattan Island are these flame-charred timbers of *The Tiger*, Captain Adriaen Block's ship that burned in 1613. They were turned up in 1916 by workmen excavating beneath the intersection of Dey and Greenwich streets, which, when *The Tiger* burned, was on the west shoreline of Manhattan. Despite various plans to dig up the remainder of the ship, its relics still repose about twenty feet beneath the World Trade Center. Length: 8 1/2′. Gift of the Department of Parks. 43.165

7–8. Half a century after the timbers of *The Tiger* were exhumed, another relic of the ship was discovered. In 1967, an excavation near Dey Street turned up a seventeenth-century bronze breech-loading swivel deck gun. On the removable breech block is the monogram "VOC," standing for *Vereenigne Ost-Indische Compagnie,* the Dutch East India Company, under whose auspices *The Tiger* sailed—the Dutch West India Company had not then been founded. The "A" forming the top of the monogram stands for the Amsterdam chapter of the company. There is every indication that the deck gun was part of Block's armament on *The Tiger*—he was later sued by the Dutch Admiralty for loss of the ship's cannon. Length: 41″. Gift of the Mrs. Winthrop W. Aldrich Fund. 76.9

Afbeeldinge van de Stadt Amsterdam in Nieuw Neederlandt.

9. Jacques Cortelyou came to New Netherland in 1652, and in five years became surveyor-general of the province. In 1660 he drew up a detailed plan of the City of New Amsterdam for Peter Stuyvesant to send the directors of the West India Company in Holland. The plan was either lost on route or mislaid in the archives and has never turned up. A watercolor copy survived, however, in Italy at the Villa Castello near Florence. Reproduction by Alinari of the Castello Plan, 23 1/2 × 31 1/2". Gift of La Biblioteca Medicea Laurenziana. 49.150. A scale model, 1" to 20', made by Charles C. Capehart and J. E. Dougherty in 1931, is on display in The Museum of the City of New York.

10. On 15 May 1664, Stuyvesant and Cornelis van Ruyven, secretary of the Council, signed this deed granting land in Brooklyn to Thomas Lambertse of Pearl Street. Manuscript on parchment, 15 × 18". Gift of DeLancey Kountze. 33.307

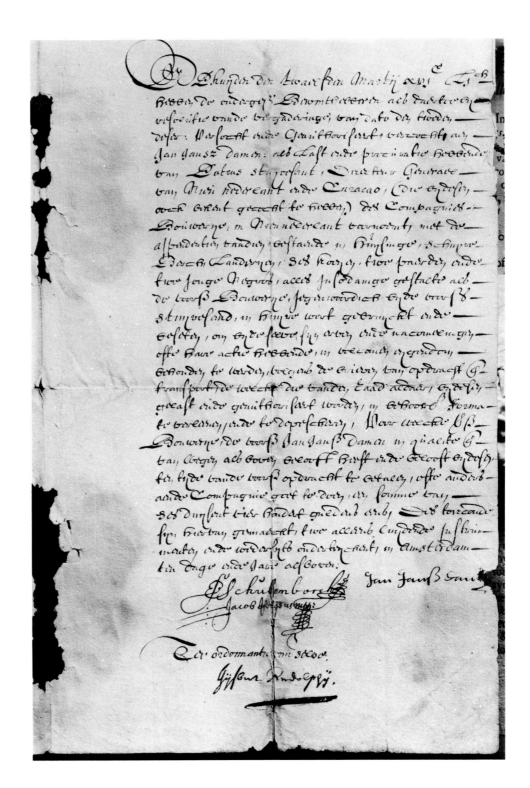

11. On 8 December 1654, Stuyvesant delivered to Martin Creiger, president of the board of burgomasters and *schepens*, a painted coat-of-arms of the new municipality of New Amsterdam. Sent by the directors in Holland, it had just arrived on the ship *Pereboom* (*Peartree*). The original painting has been lost, but this reconstruction shows the combination of the arms of Amsterdam in Holland with the insignia of the West India Company, the whole draped with the orange, white, and blue flag of the Netherlands Republic. From E. S. Wilde, *The Civic Ancestry of New York*, 1913, plate VII.

12. The earliest dated document in The Museum of the City of New York records the purchase of property by Governor Peter Stuyvesant, through his agent Jan Jansen Damen, from the West India Company, 12 March 1651. This was the company's Bouwerie No. 1, where Stuyvesant lived after the English conquest until his death in 1672. This deed gives him title to a dwelling house, barn, barrack, land (sixty *morgens*, or about 120 acres), six cows, two horses, and two young Negro slaves for the sum of 6,400 guilders. Manuscript on paper, 12 1/2 × 8". · Gift of Stuyvesant Fish, direct descendant of Peter Stuyvesant. 35.431.1

13. This earliest known impression of the seal of the City of New York displays the coronet of James, Duke of York, above the arms although (as may be seen by the last two lines of the document) he was already king of England. Stephen De Lancey is admitted freeman and citizen of the City in this document which is signed by Mayor Nicholas Bayard and dated July, 1686. De Lancey, who had arrived only that year from Caen in Normandy, married a Van Cortlandt and founded one of the most prominent New York families. Manuscript on paper, 5 1/8 × 10 1/4″. Gift of Beverley R. Robinson. 40.190.1

14. Stuyvesant planted a pear tree, imported from Holland in 1647, on his Bouwerie estate at the present-day northeast corner of Third Avenue and 13th Street. It survived not only the Director-General but his estate and became an object of veneration for New Yorkers of the eighteenth and nineteenth centuries. The diarist Philip Hone wrote sentimentally of the pear tree several times and reverently preserved one of its rather sparse blossoms under glass. This photograph by J. Gurney & Son was made on 22 August 1863, four years before the tree perished, victim of a traffic accident between two wagons. An effort in the 1950s to plant another pear tree on the spot failed when the Parks Department assured antiquarians that a pear tree could no longer survive in Manhattan's air. Mounted photograph, 23 × 19 1/4″. Gift of the Staten Island Historical Society Museum.

15. A passage in Washington Irving's comic *A History of New York from the Beginning of the World to the End of the Dutch Dynasty,* published under the name Diedrich Knickerbocker, inspired Asher B. Durand to paint *Dance on the Battery in the Presence of Peter Stuyvesant*, exhibited at the National Academy of Design in 1838. Irving told fancifully of a Saturday afternoon dance on the green-sward of the Battery in the Dutch days of New York. One young lady, recently arrived from Holland, danced in short petticoats, to the scandal of Stuyvesant and the other onlookers. Oil on canvas, 32 × 46″. Gift of the late Jane Rutherford Faile through Kenneth C. Faile. 55.248

16. The couchant-lion decoration on the handle of this tankard and the well-defined cherub's head on the handle's tip are the New York style in silver at its exuberant best in the early eighteenth century. Cornelius Kierstede, maker of the piece, was a native New Yorker and one of the most accomplished silversmiths in the history of that craft in America. This splendid tankard is engraved on the handle I S E for Isaac and Elizabeth (Underhill) Smith, who were married about 1685. Height: 6 1/2″. Gift of Mrs. Mary F. Youngs, descendant of the Smiths. 51.100

18. Jacobus van Cortlandt, merchant, member of the colonial Assembly, alderman, and twice mayor of New York (1710 and 1719), owned this tankard which is attributed to Jurian Blanck, Jr. It is initialed on the handle C over I∗E for Jacobus and his wife Eve Philipse, who were married in 1691. It is also engraved with the arms of the Van Cortlandts. Height: 7 1/2″ to the top of the cover. Gift of Augustus van Cortlandt. 57.79

17. Just six years after the first permanent settlement of the Dutch on Manhattan, the patroonship of Rensselaerwyck in upstate New York was created for Kiliaen van Rensselaer (1630). At its greatest extent it stretched twenty-four by forty-eight miles, and until the nineteenth century remained the greatest single piece of private property in America. The Van Rensselaers owned this hexagonal standing salt, which is one of a pair, the only known with a history of ownership in America. Made in Amsterdam in 1623, one of the salts bears the early initials LVW, probably for Leonora Van Wely, a relation of the first patroon, as well as the later initials M∗V∗R for Maria van Rensselaer. Each is paneled with oval medallions on which scenes represent months of the year. Height: about 5 1/2″. Gift of Mrs. Edward Robbins. 66.103b

21. Gerrit Onckelbag (or Onclebagh) made this two-handled bowl in New York about 1700; it was probably used for punch. Length: handle to handle, 12 7/8″; diameter rim: 9 3/8″. Bequest of Miss Charlotte A. van Cortlandt. 72.88.1

19. These silver casters, presumably two from a set of three, are attributed to Jurian Blanck, Jr., working in New York about 1668–1714. They came from the family of Margaret Beekman, who married Judge Robert R. Livingston in 1742. Chancellor Livingston was the son of this marriage. Heights: 7″ and 5 1/2″. Taller caster gift of Mrs. Frederick S. Crofts. 52.338. Shorter caster gift of Mrs. J. Insley Blair. 51.19ab

20. "Suckets" were preserved fruits, often eaten in an age when there was little way to keep fresh fruit. They were eaten with "sucket forks," of which this is a fine example by the New York silversmith Jesse Kip, working 1682–1722. It is engraved "Maria van Renslaer." Length: 6 1/8″. Gift of Mrs. Thomas K. Gale. 33.175.2

22. It used to be customary for mourners at a funeral to be given a *memento mori* of the occasion. Spoons such as this survive from the usage which persisted into the nineteenth century, when gloves were often given. This spoon was made by the silversmith Cornelius van der Burch, and the inscription (in translation) reads: "Dominie Nicholas van Rensselaer died 12 November 1678." Length: 7 3/8″. Gift of Nicholas G. Rutgers, Jr., Mrs. George Coe, and Mrs. Marshall J. Dodge, Jr. 62.166.1

23. Prosperous New Yorkers of the turn of the eighteenth century lived in rooms like the "Dutch Alcove" in The Museum of the City of New York. Some of the furniture and many of the household items such as the silver and the Delft dishes were imported, but the room contains a number of American products. The portrait by an unidentified patroon painter is of Mrs. Jacobus Stoutenburgh. The slat-back armchair, 1680–1700, is of New York origin and descended in the Riker family of Newtown, Long Island. The lady's armchair is also from seventeenth-century New York. Carpets, called "Turkish" regardless of their precise point of origin in the East, were usually draped on tables while white sand was sometimes used on the floors. Pet squirrels appear with children in a number of early American portraits. Portraits gift of the estate of the late Caroline T. Wells. 39 × 29″. Oak armchair height: 40 1/4″. Gift of Friends of the Museum. 40.296. Lady's chair height: 40 1/4″. Gift of Robert Swartwout Talmadge. 38.440. Rug 4′2″ × 6′10″. Gift of Mrs. Elon Huntington Hooker. 44.217

24. The finest piece of early
furniture in The Museum of the
City of New York is the Brinckerhoff
secretary, probably made in New
York about 1700. Its solemn richness
shows the persistence of the Dutch
taste after the English conquest.
Made of cedarwood, its inlay of
flowers and scrolls is of beechwood
and walnut. The fall front has many
drawers faced with the same woods,
each with a teardrop handle. The
two large drawers below are lined
with white pine and tulip. It
descended through eight generations
of the Brinckerhoff family, which
was founded in New Amsterdam by
Joris Dircksen Brinckerhoff in 1638.
Height: 67″. Gift of Mrs. Elon
Huntington Hooker. 45.112 a–c

26. This Dutch style chair of the seventeenth century with square Spanish cedar legs and posts and leather nailed on the back and seat is said to have belonged to Sarah Rapalje, one of several claimants to the honor of being the first European child born in New Netherland (1625). She married Tunis Bogaert, and their daughter married into the Brinckerhoff family. Height: 36 1/2″. Gift of Mrs. Edward S. Harkness. 45.151

25. This white oak stool with a carved apron was found in the Hudson River Valley and is probably seventeenth-century American in origin. It is a good example of the kind of furniture which might have been used in the homes of New Amsterdam. Height: 19 1/4″. Gift of Drs. C. Ray and Winifred Hope Franklin. 64.112.1

27. Substantial cupboards like this, called by the Dutch a *kas* (sometimes *kasse* or *kast*), were used to store linens, clothes, and household necessities. Like many other forms of Low Countries furniture, they were made in America in the late seventeenth century and, like other forms, they persisted throughout most of the eighteenth. This example was made in the New York region, probably in the first half of the eighteenth century and descended in the Ditmas family. The wood is cherry. The paneling and the ball feet are characteristic of the form as are the large dimensions, 80 5/8 × 67 1/2". Gift of John D. Talmadge. 42.170a–b

28. The ship *De Harinck (Herring)* arrived in New York on 28 March 1638, bearing Willem Kieft, the new director-general, and Oloff Stevensen van Cortlandt, who brought with him from Holland this portrait of his mother Katrien painted by M. J. van Mierevelt. The portrait is the oldest known painting from the days of New Amsterdam. Van Cortlandt was an ordinary soldier of the Dutch West India Company when he arrived but within two years he was commissioner of cargoes in the City; before his death in 1684 he rose to be burgomaster (mayor) twice, 1655–60 and 1662–63. His descendants were among the most notable New York families of the next three centuries. Oil on panel, 43 3/4 × 33 1/2″. Gift of John Pierrepont. 73.230.2

II: ROYAL NEW YORK

The city is thrifty and
quite commercial, and every one has an easy air.

—M. POUCHOT, FRENCH COMMANDANT AT NIAGARA

New York lived under the rule of England for 119 years, nearly three times longer than New Amsterdam was ruled by the Dutch and one-third of the entire history of the City.

The population increased very rapidly in royal New York. At the time of the English conquest there were about 1,500 New Yorkers. A census taken in 1698 shows 1,019 men, 1,057 women, 2,161 children, and 700 Negro slaves, for a total of 4,937 inhabitants. In 1723, there were 7,282 New Yorkers; 10,564 in 1737; in 1749, 13,290; and on the eve of the Revolution in 1771, 21,863. Negroes, freed or slave, formed a fairly constant fifteen percent of the population throughout the entire period, until at the time of the Revolution the percentage began to drop sharply. Although there was no longer significant Dutch immigration, there was continued immigration of French Protestants, of Germans (150 families of Protestant refugees from the Bavarian Palatinate in the time of Governor Lovelace, 1710), and Governor Dongan encouraged his fellow Irishmen to come to New York during his administration.

New York was more cosmopolitan than ever; Charles Lodwick (who was mayor in 1694), writing in 1692, said: "Our chiefest unhappiness here is too great a mixture of nations, and English the least part. The French Protestants have in the late king's reign resorted hither in great numbers proportionably to the other nations' inhabitants. The Dutch are generally the most frugal and laborious, and consequently the richest, whereas most of the English are the contrary."

New Yorkers were fortunate in their first royal governor. Colonel Richard Nicolls was moderate and tactful, and little friction marked the transition from Dutch rule to English. This may have been due in part to the relief of the populace in escaping the increasingly inept rule of the ailing Dutch West India Company. The government remained that of a proprietary province, but no longer controlled by a mercantile company; the Duke of York was its proprietor. Magistrates were appointed by the provincial government. The English form of municipal government with mayor and common council was quietly substituted for schout, burgomasters, and schepens. No representative legislature was granted to the people, but they were given the important right of appeal to the king; so far as democracy was concerned the English form of government in New York was little outward advance over the Dutch.

It was under Nicolls that New York was expanded to include all of Manhattan Island. The only considerable settlement absorbed was the village of Harlem, which thus became—unwillingly—part of New York. The City continued to be the headquarters for the whole vast province of New York.

The first mayor of New York was the Englishman Thomas Willett, who served in 1665 and again in 1667; his immediate successor was also English, but then Cornelis Steenwyck, who was Dutch, was named mayor. From then on throughout the English period the list of mayors is a roll-call of the principal nationalities in the City: Lawrence, De Meyer, Van Cortlandt, Rombouts, Dyer, Minvielle, Bayard, Delanoy, etc.

The English language was substituted for Dutch in the conduct of City government. As early as 16 November 1674, the court of the mayor and aldermen forbade any legal papers to be submitted to them in Dutch "on the penalty of having them thrown out."

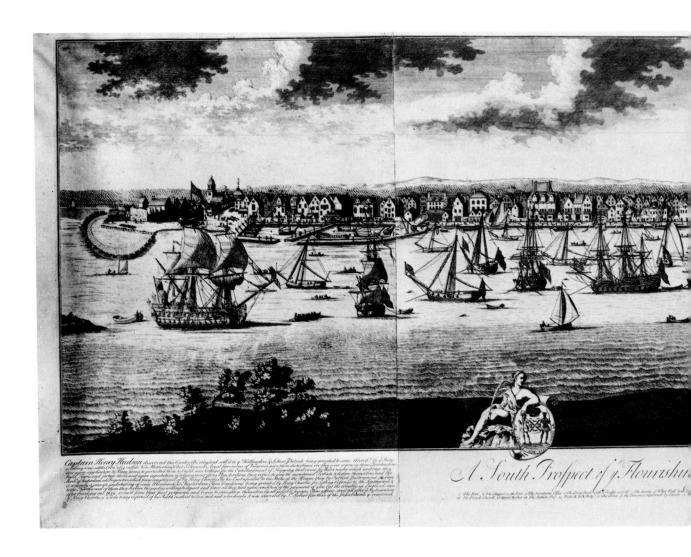

Captain Henry Hudson discovered this Coast in the year and sold it to ye Hollanders & Letters Patent being granted to some Merch.ts of ye State of Holland were settled this very called New Netherland, but Coll Nicolls, lead Governour of Virginia gave them disturbance ere they were come to their Quarters...

A South Prospect of ye Flourishu[...]

29. The most important panoramic view of the City of New York ever printed is this line engraving on copper known from the name of its engraver as "The Bakewell View." The artist was William Burgis of Boston, who originally issued his view of New York sometime between 1716 and 1718; this later issue (1747) has additions made on the plate by Thomas Bakewell of London, who was the publisher. This copy is the only recorded impression of a late state of the view. Burgis made his drawing from Brooklyn

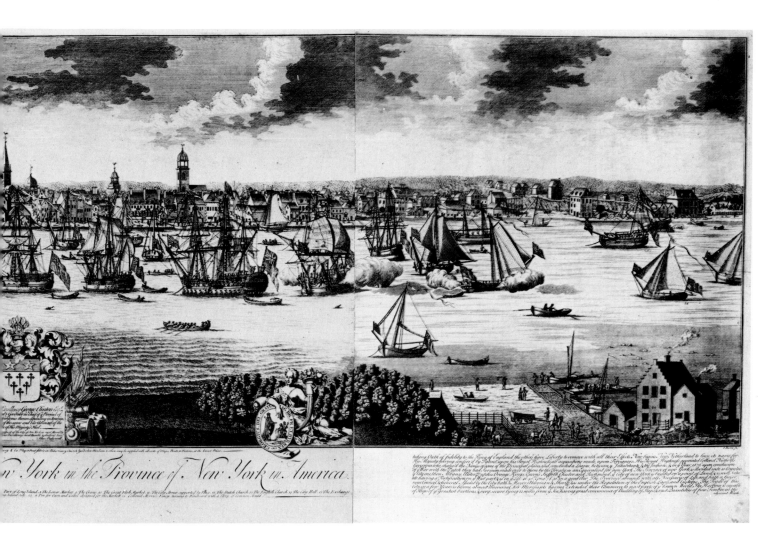

v York in the Province of New York in America.

Heights, and it shows the waterfront of New York along the East
River from the turn in State Street west of Whitehall to a point
a little north of Catherine Street. The City is evidently depicted on
some special occasion, as indicated by the large amount of
shipping in the East River, the firing of a general salute, etc.
Possibly, this was the celebration of the King's Birthday on 4 June
1717. 77 3/8 × 20 3/4". Gift of Mrs. William Sloane. 40.421.1

Dutch long persisted among part of the population as a second language. Intermarriage between prominent Dutch families and the French Protestants and English immigrants proceeded apace; for example, the Dutch Van Cortlandts with the French Jays, the English Marstons with the Dutch Philipses, the Scottish Livingstons with the Dutch Stuyvesants.

Sentimentality about New Amsterdam and Stuyvesant has stressed Dutch influence in New York; the City is rightly proud of its Dutch beginnings, but after the English conquest New York quickly and permanently focused its attention on London. Dutch influences persisted much longer in the more remote upper New York (the heart of Van Rensselaer country, so to speak) than in the City, which as a port was much more subject to new influences. Even the fifteen-month reconquest (August, 1673, to November, 1674) by the Dutch, when "New York" briefly became "New Orange" and the fort "Willem Hendrick" (both references to the stadtholder family of Holland), was only an interlude in the English domination of the City and not a lasting return to the Dutch heritage.

In religion the City became more tolerant, at least officially; by the standards of the time it was already exceedingly broad-minded. It was an age of religious consciousness; most travelers who wrote about the City began their accounts with statistics on denominations represented in New York, church buildings, and numbers of communicants. Lutherans were given permission to secure a minister of their own faith, and organized their church in 1671. The Society of Friends first met (oddly, in a tavern) the same year. The Church of England was established: Trinity Church opened for services on 13 March 1698. In 1707, when Presbyterians first tried to preach in New York, Governor Lord Cornbury imprisoned them, but they were acquitted at their trial and permitted to meet—in the City Hall. The Livingston family (descended from Robert Livingston, who was born in Rossburghshire, Scotland) were leaders in that denomination, which in the late colonial period took on political (anti-Episcopalian) overtones. The first Baptists organized in 1715.

In 1687, Governor Dongan wrote to the Committee of Trade in England: "New York has first a chaplain belonging to the fort, of the Church of England; secondly, a Dutch Calvinist; thirdly, a French Calvinist; fourthly, a Dutch Lutheran. Here be not many of the Church of England, few Roman Catholics, abundance of Quaker preachers, Ranting Quakers, Sabatarians, Anti-Sabatarians, some Anabaptists, some Independents, some Jews; in short, of all sort of opinions there are some, and the most part, none at all."

Trade with England was generally in beaver skins, whale oil, barrel staves and other lumber products, and tobacco, sent in return for numerous English-manufactured products. To the West Indies flour and bread, salted pork, and, sometimes, horses were sent; in return, rum was imported. Between 1678 and 1694 the "bolting of flour," i.e., grinding grain into flour, was the foundation of New York's commercial prosperity. In 1678, there were only three ships with New York as home port; in 1694, there were sixty. The increase was largely due to the bolting trade. When this monopoly was taken away by the Crown in 1694, it was a serious blow to the City. The new idea of mercantilism, that the home country ought to manipulate colonies for its own benefit, was flourishing, but the many English laws designed to keep the colonies in their place commercially were constantly ignored by the colonials.

New York continued to be a trading city. Merchants were the mainstay, and mercantile questions took precedence in civic considerations; for instance, in the establishment of proper weights and measures. Among the courts, one of the most important in a port like New York was that of Vice-Admiralty. Its mace, now in The Museum of the City of New York, is a surviving symbol of the English rule over New York.

The shops of this busy city were generally one-half of a dwelling house called "a double-house." The owner, although he might live very comfortably and even in considerable elegance, shared his house with his business. Cornelis Steenwyck, who served as mayor from 1668 to 1670 and from 1683 to 1684, ran a prosperous mercantile establishment (what we would call a "general store") on the southeast corner of Bridge and Whitehall streets. The street-floor front of the building was the store; the owner and his family lived at the back. Upstairs, the warehouse, was filled with fancy goods and was "the principal shopping mart of the Dutch ladies of the day."

These merchants, whether or not they lived in the back of the store, were often prosperous enough to have stately portraits painted of themselves: Benjamin Peck, John Cruger, and Moses Levy are examples.

The death of Charles II in February, 1685, brought his brother James, proprietor of New York, to the throne of England as James II. The legal status of New York changed again: it was now a royal province. Government was under the so-called "Dongan Charter," named after the royal governor. The charter provided a slightly more liberal regime than that of earlier Dutch and English governments. The choice of aldermen, assistants, and subconstables was given to voters in the six wards into which the City was divided and which long persisted in New York history.

Thomas Dongan was an Irishman and a Catholic. He was accompanied by priests, and the first Roman Catholic services in the history of the City were held in the fort under his administration. A Catholic, appointed by a Catholic—and unpopular—monarch, aroused the suspicions of the staunchly Protestant New Yorkers, but the citizens relaxed when Dongan proved himself fair and capable, few Catholics followed him, and the City prospered under his government.

Under Dongan, in 1683, counties were established in and around New York along lines which they mostly retain today: Westchester (Westchester County and the Bronx), New York (Manhattan), Kings (named after Charles II), Queens (after his queen Catherine of Portugal), and Richmond (after Charles's illegitimate son).

The "Glorious Revolution" in England (1688) led to one of the extraordinary episodes in New York history. When King James was overthrown, Lieutenant-Governor Francis Nicholson was in charge of New York, Governor Edmund Andros having departed on a visit to the Massachusetts Bay Colony. New Yorkers of "radical" (meaning anti-James and anti-Catholic) sentiments led by Jacob Leisler and Jacob Milbourne took over the government of the City.

Leisler, the son of a German Protestant clergyman, had come out to New Netherland in 1660 as a Dutch West India Company soldier, so poor he had had to acquire his gun on the installment plan (it being customary then for soldiers to furnish their own weapons), but he soon married a rich widow of the Loockermans family (one of the first families of New Amsterdam and allied with Director-General Stuyvesant himself) and became a tobacco trader. He was energetic and successful but quarrelsome and litigious—once going to court with a discharged maid over "almost a bottle of preserved strawberries and a biscuit" he claimed she had eaten while entertaining two male visitors in her master's absence at church. But Leisler made himself respected and actually was as often a referee or juryman as litigant.

He was a fierce Protestant and hand in glove with someone equally fierce, his son-in-law Jacob Milbourne. Milbourne's career before his arrival in New York did not inspire confidence; as a boy in England he had been convicted of coin-clipping and transported to Barbados. He was then sold as a bond-servant to Connecticut and finally arrived in New York at the age of twenty in 1668. There he worked (surprisingly) as a bookkeeper.

Leisler and Milbourne were able to come to the fore in New York because religious feelings ran high in the City and province, as the curious case of Dominie Nicholas van Rensselaer shows.

Although a member of the famous New York family, Van Rensselaer had lived in England, where he acquired friends in high places (he knew King Charles II during the latter's exile in Brussels), and he was an ordained minister of the Church of England. In 1674, he came to America with a letter from the Duke of York recommending that he be put in charge of one of the churches—the *Dutch* churches. This recommendation led to a heated theological row; Jacob Milbourne and other elements of the Dutch Reformed Church regarded Van Rensselaer as a divine of

30. The first print to depict a true New York City street scene is this famous engraving by William Burgis of the New Dutch Church, often called "The Rip Van Dam View" from its dedication to the president of the council of the New York colony. The copy in The Museum of the City of New York is the only one known in the first state. The view was probably taken in 1731. The street to the right of the church is Nassau and that on the left is Crown (Liberty). The language used in the church services here remained Dutch as late as 1764. The building survived use by the British during the Revolution as a prison, reopened after the Revolution, and held services until 1844, when it became the U.S. Post Office for New York. It was not demolished until 1882. The church shown in the background is the French Huguenot Church of Saint-Esprit. Carriages were rare in New York that early, and possibly Van Dam, one of the richest men of his time, owned the one pictured. Line engraving on copper, 9 3/4 × 13 3/4" including title. Gift of Mrs. James Garretson. 55.249.1

"papistical" tendencies and a tool for the English domination of the province's ecclesiastical affairs. They saw his appointment as a plot to impose Anglican rule over the old Dutch churches. The antagonism went to such lengths that Van Rensselaer was arrested and imprisoned "for some dubious words spoken in a sermon," the complainants being Leisler and Milbourne. Compromise was effected but Van Rensselaer's career was beset with similar vexations to the end of his life. His distinguished family, his important alliances (he was married to a Schuyler, daughter of another powerful family), and his learning (he owned a library of 200 volumes, said to be the largest in the province) did not preserve him from continuous attacks.

When news arrived via Barbados that James II had been overthrown and William and Mary crowned, Leisler proclaimed his allegiance to "the Protestant religion and His Royal Highness the Prince of Orange," and he and his followers celebrated the release of the colony from "tyranny, popery, and slavery." Lieutenant-Governor Nicholson, who of course had been appointed by the rejected King James, fled.

For two extraordinary years Leisler and his adherents were the government of the City. They had their opportunity largely on account of the dilatoriness of William of Orange in sending out a proper government. A new governor, Henry Sloughter, was appointed, but *sixteen months* elapsed between his appointment and his landing on American shores. In March, 1691, when he finally set foot in New York, he demanded surrender of the fort from the Leislerian forces. Leisler and Milbourne made the fatal mistake of waiting twenty-four hours before complying, thus presenting the Crown with some basis for trying them on a charge of treason. Leisler and Milbourne were in fact tried, convicted, and hanged in the midst of a terrible storm; their lifeless bodies were beheaded on 16 May 1691.

The verdict and the executions were very unpopular in both New York and England. Leisler had, at least by his own lights, filled a vacuum in the legal government of the province and had never ceased to proclaim his loyalty to the lawfully constituted government of England. In his final address from the gallows he proclaimed that he died "a martyr for King William." The charge against him and Milbourne obviously should have been sedition (not a capital offense) rather than treason. Four years later Parliament reviewed the case, reversed the decision, and cleared the names of the unfortunates. This was not enough, and from then on it is possible to see in the history of New York two parties of constantly varying names, "the Presbyterians" versus "the Episcopalians," "popular" versus "court," but one always the "American" descending from the Leislerians, and the other the "English."

But there was no more real political violence for half a century, until the first stirrings of the Revolution, and peaceful New York kept getting larger and on the whole more prosperous.

New York was not very well governed. The English governors of the province, with the exception of Dongan and a few others, were a poor lot. Edward Hyde, Lord Cornbury (governor, 1701–8), despite his distinguished family (he was grandson of the historian and statesman Clarendon and first cousin to Queen Anne) was most unsatisfactory. Although married and the father of many children, he persisted in dressing as a woman, had his portrait painted in a low-necked gown, and spent so much money (he did not distinguish very clearly between his own and the City's) that he was arrested for debt and practically expelled from the province. Lord Lovelace, his successor, arrived in New York, 18 December 1708, and died there 6 May 1709. His secretary said "he never had a well day in his government." Nearly a third of the governors died while at their post, sometimes within a short time of their arrival at New York.

Many of the governors seemed to have difficulty even *getting* to New York. Some of them waited months before embarking for America; others fell ill just after their appointment; some went to New England, presumably more salubrious, on extended stays. Interregnums when there was no royal governor in New York occurred with astonishing frequency: there were twenty-two such hiatuses in the royal rule of the colony. When a governor failed to appear, died in office, or absented himself, a lieutenant-governor was in charge of New York. Some of these were remarkable men, usually colonials themselves, sometimes New York born. They included James de Lancey, a native, longtime chief justice of the province, and founding leader of the "Episcopalian party," who served as lieutenant-governor on two different occasions, and the Irishman Cadwallader Colden, scientist, student of the American Indians, and prolific author on science and philosophy, who was lieutenant-governor no fewer than five times.

The city over which these governors presided is shown about 1717 in the Bakewell view when it was the third largest city in the English colonies, after Boston and Philadelphia. The reference key below the cartouche lists twenty-four landmarks of the City including the fort, "the ruines of White Hall" (which had been Stuyvesant's town house), the City Hall, various slips and wharfs, and of course the churches. No. 24 is a yacht, "Collonel Morris's Fancy turning to Windward. . . ." This is probably the first view showing an American yacht. In addition to the twenty-four keyed buildings, etc., close scrutiny of this remarkable engraving has enabled historians to identify numerous other landmarks. The indefatigable I. N. Phelps Stokes and his researchers were able to locate no less than 105 landmarks on this view, all of which are listed in Stokes's *Iconography of Manhattan Island*. And yet, despite the overall accuracy of the view, it is incorrectly titled "South Prospect" of New York; actually the view is from the east, looking west across the East River.

In the city shown in the Bakewell view, life was more luxurious than it had been in Dutch times. Commercial progress had brought the wherewithal for elegant living. Lamothe-Cadillac, a French visitor, wrote as early as 1692 about New York: "This town is much richer in money than Boston." Rich families were able to import items of luxury—porcelain, for example, from China. Even under the Dutch New York had always been gayer than the psalm-singing cities to the north and south, and sober visitors had long shaken their heads over the expensive dresses of New York

ladies, their carriages (always rare anywhere in the colonies), and their entertainments. Even New York dolls of the period reflect the elegance of the clothing.

New Yorkers have never been averse to displaying financial assets, and household silver of aesthetic and monetary significance was made in large amounts throughout the colonial period. It is noticeable that much silver continued to be made in the Dutch manner, and many of the silversmiths were Dutch: Benjamin Wynkoop, Adrian Bancker, and Nicholas Roosevelt. In England and in America, silversmiths of French Protestant background were noted in the eighteenth century, and in New York several of the greatest craftsmen in silver were Huguenots: Simeon Soumain and the Le Roux dynasty.

Walnut and mahogany furniture of the eighteenth century in New York has not been so highly esteemed by connoisseurs as that made in Newport and Philadelphia, but it has its merits of rich solidity and fine carving. Both the Queen Anne and Chippendale styles are well represented in the collections of The Museum of the City of New York.

John Adams visited New York in 1774 and was entertained in lavish rooms filled with fine furniture and silver. In his diary he wrote rather sourly in a famous quotation about New York: "With all the Opulence and Splendor of this City, there is very little good Breeding to be found. We have been treated with an assiduous Respect. But I have not seen one real Gentleman, one well bred Man since I came to Town. At their Entertainments there is no Conversation that is agreable. There is no Modesty—No Attention to one another. They talk very loud, very fast and alltogether. If they ask you a Question, before you can utter 3 words of your Answer, they will break out upon you, again—and talk away."

Governor John Montgomerie died in office in New York, but in his short administration (1728–31) he granted the City a new charter which remained in use until after the formation of the United States. It mainly reaffirmed the liberties, such as they were, of the Dongan charter, but the mayor was still appointed by the governor, and in general it was no advance in the right of New Yorkers to control their own affairs.

When Montgomerie died suddenly, the executive function devolved upon Rip van Dam, a wealthy merchant of Dutch descent who spoke English only imperfectly. New York's Dutch element was much pleased at his holding the city's most important office, of which the dedication to Rip van Dam of the famous print of the New Dutch Church is an indication. When the new governor Colonel William Cosby arrived in 1736, he plunged at once into a lively controversy with Van Dam over the accumulated perquisites of the office. One of the principal events of his administration was the trial of John Peter Zenger for printing a "seditious libel" against Cosby's government in his *New York Weekly Journal* newspaper. The court's verdict on Zenger of "not guilty" was a notable victory for freedom of the press in the English colonies.

In the spring of 1741, a succession of house robberies and mysterious, devastating fires attacked the most important citadels of government in New York: the governor's house, the secretary's office, the chapel, and some other buildings in the fort were destroyed. The population was apprehensive. It was believed that the City's Negro slaves were planning to seize the town with the help of certain criminal whites, notably the tavernkeeper John Hughson, a receiver of stolen goods, and possibly a few Indians under the control of Spain. There was some reason for alarm: an insurrection in 1712 had resulted in nine white men killed and twenty-one Negro slaves executed. Now, confessions by various whites and Negroes were brought before a grand jury and court, and the sinister events became "The Negro Conspiracy." There were trials of whites and Negroes. Four whites (including Hughson and his wife) and twenty-nine Negroes were executed; seventy-one Negroes were transported, fifty-two pardoned.

New York had been rather slow to develop culturally, but in the year 1754 there were two important developments: King's College (later to be called Columbia) received its first students in its building on Broadway between Church and Barclay streets, and the New York Society Library was formed by a group of subscribers who established their small collection of books in City Hall. Both institutions were formed amidst furious rows between "Episcopalians" and "Presbyterians."

"Episcopalians" and "Presbyterians" were at loggerheads when Governor George Clinton arrived in 1743. Although he appointed James de Lancey, leader of the "Episcopalians," to be chief justice of the province, as expected, governor and justice soon fell out. Clinton became extremely unpopular and eventually secured his own recall. He departed, followed by the curses of New Yorkers. His successor, Sir Danvers Osborn, arrived on the same day, 10 October 1753. Apparently the hatred with which the populace pursued the outgoing Clinton impressed Osborn's mind to the point of unhinging it. New York was too much for Osborn; four days after his arrival he went into the garden of the governor's residence and hanged himself.

On the eve of the American Revolution, New York had about 20,000 inhabitants and had passed Boston to become the second city of the colonies—after Philadelphia. The bulk of the population still lived south of Wall Street, as it had since the City's founding. Despite English regulations, the trade of the province was thriving; more than 200 ships a year cleared the port of New York. In general, the exports of New York were still those of earlier times: lumber and wood products, skins, and flour. The City manufactured surprisingly little. Some important business firms were being founded, however, and a few of these are still in existence and still operating in New York, among them Caswell-Massey (founded 1752, the oldest pharmacy in America), Devoe & Raynolds (founded 1754, manufacturers of paints), and P. Lorillard (founded 1760, the oldest tobacco company in America).

Since New York thrived and grew in commerce and in population and was the capital city of a large and important province, thousands of its citizens, despite dissatisfaction with many moves of the English government toward the colonies and chronic grumbling at London, felt no necessity of permanently rending the ties that linked them with Great Britain; that was to be the tragedy of New York during the American Revolution.

31. Samuel Vetch was a Scot who came to New York as a soldier in 1699. Just a year later he was married to Margaret Livingston, daughter of Robert Livingston, Secretary of Indian Affairs (the families had been acquainted in Scotland). He was soon deep in the Indian trade and illicit dealings with the French in Canada. Tried and fined by the general court of the Colony of Massachusetts, Vetch fled to safety in England. However, in 1711 he was back leading a military attack against the French in Nova Scotia. Governor there from 1715 to 1717, his personal affairs forced his recall to England, where he died in prison in "the King's bench for debt" in 1732. Portrait by an unknown artist, 1703. 41 × 50". Gift of Julian Ricketts Speyers and Mrs. Edith Speyers Kelley. 49.322.1

32. Harmanus Wendell,
Commissioner of Indian Affairs
in the Colony of New York, was
painted by an anonymous artist
whose "signature" was the use of
"Aetatis Sue," meaning "in a
certain year of one's age,"
followed by a date. Wendell was
forty years old when this painting
was done in 1718. Oil on canvas,
44 × 35 1/4". Gift of John
Wendell Minturn. 48.13

33. Moses Levy, shown here in a portrait in the florid British style attributed to the anonymous painter called "The De Peyster Limner," came to New York from England about 1695. His granddaughter Phila Franks was married outside the Jewish faith to the Loyalist Oliver De Lancey and fled with him to England during the Revolution. The Levy and Franks families were Ashkenazic and leaders in the small Jewish group in New York which in 1730 counted twenty-nine heads of families. Oil on canvas, 42 1/2 × 33 1/2″. Bequest of Alphonse H. Kursheedt. 36.343.1

34. John Cruger, Sr., here painted by an unknown artist, was prominent in the commerce of New York throughout most of his long life. As a young man, in 1698–1700 he acted as the agent for New York merchants in the slave trade and made a voyage to Africa to secure slaves. Forty years later he became mayor of the City (1739–44). Oil on canvas, 45 × 36″. Gift of Mrs. Bernice Chrysler Garbisch. 57.230.1

35. Benjamin Peck, shown in this solemn portrait attributed to Joseph Badger, gave his name to Peck Slip, still to be found on the East River in Lower Manhattan. Peck owned extensive water-lots in that area of New York. Badger, who never signed his portraits, was a New Englander who also painted houses and signs. Oil on canvas, 50 3/8 × 40 1/2″. Bequest of Miss Ellen A. Jarvis. 57.91

36. Abraham de Peyster was a native New Amsterdamer, born in 1657, the son of one of the City's most prosperous citizens. He was mayor from 1691 to 1694. The De Peyster home stood on Pearl Street (then Queen) between Pine and Cedar facing west. After the British evacuation of New York in the Revolution it was General George Clinton's headquarters. Amazingly, the house was not demolished until 1856, at which time it was believed to be the oldest building in the City. The bronze statue of De Peyster by George E. Bissell standing now on Bowling Green was presented to the City by a descendant in 1896. Portrait attributed to Gerret Duyckinck. Oil on canvas, 25 × 30″ oval. Gift of Miss Augusta M. De Peyster. 59.84.1

37–38. Mr. and Mrs. Philip Philipse (Margaret Marston) were painted by John Wollaston, probably at the time of their marriage in 1751. The Museum of the City of New York also owns portraits of her parents, Mr. and Mrs. Nathaniel Marston. Marston was a rich New York City landowner who gave £1,200 toward the founding of King's College (Columbia). Oil on canvas in contemporary frames, 50 × 40 1/2″. Gift of Mrs. Frederic Grosvenor Goodridge. 32.312.1–2

39. This miniature tankard was made by Charles Le Roux, who worked in New York, 1710–45. It is initialed MR, probably for Maria Rutgers, who was baptized in 1716. Height: 3 3/4″ to thumbpiece. Gift of Nicholas G. Rutgers, Jr., Mrs. George Coe, and Mrs. Marshall J. Dodge, Jr., in memory of Mr. and Mrs. Nicholas G. Rutgers. 62.166.5

41. In 1714, the corporation of the City determined to establish proper weights and measures, obviously to eliminate disputes in the market, and sent to London for a standard set certified by the lord mayor. This vessel, which is inscribed "Citey of New York 1714," is the quart measure, apparently based on the old English ale gallon. Height: 6 1/2″. Gift of Mrs. Malcolm E. Smith and Mrs. William Wickham Hoffman. 41.291

40. Benjamin Wynkoop, a New York silversmith working between 1698 and 1728, made this handsome tankard with characteristic New York features including the applied leaf band and the corkscrew thumbpiece. The exuberantly engraved arms are those of the Klock family ("klock" is Dutch for "bell"). The cypher on the top is AK, probably for Albertus Klock, and the initials on the handle, K over A∗T, are probably for him and his wife Trintje. Height: 7 1/2″ to top of thumbpiece. Bequest of Mrs. Katharine Brady Harris. 52.132

42–44. New York City was wholeheartedly in favor of the Glorious Revolution of 1689 in England which dethroned the Roman Catholic James II and elevated the Protestant monarchs William and Mary. Various anti-Catholic laws were passed, and until after the Revolution no Roman Catholic church was built in the City. Although little threatened by the events in Scotland in 1745, when Jacobite supporters of James II's son the Young Pretender rose against the British government, the colonists supported government suppression of the Jacobites. Anti-Catholic and anti-Jacobite designs are common in the English decorative arts of the time. Hugues Lossieux made this beaker in Saint-Malo, France, in 1707–8. It was engraved in New York in 1750 by Joseph Leddel or his son of the same name, both of whom were pewterers, with typical anti-Catholic and anti-Pretender verses. Height: 3 1/16″. Museum Purchase. 76.79

45. This seventeen-piece tea set of "China Trade" porcelain has an unusually early history, having belonged to Hendrick Rutgers, a shopkeeper who became freeman of the City of New York on 12 November 1734, and his wife Catharina de Peyster. The design is in black and gold, and like all such services of this period the pieces are quite small, the teapot standing only 5 1/2" high. From the Collection of Waldron Phoenix Belknap, Jr. 58.12.21a–v

46. Courts of Vice-Admiralty with jurisdiction over maritime cases were established in the American colonies under the Navigation Act of 1696. This silver mace in the form of an oar was made in New York by Charles Le Roux about 1725, and is engraved on the loom in handsome script "Court of the Vice Admiralty New York." Its function was purely symbolic. Length: 22 1/4". Deposited by the United States District Court for the Southern District of New York. L2966a

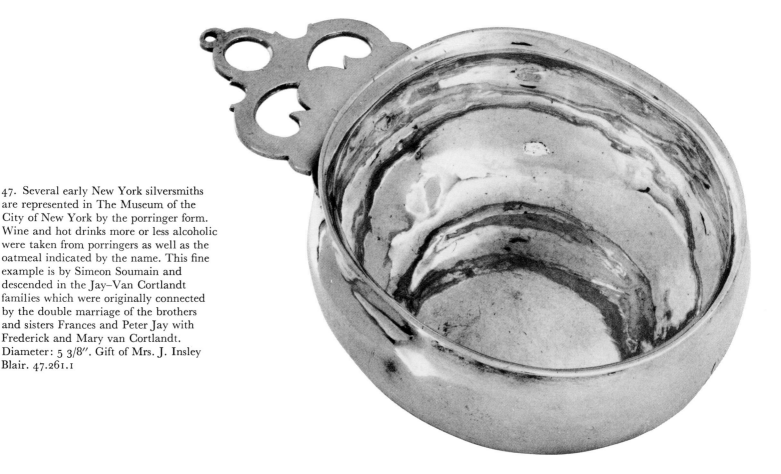

47. Several early New York silversmiths are represented in The Museum of the City of New York by the porringer form. Wine and hot drinks more or less alcoholic were taken from porringers as well as the oatmeal indicated by the name. This fine example is by Simeon Soumain and descended in the Jay–Van Cortlandt families which were originally connected by the double marriage of the brothers and sisters Frances and Peter Jay with Frederick and Mary van Cortlandt. Diameter: 5 3/8". Gift of Mrs. J. Insley Blair. 47.261.1

48. This elegant chest of drawers in the Chippendale style is typical of the simple but luxurious mahogany furniture of New York about 1760–80. 33 1/2 × 42″. Gift of Mr. and Mrs. Milton Hepner. 65.1

49–50. Samuel Prince, "joyner," made this chest of drawers of mahogany and whitewood about 1770. The top drawer is fitted with writing board, mirror, and compartments for toilet articles and writing accessories. The maker's label, which is very rare in colonial American furniture, is from his shop "At the Sign of the Chest of Drawers" located in Cart and Horse Street, later called William Street. It was also headquarters for John Sheiuble, organ builder, who advertised as the maker and repairer of "all kinds of Organs, Harpsichords, Spinnets, and Piano." 33 5/8 × 40 1/4". Gift of Mr. and Mrs. Eric M. Wunsch. 70.4

51. Bartholomew Barwell, who advertised in 1749 as being lately arrived in New York from Bath and at the service of New Yorkers for cleaning and mending clocks, made and signed the brass face of this japanned long-case clock between 1749 and 1760. The japanning (which imitates the popular oriental lacquer) may have been done by Gerardus Duyckinck, Jr. The clock once belonged to the Meserole family of Bushwick, Long Island, and Turtle Bay, Manhattan. Height: 92″. Bequest of Mrs. Henry de Bevoise Schenck. 43.91.31

52. Card games were a mania in the eighteenth century, and English New York was no exception. Games were played on handsome tables such as this one, made in New York about 1765–80. The top, which folds, has smooth square reserves for candles and inset pockets to hold coins and counters. The large scale of the table, its forceful serpentine form, and the elegant gadrooning are characteristic of New York cabinet work of this era. Height: 27 3/4″; width: 34″. Bequest of Virginia T. Nicholas. 71.72

53. The Queen Anne style in New York furniture is shown in this side chair of walnut and walnut veneer on maple, which is one of a pair made between 1730 and 1750 and originally owned by a family in Flushing, Long Island. The carved shell and flower designs on the crest rail and on the knees are typical of New York work of the period but the trifid front feet are unusual. Height: 39 1/2″. Gift of Mrs. Screven Lorillard, from the collection of her mother, Mrs. J. Insley Blair. 53.150.8

55. Whitehead Hicks, last mayor of New York before the Revolution, owned this New York Chippendale chair, which is one of a set of four. The ruffle and tassel design on the back splat is found on several sets of chairs made by an unknown craftsman for New York families. Height: 38 1/4″. Gift of Henry Rogers Winthrop, descendant of Hicks. 43.335.1a

54. Nothing could be a clearer example of the rich and dignified style of English New York than this handsome side chair of walnut which descended in the Thompson family of Brooklyn and Long Island. The design of the back splat is modeled on plate 12 of Chippendale's *Director* of 1762. Its presence in the colonies shows how quickly the new styles could arrive in New York from London. Height: 38 1/8″. Gift of Mrs. Screven Lorillard, from the collection of her mother, Mrs. J. Insley Blair. 53.150.19

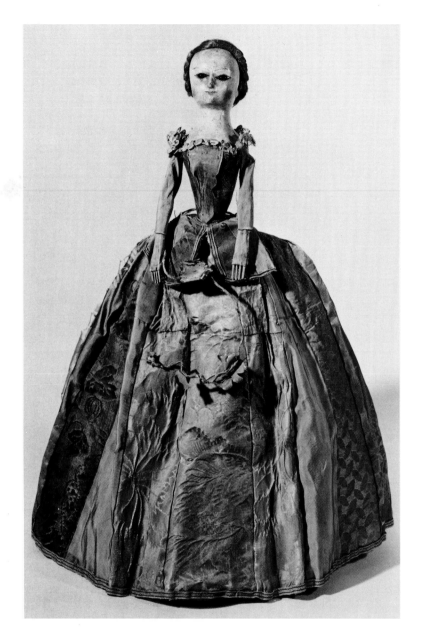

56. "Mary Jenkins" was brought to New York in 1748 as a gift for a little girl of that name, then two years old, and remained among her descendants until arriving at The Museum of the City of New York two centuries later. This English doll is outstanding for the carving of its features. The dress appears to be commercially made, the skirt being lined with paper. 21″ high. Gift of Mrs. Theodore C. Jessup and Mrs. Kenneth C. Carter. 76.82

57. "Abigail van Rensselaer," from about 1760, is also an English doll, with waxed wooden head. Like other dolls with historic associations, she is named after the little girl who originally owned her. She was re-dressed in the 1830s. Height: 9 1/2″. Gift of Mrs. Sophia S. McDonald. 63.46.3

III: THE CAPITAL OF TORY AMERICA: NEW YORK IN THE AMERICAN REVOLUTION

*Two-thirds of the property of
the city of New-York and the suburbs belongs to the
Tories. We have no very great reason
to run any considerable risk for its defence.*

—GENERAL NATHANAEL GREENE TO GENERAL GEORGE
WASHINGTON, "NEW-YORK ISLAND," 5 SEPTEMBER
1776

The twenty years between the 1763 treaty signed by France and Great Britain settling their longtime North American disputes and the final evacuation of British troops from Manhattan at the conclusion of the American Revolution in 1783 were among the most dramatic and destructive in the City's history.

Unfortunately for the Americans, and particularly for the port cities of the colonies, after 1763 England was in a better position to enforce the navigation laws which were intended to keep the trade of the colonies confined to British ships. Worse yet, trade in some commodities was restricted to Great Britain altogether or to the British colonies in the West Indies. These were the laws that had been comfortably ignored by the colonists for years without much serious effort on the part of England to enforce them. The first British effort to tighten the screws came just four years after the 1763 treaty. The Townshend Acts of 1767 were aimed at enforcing navigation laws as well as taxing the colonists to support a standing military force in the American colonies.

About 1763, a junior British officer stationed in America, Capt. Thomas Howdell, drew the prospect of New York on the eve of the Revolution known as "The Howdell-Canot South-East View," giving us a fairly accurate portrait (except for the palm trees, a typical engraver's embellishment of any American view).

In New York, where the trade of the port was the very fount of prosperity and where merchants were the most respected men and leaders, the populace was outraged by the Townshend Acts and other new moves of the British government which they regarded as high-handed. An opposition party, which descended even if remotely from the Leislerian faction, was formed. It was a sort of loose but constant underground movement in the City in these years, but it controlled the provincial assembly, which before 1763 had won a succession of privileges from the mother country relating to Indian affairs, fortifications, revenue, etc., and was now astonished to find itself rapidly losing not only privileges but rights.

In 1765, George Grenville's ministry passed the Stamp Act, laying a tax on all legal documents executed within the colonies. This unintelligent act placed a tax squarely on colonial lawyers and men of property—the best educated colonials, those most resentful of English superiority and most likely to lead opposition to parliamentary actions. Organizations called "Sons of Liberty" and "Committees of Correspondence" were immediately formed. The fact that Parliament and the government expected no opposition to the act is a good indication of how out of touch they were with the

61

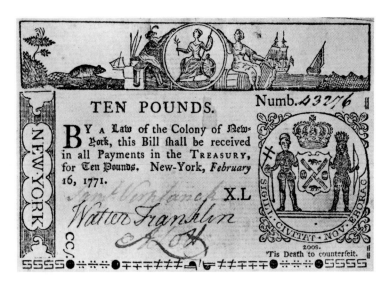

58. There was a permanent shortage of coins in British America, and all the colonies issued paper money, often in excessive quantities. This ten pound note of the New York Colony is dated 16 February 1771. Abraham Lott, who signed it along with Samuel Verplanck and Walter Franklin, was treasurer of the colony and like many other treasurers succumbed to temptation. A year after this note was issued the Assembly found that Lott had been "imprudent but not dishonest." Engraving, 2 3/4 × 4". Gift of Mrs. de Peyster Hosmer. 41.33.2

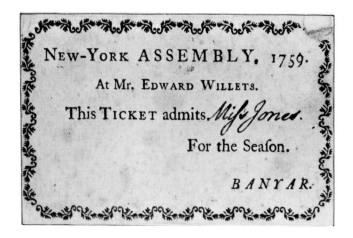

59. Dances were held at public taverns in colonial New York by groups who rented the rooms. This is a season ticket for "Miss Jones" to balls at Mr. Edward Willet's, a tavern formerly located at 115 Broadway. Engraving, 2 × 3 1/4".
The J. Clarence Davies Collection. 29.100.3512

colonies or disdainful of their opinion; little attention was paid to its passage in Parliament. Shortsighted monetary policies on England's part had already helped set the stage for rebellion.

Colonial indignation at the Stamp Act is shown in the speed of reaction. As quickly as October, 1765, a general congress of delegates from all but five of the English colonies met at the City Hall in New York and drew up petitions and memorials to the king, the House of Lords, and the Commons.

The merchants of New York strenuously objected to the act. As Evert Bancker wrote: "The merchants of this City are come to a Resolution to which above 400 of us have set our hands that unless the Stamp Act is repealed that we shall not sell any European goods that are shipped after the 1 January 1766."

When the inflammatory stamps actually arrived in New York, great meetings were held, and there were parades not only of merchants, but of "tradesmen, mechanics, and other workingmen." The effigy of Lieutenant-Governor Cadwallader Colden (complete with gray hair—he was seventy-seven years old) was gleefully burned. The use of the stamped paper was successfully refused; the Stamp Act was repealed 18 March 1766. The prestige of His Majesty's government never really recovered. Various new and almost equally irritating taxes were then ordered by England, including the celebrated import duty on tea (paint, paper, and glass were also covered, but that is now forgotten).

The Sons of Liberty in New York were divided among themselves now in their attitude toward the British government. The organizers of the Sons had included men such as William Smith, William Livingston, and Evert Bancker, men of substance and basically conservative. These leaders were now challenged by men like Alexander McDougall and Marinus Willett who were full of fury at the British and already talked of revolution, independence, and republicanism. When the election for a committee was held on 19 May 1774, the "radical" element was defeated, a sign of "Tory" strength in New York.

In the meantime, relations between New Yorkers and British troops stationed in the City had become constantly abrasive. A "Liberty Pole" after the model of Roman times (evidence of the classicism in the minds of eighteenth-century men) was erected by the New Yorkers; it was promptly blown up by the soldiers. The patriots then put up another in "The Fields" (now City Hall Park) near the encampment of the British troops. Next, on 18 January 1770, soldiers and citizens clashed at the little rise on John Street known as "Golden Hill" in what is sometimes called (mostly by New Yorkers) "the first engagement of the American Revolution" because it occurred several days before the Boston Massacre. One man was killed at Golden Hill and several wounded.

The other colonies continued to import dutiable British goods; the merchants of New York did the same, with the exception that when tea was consigned it was not accepted. Because of the uproar over tea, the British government closed the port of Boston to commerce. When Boston asked support from New York, another serious division arose among the citizenry. Again, the conservatives won; they sent Boston their sympathy but declined to enter into a nonimportation agreement, an additional indication of the New York determination not to rush headlong into rebellion.

News of the battles at Lexington and Concord reached New York on Sunday morning, 23 April 1775. There was exuberant reaction to these events on the part of the "rabble" of New York, i.e., the radical faction among the lower classes. A mob broke into the arsenal and seized 600 muskets. The keys of the Customs House were taken, as were all public stores. Having done this much the patriots were somewhat at a loss. "The armed citizens were constantly parading about the City without any definite object," wrote Marinus Willett, a radical himself but scornful of this undirected energy.

In June, delegates from the different counties of the New York colony met in New York and authorized the enlistment of troops for the defense of the colony. But during the summer a strange quiet fell over the City. It was a sort of "phony war." George Washington passed through New York on 27 June on his way to take command of the army assembling near Boston, and

on the very same day the royal Governor William Tryon, returning from a visit to England (even in this critical time royal governors were away from their posts), arrived in New York. Both were greeted enthusiastically by their followers, "Whigs" for Washington, "Tories" for Tryon, but there was no violence.

British ships were lying in New York harbor while the New Yorkers were choosing sides, and by October the City was so restless that Tryon, alarmed, went on board one of the vessels and governed the City from it. During the following bitter-cold February the American general Charles Lee arrived, sent by Washington to supervise the construction of defenses for New York, including a fort on the East River at the foot of present East 88th Street. Washington entered New York on 13 April and headquartered at the "Richmond Hill" house in Greenwich Village on the block now bounded by King, Varick, Charlton, and Macdougal streets. He was accompanied by his aide Alexander Hamilton, a former King's College student, and a band of young, officers who were already beginning to wear the American uniform of blue and buff (as opposed to the British red and white) of which a rare example is preserved in The Museum of the City of New York.

By this time many fearful New Yorkers, regardless of their political loyalties, had fled the city. General Sir William Howe, his brother Richard Admiral Lord Howe, shortly followed by General Clinton and Lord Cornwallis, now arrived at New York. Their ships and men took up positions nearly surrounding New York, and about 25,000 British troops now faced the terrified City. General Washington had scattered about at New York, Governor's Island, Paulus Hook, and the nearer parts of Long Island about 18,000 men; of these only about 10,500 were considered fit for duty.

The provincial congress of New York approved the Declaration of Independence (or "Independency" as it was referred to then) on 9 July 1776, and on the 18th it was publicly proclaimed from the City Hall on Wall Street. The large crowd gathered before the Hall "signified their approbation of it by loud acclamations." The royal coat-of-arms was torn to pieces and the new

American flag raised for the first time over the seat of New York's government. Patriots ran about the streets tearing down royal arms wherever they were displayed, even on tavern signs. The Committee of Safety ordered churches to omit the prayers for the sovereign in their services, but the vestry of Trinity Church closed the church rather than comply.

Hospitals were set up, earthworks thrown up, and batteries planted on both the North and East rivers. General Washington, addressed now as "His Excellency," took up residence at the Kennedy House, No. 1 Broadway. The general was much concerned about the civilians remaining in the City and wrote to the provincial congress: "When I consider that the City of New York will in all human probability, very soon be the scene of a bloody conflict, I can not but view the great numbers of women, children, and infirm persons remaining in it with the most melancholy concern. When the men-of-war passed up the river, the shrieks and cries of these poor creatures, running every way with their children, was truly distressing; and I fear will have an unhappy effect on the ears and minds of our young and inexperienced soldiery. Can no method be devised for their removal?" The congress gave orders for evacuating many of these noncombatants.

The British and American armies met on 27 August at the engagements known as the Battle of Long Island. The British were everywhere victorious. If a heavy rain followed by an unusually dense fog had not fallen, Washington and the entire American army might have been captured, but under the cover of rain and fog Washington succeeded in removing his entire surviving force across the East River into Manhattan.

There was no possibility that Washington's forces could hold New York. In the early weeks of September the many sick and wounded American soldiers were taken out of the City, followed by the able troops, thousands of patriots, their belongings and livestock. They straggled up what is now the East Side between Third and Fifth avenues to the Harlem River at 130th Street and up Broadway to Union Square and along the Bloomingdale Road as far as Kingsbridge. Hugh Gaine, publisher of the patriotic *New-York Gazette*, fled to Newark with his press. Augustus van Cortlandt, the city clerk, saved the City's records by placing them in the family vault near his family's mansion in the Bronx. The bells of the churches and the brass knockers from doors were taken down and removed from British range for fear they might be captured and melted into cannon. Some patriots took advantage of the confusion to beat up and rob Loyalists before leaving. It was a sad period in New York's history, and according to one of Washington's own generals "a miserable, disorderly retreat."

Washington now took up his headquarters at the Morris Mansion. It was at this time that the celebrated capture and trial of Nathan Hale occurred and gave New York City and the country one of their most durable heroes. The British troops took up their position on a hill commanding McGown's Pass at present-day 107th Street, just a few blocks north of The Museum of the City of New York. On 16 September the British and American troops were engaged again, at the Battle of Harlem Heights on the high ground now occupied by Grant's Tomb and Columbia University. The Americans won, at least to the extent of holding their own, but Washington retreated to White Plains, and the scene of further battles of the Revolution shifted away from New York City.

The British had now taken possession of New York City, to the joy of Tories who expressed their satisfaction in the famous "Loyal Addresses" to the Howes. Returning Loyalists came back to a melancholy sight. One wrote that he found New York on his return "a most dirty, desolate, and wretched place." Another, that New York presented "a most melancholy appearance, being deserted and pillaged." A military establishment now ruled the City although the office of mayor was continued in the person of the Loyalist David Mathews (the mayor at the outbreak of the Revolution, Whitehead Hicks, having wisely resigned). From late 1776 until 1783, New York was the capital of Tory America and the mecca and refuge of Loyalists from all over the colonies.

A series of fires, possibly accidental (after all, New York was notoriously subject to conflagrations) but at the time supposed to have been deliberately set either by "rebels" or "Tories" (depending on which side was telling the story), ravaged the City in these years. The fires began on 21 September 1776, when one of the worst disasters in the City's history began near Whitehall. British soldiers were sent in to fight the fire but about a quarter of the City was wholly demolished. King's College and St. Paul's Chapel were saved, but Trinity Church, the Lutheran Church, and over 1,000 houses were not. The fire was thought to have been set by departing American troops; one writer said that the burning was ascribed to the rebels "as that of Rome was to the Christians."

Less than two years later, another fire, although not nearly so bad as that of 1776, did further damage to the already devastated City, and on the following day, 4 August 1778, an ordnance ship with 260 pounds of gunpowder on board blew up in the East River and damaged many more buildings.

Outside New York, the civilian government of the new state of New York was meeting in Kingston, where a constitution was adopted on 20 April 1777. George Clinton was elected governor, John Jay chief justice, and Robert R. Livingston, Jay's former law partner, chancellor.

One of the curiosities of the British occupation of the City was that since most of the departed patriots were Dissenters their churches (Presbyterian, Dutch Reformed, and Huguenot) were used by the British for prisons, stables, hospitals, riding schools, etc., while the Anglican churches (except for the burned Trinity) continued and flourished. The few students of King's College, an Anglican institution, took up their studies in a house on Wall Street since the College building had become a hospital. Life in New York was nervous but strangely jolly, perhaps because the Dissenter element had left; plays were presented at the little theater in John Street, an orchestra performed in Trinity Churchyard, and cricket was played near the Jews' Cemetery in Chatham Square.

But the poorer citizens suffered much. The fires and the terrible winter of 1776–77 made their life almost unbearable. Worse still, captured American troops

60–61. King's College (Columbia) gave Benjamin Moore this silver medal for literary excellence, probably at the time of his graduation in 1768. His distinguished undergraduate career was a token of future success, for he became professor of rhetoric and logic at his alma mater and served as president of Columbia from 1801 to 1811, while he was also Episcopal Bishop of New York. He retired to his house in Greenwich Village (called "The Pulpit") on present-day 20th Street between Eighth and Ninth avenues. Diameter: 2 1/2″. Gift of Mrs. Robert Le Roy. 46.354.1

numbering in the thousands were languishing in makeshift prisons or even prison ships in the harbor or in Wallabout Bay, where horrible conditions and disease carried them off by the hundreds.

After Cornwallis surrendered in October, 1781, Washington returned to the neighborhood of New York, but there was little military action while the English made up their minds whether to continue the war. News of the negotiation for peace and the king's proclamation of the cessation of hostilities reached New York and was read at noon, 8 April 1783, from the balcony at the City Hall.

This news was received in a wholly unexpected manner by the people of New York. Instead of noises of approval, the Loyalist crowd groaned and hissed and heaped "bitter reproaches and curses upon their King for having deserted them in the midst of their calamities." Loyalists from all over the colonies had poured into New York during the previous six years; throughout the summer of 1783, more thousands were concentrated by the British in the City. They petitioned the king for resettlement in Nova Scotia, the British West Indies, or England itself. In the autumn of 1782, the first group left for Nova Scotia, 460 families. In September, a whole fleet of British ships carrying more than 8,000 Loyalists left for the same destination. Thousands more followed, including about one-third of the population of New York, the mayor, many officials, representatives of many notable New York families, including Philipses, Morrises, Robinsons, De Lanceys, Whites, and scores of others, bag, baggage, and slaves.

Passage for the Loyalists was one of the many arrangements made by Sir Guy Carleton, British commander at New York, who also was arranging through the summer and autumn for surrender of the City to General Washington, who was waiting on the outskirts.

On 25 November 1783, Carleton called in the British troops from McGown's Pass and Kingsbridge. General Washington, accompanied by Governor Clinton and troops commanded by General Knox, marched from Harlem to the Bowery Lane. The British troops retired from the post there. When the Americans marched in, they took possession of the City of New York, again raising the American standard. A salute of thirteen guns was fired from the fort at the Battery while the British troops embarked on ships waiting in the harbor. Washington and his followers then made their public entry into the City on horseback. Perfect order and quiet, ever the mark of Washington's arrangements, prevailed from the beginning to the end of the Evacuation. "Evacuation Day" became a patriotic holiday in New York second only to July Fourth and was celebrated for decades.

After a stay of less than two weeks in New York, General Washington assembled his officers at Fraunces Tavern on Pearl and Broad streets, 4 December 1783. He drank a glass of wine with his old comrades and told them: "With a heart full of love and gratitude, I now take leave of you: I most devotedly wish, that your latter days may be as prosperous and happy as your former ones have been gracious and honorable." After shaking hands with each officer, he passed through two lines of the Corps of Light Infantry to Whitehall dock and there took ship for Annapolis, where he resigned his commission into the hands of the Continental Congress from which he had received it.

64. Nicholas Roosevelt, grandson of the first Roosevelt to settle in New Amsterdam, had a long career (1737–67) as a silversmith in New York and this salver is typical of his work. From Nicholas's brothers descend the presidential Roosevelts. Diameter: 6 1/4″. Gift of Mrs. Elon Huntington Hooker. 42.189

65. Mr. and Mrs. Nathaniel Marston owned this pair of silver candlesticks made by William Anderson, who served his apprenticeship with Simeon Soumain, in whose molds these candlesticks may have been cast. The engraved initials M over N*M on the stems are for Nathaniel and Margaret Marston. Height: 7 1/4″. Gift of Mrs. Frederic Grosvenor Goodridge. 32.310.1ab

62. Samuel Tingley, in 1767, had his silversmith's shop in the Rotten-Row (Hunters Key), on Water Street below Wall, and is believed to have made this pair of candlesticks for the Delafield family. Height: 10″. Gift of Mrs. Elon Huntington Hooker. 43.78.1a–b

63. Mr. and Mrs. Philip Philipse owned this elegant silver salver engraved with the Philipse crest and on the base P over PM. It was made for them by Bartholomew Le Roux, working 1738–63, grandson of the founder of the Le Roux dynasty of silversmiths in New York. Diameter: 7 1/2″. Gift of Mrs. J. Insley Blair. 49.135

68. For many years this set of three ▶ casters for sugar, dry mustard, and spices was the only one known to have survived from colonial America. It was made by Adrian Bancker, whose father was mayor of Albany. He, however, worked in New York from 1725 to 1772. In 1766, when he advertised in *The New-York Journal*, his shop was in "Bridge-Street, near the Exchange." Height of central caster: 7 1/8"; the others: 5 3/4". Gift of Herbert L. Pratt. 43.10.1ab–3ab

69. This pair of tea caddies by Thauvet ▶ Besley, who was admitted freeman of the City in 1727 and kept a silver shop on Golden Hill, were long separated before being united in The Museum of the City of New York. They are initialed on the bottom CMP for Catherine McPhaedres who married Robert G. Livingston in 1740. The initials on the front, RLR and CLR, are for her grandchildren Robert and Catherine Livingston Reade. Catherine married into the Stuyvesants and lived on the ancient Bouwerie Farm. Height: 5 7/8". The caddy marked "Bohea" is the gift of a descendant, Miss Margaret S. Dart. 42.303.1ab. The "Green" caddy is a gift of Andrew Varick Stout. 52.25ab

66. Myer Myers, a freeman of the City from 1746 and active in Jewish affairs, was president of the New York Silver Smith's Society for fourteen years, including the entire Revolutionary period. He and his partner Halsted advertised in 1763 their "neat assortment of ready made plate, chased and plain," rings, brooches, buttons, earrings, "etwees" (i.e., *etuis*, small boxes), toothpick cases, glassware, and tools for watch and clock makers. Silver coffeepot by Myers with former owner's initials "CC" on the inside of the foot. Height: 12". Given in memory of Wendell Davis by his children. 76.107

67. New York had coffeehouses at least as early as 1709, and coffee was a popular beverage. The silversmith Cary Dunne made this fine coffee pot which belonged to John Jay, first chief justice of the United States, and his wife Sarah Livingston. Height: 11 5/8". Gift of Mrs. J. Insley Blair. 47.261.4

70. Peter De Riemer, working in New ▶ York from 1763 to 1796, made this silver tea set for Philip Schuyler van Rensselaer. Each piece is engraved with Van Rensselaer's initials beneath the crest of his family, an iron basket out of which flames are issuing. The Van Rensselaer motto, not shown on these pieces, was "omnibus effulgeo" ("I outshine all"). Height of teapot: 6 3/4"; sugar: 4 5/8"; creamer: 5 1/2". Gift of Mrs. Francis P. Garvan. 51.304a–d

69

71. The earliest valentine in The Museum of the City of New York, among more than 800 examples, is this white paper cutout dated 1790, in which hearts and birds with outstretched wings alternate. It is one of the finest early American valentines known. The message, written across the bird's wings and through the center, with its lines numbered in proper order, reads in part: "The rose is red the violet blue / Lilies are fair and so are you / Round is the ring that has no end / So is my love for you, my friend." Paper, 11 7/8″ square. Gift of Mrs. Charles Marvin Porcher. 43.401.1a

72. Evert Bancker was presented with this white enamel snuff box to commemorate his energetic organizing of the New York merchants' boycott of British goods at the time of the Stamp Act in 1765. After the Revolution Bancker was rewarded with the important post of city surveyor, and in 1794 had the responsible job of numbering all the houses in the City. Length: 3 1/2″. Gift of Mrs. Gordon Wightman, Mrs. John Cadwalader, and William L. Nicoll. 48.250.2

73. This steel tobacco box was owned by William Smith, chief justice of the province of New York and its historian (*The History of the Province of New-York from the First Discovery*, 1757). When the Revolution came he fence-sat for as long as he could, but he left with the British troops at the evacuation of New York. Length: 5 1/8″. Gift of Francis H. Cabot. 69.22

75. To judge from the number of notices he inserted in New York newspapers between 1763 and 1776, the silversmith Charles Oliver Bruff was a go-getting craftsman. In 1763, Bruff advertised that he had "put himself to a great expence in sending to London for diamonds and all manner of precious stones" to use in jewelry for the ladies and gentlemen of the City. In 1767, annoyed by having his work undervalued by rival silversmiths, he published his prices (unusual in advertisements then). For making a silver tankard he charged at the rate of three shillings per ounce; for making a teapot, four pounds; for a pair of silver buckles, eight shillings. In 1772, he was urging buttons, for which he had "finished some of the neatest dies." In 1775, two days after Bunker Hill he advertised that "gentlemen forming themselves into companies in defence of their liberties" and others not provided with swords "may be suited therewith by applying to Charles Oliver Bruff, in Maiden Lane, near the Fly-market." This attractive sugar bowl, made like many of the time to a Chinese porcelain model, is initialed E R, possibly for Elizabeth Rutgers. Height: 4 1/16". Gift of Nicholas G. Rutgers, Jr., Mrs. George Coe, and Mrs. Marshall J. Dodge, Jr. 62.166.4

74. Elias Pelletreau, who was trained by Simeon Soumain and had a long career as silversmith in New York City and on Long Island, 1748–1810, made this substantial tankard. It is engraved with the arms of the Dunscomb(e) family and initialed MD on the lid for Mumford Dunscomb(e). It was quite common in the later nineteenth century for families to have their silver heirlooms engraved with the names of later generations. The inscription on this tankard was added thus. Height to top of thumbpiece: 7 1/8". Gift of George Elsworth Dunscombe. 32.237.1

76. The Museum of the City of New York owns twenty-one letters written between 1800 and 1803 by Thomas Jefferson, then President, to Chancellor Robert R. Livingston. In this one Jefferson asks Livingston to serve as minister plenipotentiary to France. Livingston left his post as chancellor of the State of New York, remained in France for three years, and while there concluded his notable career as public servant by scoring the greatest success in the history of American diplomacy when he seized the opportunity to buy Louisiana from France. Manuscript on paper, 9 5/8 × 7 7/8″. Gift of Goodhue Livingston. 47.173.252

77. Plays were performed at the John Street Theatre beginning in 1767. The playhouse was located about sixty feet back from the north side of John Street near Broadway. There was vigorous and continuing opposition on the part of the pure-minded to its opening at all since there was even in gay New York a persistent religious horror of the stage. The protestors were not mollified even by the attendance several times of the revered President Washington, who loved plays. Ever mindful of the dignity of his high office, Washington used to attend in great state; when he saw *The School for Scandal* in 1789, his box was decorated with the arms of the United States. This playbill is for 30 November 1785. "Mr. Wignell" is Thomas Wignell, celebrated as a comedian and later as a theatrical manager who operated the first theater in Washington, D.C. 17 × 11″. Gift of J. F. Mulrein. 31.141.1

78. Some eighteenth-century New Yorkers in miniature. From top, left to right:

Beverley Robinson by an unknown artist. Robinson, who married into the Philipse family, was a great landowner and an ardent Tory. He left New York with the British troops in 1783, and died in England. Oval miniature on ivory, 2 × 1 3/4″. Gift of Beverley Robinson and Adeline King Robinson, descendants. 34.200

James Duane painted by John Ramage. Duane was mayor of New York between 1784 and 1789. Oval miniature on ivory, 2 × 1 1/2″. Gift of Mrs. Elon Huntington Hooker. 39.207

Cornelius Ray by an unknown artist. Ray was first president of the Bank of the United States (founded 1791). Oval miniature on ivory, 1 × 1 1/4″. Purchase, Mrs. Elon Huntington Hooker Fund. 42.269

Alexander Hamilton by (?) Chartres. This miniature was taken to France by Prince Talleyrand in 1794, but it was returned to Mrs. Hamilton after her husband's death. Oval miniature on ivory, 2 3/4 × 2 1/2″. Gift of Mrs. Alexander Hamilton and General Pierpont Morgan Hamilton. 71.31.4

Alexander McDougall by an unknown artist. McDougall was a Scottish-born New Yorker and a general during the Revolution. In 1784, he became the first president of the Bank of New York. Oval miniature on ivory, 1 7/8 × 1 3/5″. Gift of Elizabeth Mary Frelinghuysen. 67.113.2

J. H. Remsen by an unknown artist. Remsen engaged in the dry-goods business, at the time of the Revolution, in Hanover Square. Oval miniature on ivory, 3 × 2 1/2″. Gift of Miss Barbara Mercer Adam and Mrs. Charlotte Adam Coate. 68.62.2

Richard Varick by an unknown artist. Varick was Federalist mayor of the City, succeeding James Duane in 1789, and retained the office until 1801. Oval miniature on ivory, 2 3/4 × 2 1/2″. Gift of the Misses Maria and Amy Reid Knox. 62.111.23

79. Firemen have always been important in the history of the City of New York; from the earliest times the City has been afflicted with terrible conflagrations. The firefighters of colonial times were volunteer forces with a spirit and pride all their own. In 1787, three hundred firemen were appointed by an act passed "for the better extinguishing of Fires in the City of New York," and a handsome engraved certificate of which this is an example was issued to each of them. The scene, which was engraved by Abraham Godwin, shows a New York street scene with a Newsham fire engine in action. Engraving, 11 1/2 × 9 3/4". Gift of the Brooklyn Volunteer Firemen's Association. 34.419.33

80. John Durand, an artist probably of French origin, painted portraits in New Yòrk beginning about 1766. The Beekmans, the Rapaljes, and the Rays were among the rich families for whom he did portraits. This is Robert Ray, who was born in 1759 and died at the age of twenty-three, with his dog. Purebred dogs were seldom introduced into the colonies; the amiable mongrel shown here is typical of those whose portraits survive. He must have had plenty of companions, for about this time an irate newspaper writer estimated at least one thousand dogs in New York and urged the corporation to pass a law "securing the perpetual exile" of this canine horde. Oil on canvas, 30 × 25 1/2". Bequest of Gherardi Davis. 41.304.1

81–82. Mr. and Mrs. Richard Bancker also had their portraits painted by John Durand. Mrs. Bancker was born Sarah Duyckinck, a member of the family of craftsmen-artists who engaged in "limning, painting, varnishing, japanning, gilding, glazing, and silvering of looking glasses," according to one of their advertisements. Oil on canvas, 39 1/2 × 34 1/2". Gift of Mrs. Albert S. Fehsenfeld. 67.83.1–2

83. Robert R. Livingston was one of the great men of Colonial, Revolutionary, and Federal New York. Descendant of the lords of Livingston Manor, one of the committee of five who drafted the Declaration of Independence, and first chancellor of the State of New York, he was also deeply interested in experimental agriculture and assisted Robert Fulton in his steamboat development. As chancellor, he administered the oath of office as President to George Washington. This important portrait of Livingston is by Gilbert Stuart. Oil on canvas, 36 × 28 1/4". Gift of Evelyn Byrd Hawkins in memory of her husband, Dexter Clarkson Hawkins. 66.65

84. The most famous paintings in American history, Gilbert Stuart's portraits of George Washington, were produced under rather adverse circumstances for the artist. Stuart, who needed commissions badly, having recently left Dublin on account of his debts, had difficulty in getting Washington to sit at all since the President did not like having his portrait painted. Stuart liked to chat with his sitters; Washington rebuffed all efforts at conversation. A rival painter, John Trumbull, wrote: "Mr. Stuart's conversation could not interest Washington; he had no topic fitted for his character; the President did not relish his manners." Nevertheless, Washington was painted from life three times by Stuart; the resulting portraits (of which various copies were made) fall into three types: the "Vaughan," the "Landsdowne," and the "Athenaeum Head," which was painted in Stuart's studio in Germantown, Pennsylvania, in 1796. The name of the last derives from its being given to the Boston Athenaeum in 1831. The replica of the Athenaeum Head in The Museum of the City of New York is considered one of the finest portraits of Washington that Stuart painted. Oil on canvas, 35 × 29". Gift of John Morgan Hill. 46.1A

85. John Gerard Coster wore this elegant purple velvet suit and waistcoat embroidered with multicolored silk to the ball given in honor of the inauguration of George Washington on 7 May 1789 by the "Dancing Assembly" of New York. Over three hundred guests, including Baron von Steuben and other distinguished foreigners, were present. The new President danced in two cotillions and performed a minuet with a Mrs. Maxwell. Coster was a recent arrival in New York, having immigrated with his brother only three years before from Amsterdam. They were soon successful merchants and owners of a great mansion at Kip's Bay. Gift of E. Coster Wilmerding. 50.256a–c

86. Among The Museum of the City of New York's most important relics of the American Revolution is this blue-and-buff uniform of the type worn by American officers. Very few examples of these uniforms have survived. This one, in excellent condition, was worn by Colonel Lewis Morris, son of the signer of the Declaration of Independence from New York and descendant of the family that established Morrisania. Gift of Henry L. Rutherford. 36.476.14a–c

87. Alexander Hamilton saw considerable military action during the Revolution. He was an officer in the New York Artillery Company from early 1776 and fought in the famous engagements on Long Island, at Harlem Heights, and at White Plains. Alonzo Chappel (1828–87), a New York artist and illustrator of historical works, here shows Hamilton in the uniform of an officer of the Artillery Company about 1776. Oil on canvas, 17 3/4 × 13 3/4″. Gift of Mrs. Alexander Hamilton and General Pierpont Morgan Hamilton. 71.31.5

88. In England there persisted throughout the Revolutionary War a strong sympathy for the American cause. There was also great admiration for General Washington as soldier and leader. In 1791, the Scottish artist Archibald Robertson, who had been commissioned by the Earl of Buchan to paint a portrait of Washington, arrived in New York to carry out his assignment. The portrait he did has disappeared, but this watercolor has survived and is believed to be one of the most accurate likenesses of Washington to have come down. While not so adeptly painted as a Stuart or a Peale, it has an immediacy which still catches the dignity so characteristic of Washington. Watercolor, 16 1/2 × 11 1/2″. Gift of Stephen C. Clark. 35.408.92

89. John Singleton Copley painted the prominent New York Loyalist Henry White in London between 1782 and 1786. White was a merchant who signed the Loyal Address to Admiral and General Howe and was used by the British as an agent for selling ships taken as prizes. By the Act of Attainder, 1779, his property was confiscated, and he removed to London. His wife was Anne van Cortlandt, and by family agreement their heirs assumed that name. Oil on canvas, 30 × 25". Gift of Augustus van Cortlandt, direct descendant of White. 55.95.1

90. Whitehead Hicks was serving his tenth year as Mayor of New York when the Revolution broke out. On Valentine's Day, 1776, he resigned, perhaps wisely, from the mayoralty, saying he was tired and "desirous to retire from the Town." His place of retirement was Flushing, Long Island, where he died in 1780. This portrait of Hicks has been attributed to John Singleton Copley. Oil on canvas, 41 1/4 × 28 1/4". Gift of Henry Rogers Winthrop. 43.335.3

91. The earliest significant New York view painting in The Museum of the City of New York is *View of New York From Le Jupiter of 74 guns lying at Anchor in the North River. New York, February 1794,* probably done by Archibald Robertson or one of his pupils. The *Jupiter* was part of a French fleet visiting New York. The view shows the lower part of Manhattan from Trinity Church at the left to the tip of the Battery, with the large Government House built in 1790 facing Bowling Green at the foot of Broadway prominent in the center. Watercolor, 24 × 30 1/2″. Bequest of Mrs. J. Insley Blair. 52.100.1

92. On 25 November 1783, General Washington entered the City as the last British troops were leaving it. On this "Evacuation Day," he was accompanied by George Clinton, six-term governor of New York State. Governor Clinton took up residence in one of the City's great houses, the De Peyster Mansion, on Queen (now Pearl) Street. Although the City was in social and economic shambles, a third of its population having left with the British, and physically damaged by a series of dreadful fires, there was still spirit enough to entertain the victors. A few days later a dinner at Cape's Tavern was proffered to the governor and council which was attended by about three hundred gentlemen, including Washington. This reconstruction of Clinton's headquarters was done in the mid-nineteenth century, probably by Abraham Hosier. Watercolor, 5 7/8 × 6 3/8″. The J. Clarence Davies Collection. 29.100.1632

93. "The Carwitham View" is named after its engraver and is fully titled *A View of Fort George with the City of New York from the S. W.* The time depicted is about 1731–36. "Fort George" is the name given at that period to the fort originally called Fort Amsterdam and later named for various British royalty. The line of trees along the shore at left marks present-day Church Street. The numbers near the steeples indicate churches for the most part, beginning with Trinity at number one. Line engraving on copper, 15 1/2 × 20". Bequest of Mr. and Mrs. J. Insley Blair. 52.100.30

94. A British Army officer, Capt. Thomas Howdell, did two fine "Views of the City of New York, in North America" about 1763. This is the southeast view. The huge edifice (exaggerated) with the cupola is King's College (Columbia). Next to it, with the tallest steeple, is Trinity Church. New York was still a fortified city: at the right are palisades and a blockhouse. Between the blockhouse and Trinity Church is Vauxhall, a garden and tavern which was a popular place of amusement. Line engraving on copper, 19 3/4 × 12 1/2". Gift of Miss Edith Allen Clark in memory of her brother, P. A. Clark. 51.48.2

95. John Banvard spent most of his life as an artist painting panoramas (huge rolled canvases) generally depicting some natural wonder, which slowly unfurled before an audience stationed before them. He traveled much preparing sketches for popular panoramas of the Mississippi and the Nile. In his old age he favored New York, where he had been born, as the subject for his paintings and did a series of watercolors of old houses, some remembered, some reconstructed. *"Brother Banvards" 1776* shows a house which stood just below Fair (now Fulton) Street facing the Hudson River. It was old even in 1776 and was said to have been built of bricks and tiles brought from Holland. During the Revolution a cannonball fell on the house. The drawing was done by Banvard about a century later. Watercolor, 5 1/8 × 8 1/2". Gift of Miss Edith M. Banvard, daughter of the artist. 46.282.4

96. The first Methodist church in America, at 44 John Street, was dedicated in 1768. The artist Joseph B. Smith, who rather specialized in views of ecclesiastical structures in New York, did this watercolor of the building about 1844. The area called "Golden Hill" was bounded by present William, John, Fulton, and Cliff streets, and it was there that the so-called "Battle of Golden Hill," a riot between British soldiers and the New York Sons of Liberty took place in 1770. Watercolor, 21 × 28 1/2". Bequest of Mrs. J. Insley Blair. 52.100.9

◀ 97. The second year of the Revolution, while the British under General Howe occupied New York, Nathan Hale, a twenty-two-year-old Yale man and schoolteacher who had been commissioned captain in the Revolutionary army, volunteered to spy on the British forces on Long Island. Returning to the American position on Harlem Heights, he was captured by the British and on 22 September 1776 hanged without a trial. About five years later a newspaper reported his final words: "I am so satisfied with the cause in which I have engaged that my only regret is, that I have not more lives than one to offer in its service." Hale only gradually became a folk hero, but by the late nineteenth century he was *the* martyr of the Revolution, and his final words in somewhat abbreviated form had become a great American slogan. In 1893, the Sons of the American Revolution gave the City the life-size bronze statue of him by Frederick MacMonnies which stands in City Hall Park. This model was made by the artist in 1890, and cast in Paris. Bronze, height: 21 1/2". Gift of Howard Phipps. 46.289

98. Giuseppe Ceracchi, born in Corsica and trained as a sculptor in Rome, visited the new United States twice, about 1790 and 1793, and executed likenesses of several of the great American revolutionaries. The marble bust of George Washington shows him at the time of his presidency when Washington was in his late fifties. Marble, height: 26″. Gift of Henry Rogers Winthrop. 42.10

99. This bust in marble of Alexander Hamilton was made by Ceracchi about 1791, in New York. After Hamilton's death from Aaron Burr's bullet in the celebrated duel of 1804, an entrepreneur exhibited a plaster cast from "the celebrated bust by Ceracchi" at the Tontine Coffee House on the northwest corner of Wall and Water streets. The sculptor had come to an unfortunate end: in 1802, his fellow Corsican Napoleon had him executed on a conspiracy charge. Marble, height: 23 1/2″. Bequest of Mary Trumbull Morse in memory of her mother, Ann Church Morse. 35.214

100. The portraits and furniture of Alexander Hamilton and his family in The Museum of the City of New York came either from his lower Manhattan residence or his country seat on Convent Avenue called The Grange. The portrait of Mrs. Hamilton (Elizabeth Schuyler), who survived her husband more than fifty years, is by Ralph Earl. The diarist George Templeton Strong handled her affairs when he was a young lawyer. At the age of eighty-two she would *walk* from her home on St. Mark's Place to Strong's office on Wall Street to make, as he wrote irritably, "the fortieth alteration" in her will. When she was ninety-one Strong wrote in amazement: "I don't believe that old body has the slightest intention of ever going to a better world: such a specimen of juvenile antedeluvianism I never encountered." Finally, this living link with English New York and the Revolution died in 1854, at the age of ninety-seven. Oil on canvas, 31 3/4 × 26 7/8". The portrait of Hamilton is by John Trumbull, painted posthumously, using the Ceracchi bust as a model. Hamilton used the cylinder desk of mahogany and satinwood, made about 1800, late in his public career. Height: 51 1/2"; width: 47". Gifts of Mrs. Alexander Hamilton and General Pierpont Morgan Hamilton. 71.31.2,13–15.

IV: GOTHAM: NEW YORK IN THE EARLY REPUBLIC

This city is esteemed the most eligible situation
for commerce in the United States. . . .

—JOHN PAYNE, *Universal Geography*, 1799

New Yorkers returning on Evacuation Day must have seen the future of their City as far from cheerful. Even with General Washington and his victorious troops in the City and continued public rejoicings, the confusion was terrible. At the Merchants' Coffee House a registry was opened in which citizens could list their names and new or temporary places of residence to help their returning relatives and friends locate them. Within three years this registry had led to the printing and distribution of a City directory, published in 1786. New York was the second American city to have a directory; its rival Philadelphia published the first in 1785.

Since New York had been held by both sides during the Revolution and occupied for years by a foreign force, titles to land and houses long out of their owners' hands were subject to dispute. Tory property, land and business, was now confiscated and sold; since so many New Yorkers had been Loyalists this property was extensive. Entire estates, for example that of James de Lancey bordered by the Bowery and the East River, and between Rivington and Division streets, were forfeited. The large holdings of the British Crown, which included Fort George and other fortifications, the Customs House, and other government buildings, now became the property of the new State of New York. The solution of what to do with Fort George was simple: it was completely demolished and the debris used for landfill at the Battery, creating a pleasant promenade alongside the Bay which has been there ever since, although continued extensions have taken the shoreline out many yards.

Over protests that the act was childish revenge, the Common Council ordered streets with royalist names to be turned republican. Thus, King Street became Pine, Little Queen Street became Cedar, Crown became Liberty, etc. New streets were laid out under the supervision of Anthony van Dam in the section devastated by the fires of 1776 and 1778. Van Dam's regular job was dealing in wine and liquors at No. 13 Nassau Street, but he was also secretary of the Chamber of Commerce of New York, founded under the Crown rule in 1768 but now republicanized. For the control of fires a new force was organized. A hospital, at first housing only patients with contagious diseases during New York's frequent epidemics, was opened in 1794, when the City purchased "Bellevue," an estate on the East River leased at that time to Brockholst Livingston.

Financially, New Yorkers had suffered great losses through the depreciation of paper currency and public securities. Many were left holding worthless bonds issued by various Revolutionary authorities, including the Continental Congress and the states. The lack of proper banking arrangements—for New York still had no bank—aggravated this problem. But commerce, especially the maritime trade with the Caribbean islands, recovered rapidly.

New York (or New-York as it was usually written) was the capital of the state of New York, but its legal status as a municipality was somewhat uncertain. During British occupation the City had been governed by military law. Presumably at the conclusion of the occupation it reverted to its old charter (the Montgomerie Charter of 1731), but that had the taint of royal origin. In any event, the old charter was serviceable, patched-up with certain modifications. The governor of the state now appointed the mayor, the sheriff, and other executive officers. Aldermen, assistant aldermen, and constables were elected by the freemen of the City, who had to meet fixed property qualifications. The aldermen, called "the Common Council," were the local legislature.

The first mayor after the Revolution (1784–89) was James Duane, then a fifty-one-year-old lawyer. His attitude toward colonial affairs before the Revolution had been conservative, but eventually he joined the rebels. His farm, purchased in part from descendants of Peter Stuyvesant, was east of Fourth Avenue between 20th and 21st streets at what is now Gramercy Park. He was allied with the ubiquitous Livingstons: his wife was Maria Livingston, cousin of the chancellor and of Mrs. John Jay, and aunt by marriage of Robert Fulton.

In 1785, the U.S. Congress decided to meet in New York, which meant that the City was now and for five exciting years simultaneously seat of government of the United States and of the state and municipality of New York.

New York State ratified the U.S. Constitution 26 July 1788, rather tardily; it was the eleventh state to ratify. Alexander Hamilton, New York's most influential citizen, led the fight for ratification. Opposition to the Constitution was led by Governor George Clinton. Briefly put, Clinton advocated "states rights," against the Hamiltonian idea of a strong federal government. Clinton and his allies including Chancellor Livingston and Aaron Burr were strongest upstate, the Hamiltonian Federalists strongest downstate, the beginning of a division which has become practically solidified in the history of public affairs in New York State.

The United States Congress met from 1785 to 1790 in the City Hall of New York, repaired and much altered after designs by Major Pierre Charles L'Enfant, who later planned Washington, D.C. It was subsequently referred to as Federal Hall. Like most architectural projects, especially L'Enfant's, the cost of these changes was much greater than anticipated; in the end £15,000 was spent. (New York continued to have "pounds" and "shillings" in its currency until well into the nineteenth century.) In the first flush of republican

enthusiasm prominent citizens advanced large sums for the work, expecting to be repaid by the state legislature. As the expense of the "improvements" mounted, they refused to advance more. The question of their reimbursement was pending for a long time, and lotteries finally had to be held to pay for L'Enfant's labors.

Congress was pleased with its accommodations, but even then New York street traffic created such a din that the Common Council of the City ordered chains suspended across the street during congressional business hours to stop the noisy flow of carts and carriages. There were already hackney carriages for hire with published rates; to Bellevue, for instance, sixteen shillings, with waiting time charged at four shillings the hour.

Down Broad Street from Federal Hall, the New York State Legislature met at the Exchange Building between 1784 and 1796 except for a few sessions when it met at various other cities including Albany, to which it finally removed.

The first Congress under the Constitution (assembled 4 March 1789) elected Washington president of the new republic and John Adams vice-president. Washington arrived at New York on 23 April for the ceremony of his "introduction" into the highest office, having been rowed from Elizabethtown, New Jersey, in a barge made for the occasion. The inauguration took place on the balcony of Federal Hall. Artillery discharges, the ringing of bells, fireworks, and a great ball followed the inaugural ceremony.

During his year of residence in New York, Washington and "Lady Washington," as she was often called (but never by the fiercer republicans), liked to walk in the evening "round the Battery." There were persistent complaints about "the spectacle of naked swimmers who frequent the place" and prevent the more timid ladies of New York from enjoying the air and exercise there. Presumably the swimmers stayed away when the presidential couple promenaded the Battery. Sometimes the President and Mrs. Washington and his Custis stepgrandchildren who lived with them at No. 39 Broadway took long drives, "the fourteen miles round Manhattan" being covered between breakfast and dinner time. Their invariable tour was up the

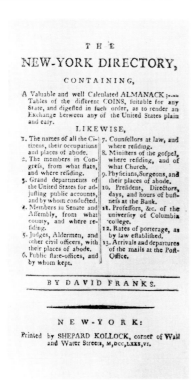

101–102. David Franks began advertising his *New-York Directory*, the first printed for the City, in December, 1785. It was sold at his shop, 66 Broadway, beginning in February, 1786, at a price of six shillings. Examples are now among the rarest New York books. The copy illustrated previously belonged to the great American book-collector Robert Hoe, at whose sale in 1912 it brought the then-unheard-of price of $2,750. The compiler was a "conveyancer and accountant" who came to New York from Dublin. The page of listings shown is of "Lawyers, Attornies, and Notary-Publics, etc.," of which there were forty-two in a city of about 24,000. Notice the law offices of Alexander Hamilton and Aaron Burr in ironic conjunction. The J. Clarence Davies Collection. 29.100.790

Bloomingdale Road to Harlem Heights, then across to Kingsbridge, and back along the Boston Post Road on the East Side. At least once Washington returned for a meal to the Morris Mansion, his former headquarters. It had become a tavern (even then New Yorkers showed little concern with historic preservation). Sometimes he went fishing at Sandy Hook.

Meetings of Congress shifted to Philadelphia in August, 1790, but the state legislature remained in New York until 1797, when it moved to Albany. The first Federal census, made in 1790, showed the population for New York at 33,131, the second largest city in the new republic, after Philadelphia. That figure is, of course, only for what was then called "New York," i.e., Manhattan Island. The areas that a century later became part of "Greater New York" were still very sparsely populated: the Bronx, 1,781; Brooklyn (Kings), 4,495; Queens, 6,159; and Richmond, 3,855.

James Duane was succeeded as mayor by Colonel Richard Varick, who had acted as one of Washington's secretaries during the Revolution. His country place, which he called "Tusculum" with a touch of the classicism of the times, stood on what is now Varick Street between Bleecker and Houston. He served as mayor from 1789 to 1801, one of the longest terms of any mayor in New York's history. The City over which he presided was beginning to prosper, and Varick was capable, but the familiar municipal problems were still very much in evidence.

As usual, the streets were filthy, and pigs still roamed highway and byway, their owners ignoring a century of laws passed against them. The pigs even had their advocates among New Yorkers who claimed that they actually kept the streets clean. But an observer noted: "The opinion of the majority is that, as the pigs only serve to scatter the dirt already collected in heaps the law should be strictly executed." Pigs, horses, and other livestock were freely kept by householders then and for many years to come in pens and outbuildings behind residences. Goats at least were effectively driven from the streets by a finders-keepers law which authorized anyone who found a goat at large "to take and appropriate such goat."

The houses of Federal New York were not jammed together. In the early republican period they were still quite often surrounded by private gardens which were surprisingly extensive. Chancellor Robert R. Livingston, who lived at No. 3 Broadway, for instance, had a garden which extended down to the Hudson. His neighborhood, according to the first directory, was egalitarian and showed the cozy combination of residence, business, and recreation which is the mark of urban civilization. Don Diego de Gardoqui, the popular Spanish ambassador, lived at No. 1 Broadway and a Van Cortlandt lived at No. 5, but at 2 there was a shoemaker, at 13 a carpenter, and No. 15 was a tavern. A similar mix prevailed throughout the City. There can hardly have been a block without its tavern. A census about this time showed a total of 3,340 buildings in the City. Mayor Duane reported to the Common Council that between the first of March, 1789, and the first of March, 1790, he granted 330 tavern licenses, which means that at least ten percent of the buildings sold liquor, a decline, it is true, from Dutch days when every fourth house was said to be a bar, but still a sobering statistic, so to speak. The licenses, incidentally, cost thirty shillings, of which the mayor kept six and the city clerk six; the rest went to the City treasury.

The house styles of New York were changing. A visitor commented that the "sharp-sloping houses of the Dutch" were being replaced by elegant buildings in the English style. "On all sides houses are rising, and streets extending; I see nothing but busy workmen building and repairing."

One of the few surviving houses of the period is that of the shipowner Archibald Gracie opposite the Hell Gate in the East River on a point of land known as "Horn's Hook" (after Hoorn in the Netherlands). Gracie either rebuilt an earlier house or constructed anew, but the style is apparently of about 1800. "The Gracie Mansion" was famous for its hospitality, described by many notables including John Quincy Adams and Washington Irving. After passing through many hands and enduring sad dilapidation, the house and its land became part of the new Carl Schurz Park in 1891. From 1923 to 1932, it served as the first home of The Museum of the City of New York. In 1942, it became official home of the mayor of the City.

In New York's houses the style of furnishings gradually was shifting in the late eighteenth century from Chippendale to the "Federal" or "American Empire" style. In 1792, the most famous of all New York cabinetmakers, Duncan Phyfe, established himself in New York. He is the "hero" of the history of the decorative arts in New York, and the only American furniture-maker who has given his name to an entire style.

A Scot by birth, Phyfe settled in New York on Partition Street. He changed his name (it was originally the inelegant "Fife") and prospered, producing chairs, tables, sofas, and sideboards in the prevailing English Hepplewhite and Sheraton styles. After the turn of the century he began to work in the so-called "Classical style" which had been transmitted from France and was in fact a grafting of the Directoire style on the Empire. This is the style we now call "Duncan Phyfe."

After 1816, Partition Street became Fulton to honor the inventor of the steamboat. Phyfe acquired four buildings on the street, three on the downtown side for his workshops and showrooms and one on the uptown side for his home. These buildings were all in the first block off Broadway within sight of St. Paul's Chapel and not far from City Hall. It is obvious that such an extensive enterprise could produce a lot of furniture, and it did. The Museum of the City of New York has one of the finest representations of Duncan Phyfe's work. Among other New York furniture-makers of the period whose work is in the museum are Slover and Taylor, who made an armchair for Mayor De Witt Clinton. The "American Empire" style is exemplified in the console table of the Sands family also in the museum.

The silver used in the houses of well-to-do New Yorkers at the end of the eighteenth century was moving away from the late colonial style toward the "Federal" style. Dishes were still often of "China Trade" origin, especially after the ship *Empress of China* made the first voyage from New York to Asiatic waters in 1784–85. Her owners proudly wrote to John Jay, then U.S. Minister for Foreign Affairs, describing her "as the first vessel that has been fitted out by the inhabitants of the United States of America for essaying a commerce with those of the Empire of China." Her voyage returned twenty percent profit on the capital invested.

New Yorkers who could afford it lived luxuriously in a manner copied by some who couldn't afford it. Many of the great men of the day were extravagant. De Witt Clinton, for example, was in debt much of his life because of his taste for show. As for Nathan Sanford, his predecessor as Chancellor of the State of New York, James Kent, described him as nearly ruining himself putting up a mansion at Flushing: "He spent his last years in building a most extravagantly expensive but inconvenient House. He is supposed to have exhausted upwards of $100,000 on his Buildings and diminished his personal Estate greatly."

In 1784, the Bank of New York, the first banking institution in the history of the City, was organized. Alexander McDougall was its first president, and Alexander Hamilton served on the first board of directors, which also counted some other famous New York names: Bowne, Low, Roosevelt, Randall, and Vanderbilt. In the bank's branch office at 360 Park Avenue, a facsimile of the first notice of its plan to organize, which appeared in the *New-York Packet*, 12 February 1784, is inscribed in gold on black marble.

The facade of the Bank of the United States, which survives as an element in the American Wing of the Metropolitan Museum of Art, is a good example of the bank architecture of the period.

Other businesses still active in New York founded before the year 1800 include the Cruikshank Co. (1794), believed to be the oldest real estate firm in the U.S.; Schieffelin & Co., the oldest drug house in America, also 1794; and the American Bank Note Co., founded in 1795.

The Manhattan Company was founded in 1799 by Aaron Burr and others to supply the City with water, the supply from the Collect Pond having become sparse and so repulsive that even horses sometimes refused to drink it. Like many such companies it did not accomplish what it was formed to do and was very busy doing things (namely banking and speculating in stocks) which had nothing to do with its original purpose. From the New York State Legislature it received an unusual charter which gave it not only a monopoly on supplying the City with water but permitted it to purchase stock and engage in banking—practically an unlimited act of incorporation. Wooden (later iron) pipes were laid, but there were complaints about the sluggishness of the flow and the quality of the water. Many New Yorkers continued to buy their "tea-water" from pumps and springs which were privately operated. By 1800, the Manhattan Company had erected a reservoir and steam pump at the corner of Reade and Centre streets, where the reservoir was maintained until 1915, to guarantee the validity of the Company's charter.

The lack of a good water supply and the dirty streets and waterfronts contributed, of course, to the frequent epidemics of cholera, yellow fever, and other diseases which swept the City. The yellow fever visitation of 1803 was especially bad. Bellevue Hospital was filled with victims, and it was reported that 40,000 (two-thirds of the population) had fled the City for Greenwich Village and other spots in the country where the air was purer. The fever struck 1,628 New Yorkers, and 596 died of it. The failure of the Manhattan Company to supply the City with an adequate and safe water source was only one of many such attempts. The problem of New York's water supply was not solved for years to come.

The Manhattan Company was large and flourished for decades, but in the history of the City by far the most important new financial establishment in early republican New York was that covered by the agreement between "Brokers for the Purchase and Sale of Public Stock" declared on 17 May 1792, in which the money men agreed to give each other preference in trading and fixed rates of commissions. This was the first step in the formation of the New York Stock Exchange. The brokers met at various places including coffee houses and taverns but usually out-of-doors under a buttonwood tree on the north side of Wall Street between William and Pearl streets. This buttonwood tree, which was believed to have been on the site since the days of Director-General Wouter van Twiller, was nearly as famous to New Yorkers as Stuyvesant's pear tree. It was not until 1817 that the name "New York Stock and Exchange Board" and a constitution were adopted.

In 1800, the second Federal census showed New York had an amazing 60,515 people. Visitors were staggered by the progress of the City. Senator Jonathan Mason of Massachusetts, a critical Yankee, wrote in his journal: "The progress of this city is, as usual, beyond all calculations—700 buildings erected in the last twelve months; and Broadway, beyond all dispute, is the best street for length, width, position, and buildings in America." He could not resist adding, however, of the citizenry: "They have not so much information so generally diffused as the New England States have, and their present paucity of characters to fill their offices shows it."

At the turn of the century, until he was killed by Aaron Burr in the famous duel at Weehawken in 1804, Alexander Hamilton, although no longer Secretary of the Treasury, was undoubtedly New York's leading citizen. He founded a newspaper, the *New York Post*, to expound ideas of Federalism, and its first issue appeared 16 November 1801. By 1817, New York had seven major daily newspapers, five semiweeklies, and five weeklies. The *Post* has outlived all of these and dozens of others besides. It is now New York's only afternoon newspaper; its masthead proclaims it "the oldest continuously published daily in the United States." Hamilton's statue in chromium bronze by A. A. Weinman (1941) is one of two placed in niches on the facade of The Museum of the City of New York. Weinman used as his model one of the surviving plaster models—also in the museum's collection—of the statue of Hamilton by Ball Hughes. The marble version of Hughes's statue of Hamilton perished in the Great Fire of 1835.

In 1801, George Clinton, a follower of Jefferson and an opponent of Hamilton, was elected governor of New York. He belonged to the political party then called Democratic-Republican. For the first time, this party controlled the nation (Jefferson was president), the state, and the City (Edward Livingston, the Chancellor's brother, was mayor). Clinton was later vice-president in the first administration of Madison until his death in 1812. He established a family of continuing prominence in New York. His daughter was married to Major-General Pierre S. van Cortlandt. His nephew De Witt Clinton was mayor from 1803 to 1807, 1809 to 1810, and 1811 to 1815, and was undoubtedly New York's best nineteenth-century chief official, active in forwarding education, sanitation, and defense (during the War of 1812). He became governor of New York in 1817, and from that position was able to promote the plan nearest his heart: the Erie Canal. His statue by A. A. Weinman stands on the facade of The Museum of the City of New York, opposite that of the political enemy of his family, Alexander Hamilton.

It was Mayor Edward Livingston—of whom Chancellor Kent said, he was a man "of a good deal of Talent & learning but rather speculative & ingenious than solid"—who laid the cornerstone of City Hall on 26 May 1803. This distinguished building, still New York's seat of government, was completed in 1811. It is shown in its early days in a watercolor by Thomas J. Stansbury, the Klincköwstrom watercolor of 1818, and an unusual kerchief showing cries of street vendors—all in The Museum of the City of New York.

Robert Fulton's steamboat, which was known at the time as the "North River Steam Boat" (only later was "of Clermont" added, referring to its formal home port), was put in operation for the first time in 1807. "Clermont," which gradually became its name, referred to Chancellor Livingston's ancestral home on the Hudson. Livingston had greatly assisted in Fulton's work, and Mrs. Fulton was a member of the mighty Livingston clan. There had been previous attempts in New York at steam navigation, John Fitch having experimented with his steamboat on Collect Pond in 1796. One wag (steamboat experimentation seemed to bring out wits) said on hearing the machine that he mistook its noise "for the blowing of a shoal of porpoises which had found their way from the River."

At the time of the celebration of the "Second Centenary Anniversary of the Discovery of this part of America by Henry Hudson" on 4 September 1809, the population of New York City was just under 100,000, and it was the largest city in the United States, having overtaken Philadelphia between the censuses of 1800 and 1810. During the following spring, between 600 and 700 dwellings and stores were under construction. In a watercolor of the period, the French visitor Baroness Hyde de Neuville caught the busy City under the snow. It was just about this time that Washington Irving, who was born in New York at 141 William Street, called New York "Gotham," referring to an English legend about a village which avoided royal taxes by having its inhabitants run about acting demented. In the bicentennial year of 1809, Irving published his famous mock history of the City entitled *A History of New York from the Beginning of the World to the End of the Dutch Dynasty* supposedly written by Diedrich Knickerbocker, the last descendant of one of the original Dutch families of New Amsterdam.

The Embargo Acts (1807 on), which led to the War of 1812, hit New York hard since maritime traffic was its basis of prosperity. The citizens were greatly opposed to the war, and rightly, because their commerce suffered severely. The increase in the City's population slowed down strikingly while the war was on: between 1810 and 1816 there was an increase of only 4,200.

Aside from these few years of war, however, the City continued its rapid growth, and concern was expressed about the further development of the Island since residences were gradually moving "uptown." Eighteen-eleven was the year in which the great Randel Plan for the development of the City was promulgated. From the point of view of today's New Yorker, his daily life is more affected by the Randel Plan than almost any other event in the City's history. Homes, businesses, and especially transportation have had their locations directly fixed by this plan for the last century and a half.

The Commissioners' Plan, as it was also known, divided the Island of Manhattan above 14th Street into rectangular blocks through which avenues one hundred feet wide extended from south to north. Some of these avenues were extended as far north as the village of Harlem and numbered consecutively from one to twelve, beginning with the most easterly, which passed west of Bellevue Hospital and east of the Harlem Church. East of First Avenue were four short avenues lettered A, B, C, and D. The cross streets were laid out as far north as 155th Street.

When the plan was criticized—and it was criticized by nearly everyone—the commissioners explained in defense of their work that they chose a rectangular plan because a city "is to be composed principally of the habitations of men," and that straight-sided and right-angled houses were cheapest to build, and the most convenient for living.

New Yorkers greeted the Randel commissioners and their plan with suspicion, hostility, and even violence. John Randel, Jr., later spoke feelingly of his experiences while engaged in this work. He was arrested by the sheriff in numerous suits instituted against him as the agent of the commissioners for trespass and damage committed by his workmen in passing over grounds and cutting off the branches of trees while surveying. The Common Council had to obtain an act of the legislature, dated 24 March 1809, authorizing the commissioners and all persons under them to enter upon grounds to be surveyed and cut down trees and do other damage subject to compensation within a specified time. When the work of opening streets began, opposition was even stronger, but it was carried through, and the present-day plan of upper Manhattan emerged.

The bill for Randel's work was $32,484.98, and he had difficulty collecting. Randel's survey was printed by William Bridges without so much as a by your leave or reference to its true author, but Randel's accomplishment stands, like Olmsted and Vaux's Central Park, as a monument of city planning.

The great harbor of New York, more bustling than ever, was the scene from about this time of many historic welcoming ceremonies, such as the famous ovation given to General Lafayette on his return to this country in 1824. The following year, 1825, the opening of the Erie Canal was celebrated with even more gusto. Ground had been broken at Rome, New York, on the Fourth of July, 1817, and work connecting Lake Champlain and Lake Erie with the Hudson River was completed in 1825, mainly through the continuing enthusiasm of De Witt Clinton, at a cost of $7,000,000. The significance of the Erie Canal in their economic future was not lost on New Yorkers, and they celebrated accordingly.

103. The marriage in 1801 of Governor George Clinton's daughter Catherine to Major-General Pierre S. van Cortlandt was one of the most important in a long series of alliances which united the old Dutch aristocracy, rich in land and money, with the newer English families who were politically influential. Ezra Ames, who painted this portrait of Catherine, has nearly 500 known portraits to his credit, mostly governors of New York, legislators, and members of aristocratic families. Oil on canvas, 30 1/2 × 24 1/2". Bequest of Joseph B. Brenauer. 46.229.11

104. This portrait of the important New Yorker De Witt Clinton is attributed to Samuel Lovett Waldo, who in 1820 founded the firm of Waldo & Jewett with his former pupil William Jewett. For more than thirty years the firm painted portraits, mainly of prominent New Yorkers, with Waldo specializing in heads and hands and Jewett in costumes and backgrounds. Oil on canvas, 45 1/2 × 57 1/4". Gift of Mrs. Leonard W. Bonney. 37.404

105. In 1780 Lieutenant-Colonel Richard Varick was made aide to Benedict Arnold, then commanding at West Point. Despite the fact that a court of enquiry acquitted Varick of all blame in the subsequent treason of Arnold, a slight cloud remained over the New Yorker until General Washington demonstrated his confidence by appointing Varick his confidential secretary. As such, he was in charge of the correspondence and records of the Continental Army, with headquarters in Poughkeepsie. After the Revolution, Varick became recorder of New York City and mayor from 1789 to 1801. A civic leader, he was also a founder of the American Bible Society, which still has its headquarters in New York. Portrait by John Trumbull. 28 1/2 × 36". Gift of Miss Amy Reid Knox. 68.104.1

106. Andrew Jackson was serving his second term as President when this remarkable wooden figurehead was created by the noted Boston woodcarver Laban S. Beecher in 1834. It served as the figurehead of the U.S. Frigate *Constitution* ("Old Ironsides"). During the summer of 1834, a determined Anti-Jacksonian, Capt. Samuel Dewey, climbed aboard the frigate in Boston harbor one stormy night and in spite of heavy guard succeeded in sawing off the figure's head and sneaking away with it in a canvas bag. The *Constitution*'s captain, Jesse D. Elliott, sailed to New York with the figurehead flag-draped, and a new head was carved by Dodge and Son. The repaired figure remained on the historic ship for more than forty years and is today considered one of the most important objects of American naval memorabilia. Height: 12'. Gift of the Seawanhaka Corinthian Yacht Club. M52.11

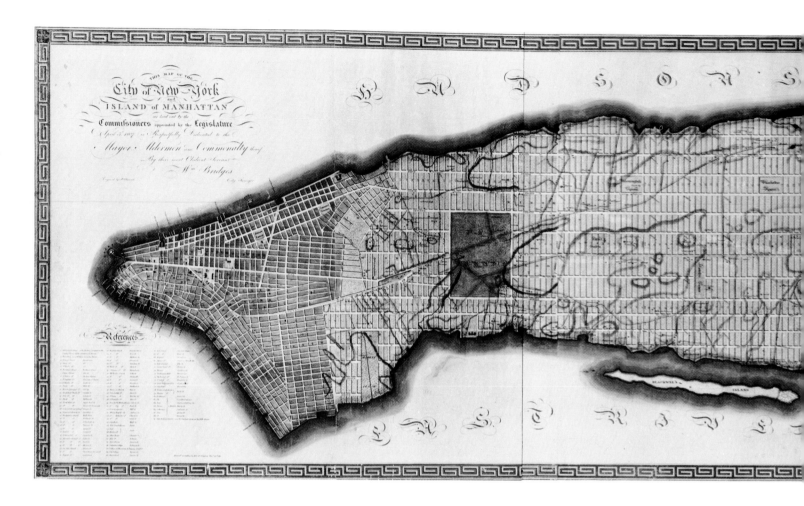

107. In 1806, the Common Council of the City ordered a survey to be made with the purpose of organizing a street system for New York north of 14th Street. From that street to the upper end of Manhattan there were only scattered settlements, a few estates, and open country. Although it did not believe that for "years (possibly centuries)" the population could possibly fill that vast area, the council decided that it should all be laid out in streets and marked for lots. When the City itself was unable to get the survey completed, it asked the aid of the state legislature. In 1807, Governor George Clinton appointed three commissioners to carry out the assignment: Gouverneur Morris, John Rutherfurd, and Simeon De Witt. The commissioners in turn engaged John Randel, Jr., to prepare the map. The survey itself took Randel's name; this map, which was adapted by William Bridges from the Randel Survey and engraved by Peter Maverick, is called "The Commissioners Map" and it was published in 1811. It depicts the most important city-planning step ever taken in the history of New York. The laying-out of a future city and especially the division into lots encouraged the systematic development which has led to present-day New York. The year 1811 marks the end of "Little Old New York" and the beginning of the metropolis. The areas below 14th Street including the present financial district and Greenwich Village were not included in the plan because they were too much developed to be tampered with, but above them symmetry was imposed. Then and later there has been criticism of the Randel Survey: no new parks were planned, an error which cost New York taxpayers millions at a later period; hills were to be leveled, forcing a man-made skyline on Manhattan; there was no variety, all was direct and simple. These "weaknesses" are of course simultaneously its particular strengths and have in fact become the very hallmarks of the modern City. Line engraving on copper, 22 3/4 × 89 1/2". The J. Clarence Davies Collection. 29.100.2730

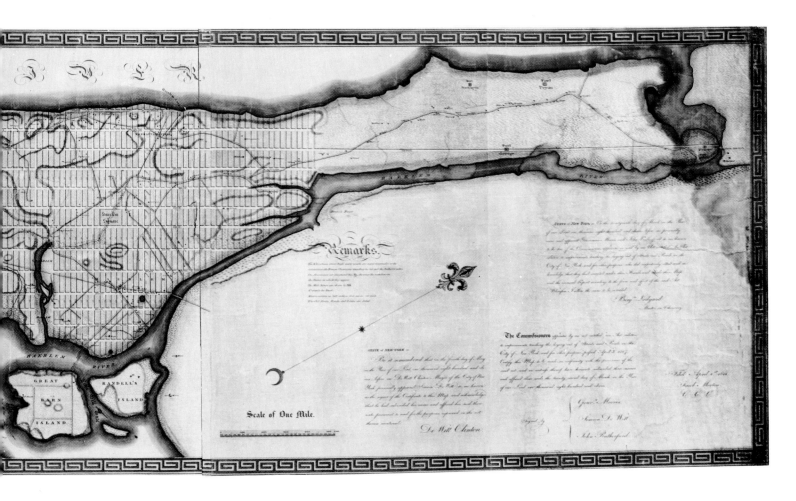

108. The building of the Croton Aqueduct, which
assured New Yorkers of a regular supply of plentiful
and potable water, was a major step in making New
York a true metropolis. This was recognized at the
time, and the opening of the aqueduct inspired civic
rejoicings. There was a great parade on 14 October
1842. To commemorate the celebration this silver medal
was struck. The side shown here has a view of the
distributing reservoir at 42nd Street (on the site of
the present New York Public Library) with figures on
its capacity; the reverse shows a section of the
aqueduct. Diameter: 2 1/2″. The J. Clarence Davies
Collection. 34.100.217

109. The arrival of General Lafayette at New York in August, 1824, was the signal for one of the most elaborate welcomes ever given by New York to a distinguished visitor. This dark-blue Staffordshire pottery platter by J. & R. Clews shows the scene at Castle Garden on the 16th of August when Lafayette was welcomed by a committee of important citizens and thousands of the populace. 14 1/4 × 19". Gift of Mrs. Harry Horton Benkard. 34.508.2

110. The steamboat *Clermont* left on its maiden trip (the first ever for a steam vessel) up the Hudson to Albany on 4 September 1807. There were twelve passengers, who paid $4.00 for the trip to Poughkeepsie, $4.50 to Esopus, or $7.00 to Albany, and there was much local scoffing at these foolhardy travelers. Thousands of spectators lined the banks of the Hudson and cheered as the little steamer passed; at West Point the entire garrison turned out. This print by J. H. Sherwin was done in the mid-nineteenth century. Lithograph, 4 3/8 × 7 7/8". Museum Purchase. 38.299.2

111. Thomas Birch painted this *View of New York Harbor from the Battery* in 1827, looking toward Staten Island with Castle Williams on the left. The "Castle" was built on Governor's Island in 1811, and was often referred to as "The East Battery." It served to fortify New York harbor for the War of 1812, and still stands guard. Oil on board, 42 1/2 × 26 1/4". Gift of the Women's Committee in honor of Hardinge Scholle, Director 1926–51. 51.261

112. Anthony Imbert, a French-born naval officer who became one of the pioneers of American lithography, prepared a series of plates for Cadwallader Colden's *Memoirs of the Erie Canal*. This painting shows the canal boat *Seneca Chief* receiving the official welcome of the City of New York. It was from the *Seneca Chief* that Governor De Witt Clinton poured the keg of Lake Erie water into the Atlantic to symbolize the linking of the Great Lakes with New York harbor. Oil on canvas, 24 × 45". Anonymous gift. 49.415.1

113. Because the drinking water in New York was barely potable for so long a time, bottled waters had considerable popularity. A man named George Usher was said by his family to be "the inventor of the distillation and preparation of mineral waters" in New York about 1811. His widow was granted permission by the Common Council to sell the product "in the vestibule of City Hall." There were soon rival establishments including "Bostwick's Bottled Soda-Water," shown in this advertisement (1843), whose waters were dispensed from 105 Muxray Street. Lithograph, 13 1/2 × 17 1/2″. The J. Clarence Davies Collection. 29.100.2488

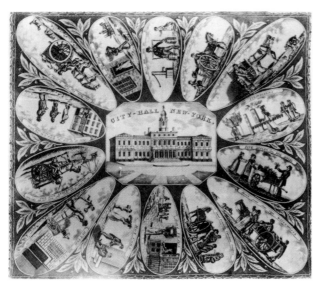

114. The cries of street vendors in New York about 1814 surround City Hall on this unusual printed toile scarf or handkerchief. Most of the vendors are selling comestibles: baked pears, hot corn, sweet potatoes, watermelons, pineapples (probably from the West India trade), strawberries, clams, oysters, milk, tea rusk (a sweet biscuit), and buttermilk. The clams are shouted as coming from Rockaway, which also supplies beach sand, "lily white and choise," for use on wooden floors. The solicitors also include chimney sweeps and a man selling cattails (marsh grass) for stuffing mattresses. 23 3/4 × 21 1/2″. The J. Clarence Davies Collection. 29.100.613

115. Alexander Jackson Davis, later famous as an architect, drew this view (about 1825) of the Branch Bank of the United States at 30–32 Wall Street. It was lithographed by Anthony Imbert. In 1915, when the building had been occupied for half a century by the assay office, it was demolished, but the facade after years in storage was bodily incorporated into the American Wing of The Metropolitan Museum of Art. Lithograph, 12 1/8 × 9 7/8″. Museum Purchase. 38.299.7

116. From Dutch times to the first quarter of the nineteenth century most New Yorkers got their drinking water from a large freshwater pond called The Collect, around present-day Centre Street. As the City grew larger, one of the new suppliers was the Manhattan Company, whose reservoir in the popular Egyptian style is shown in this watercolor by G. P. Hall dated 1825. The reservoir stood on the north side of Chambers Street between Broadway and Centre Street, but its output was not popular with New Yorkers; of some disillusioning matter George Templeton Strong wrote: "The whole affair was as flat as Manhattan water." The figure over the entrance was a bronze Aquarius. Watercolor, 12 7/8 × 7 1/8". The J. Clarence Davies Collection. 29.100.1579

117. City Hall Park from the back or uptown side was drawn in this watercolor by Thomas J. Stansbury in the 1820s. The building with the weathervane was the City Jail. "The American Museum" at left was the collection of natural history oddities (a shark caught in one of the New York slips, "a white Arctic bear," etc.) bought by P. T. Barnum in 1841 and reopened as the basis of his celebrated "Museum." In the building with the cupola at far left John Vanderlyn and other artists exhibited their mammoth landscape panoramas. Water-color, 15 × 20". Bequest of Mrs. J. Insley Blair. 52.100.16

118. Ice as well as water had once come from The Collect, but by the beginning of the nineteenth century it, too, had to be supplied from springs north of the City and even from the northern counties. The Columbia Garden, a place of popular entertainment at the Battery, advertised in May, 1806, a new service: ice for the summer season, eight pounds per family per day, for $15, the subscription to end in September. (Columbia Garden a few years earlier—in 1799—had been the first place in New York to advertise ice cream.) Nicolino Calyo, who drew this watercolor of an ice cart, came to the United States from Naples in the early 1830s. Watercolor, 10 1/4 × 14″. Gift of Mrs. Francis P. Garvan in memory of Francis P. Garvan. 55.6.13

119. St. Thomas's Church (Episcopal) at the intersection of Broadway and Houston Street was consecrated in 1826, and like so many New York buildings of the time, burned in 1851. During its relatively short existence George Harvey drew the early Gothic Revival building at nightfall about the year 1837. Watercolor, 22 1/2 × 18″. Bequest of Mrs. J. Insley Blair. 52.100.11

120. The Swedish Baron Axel Leonhard Klin006wstrom, a lieutenant in the navy of his country, visited New York in 1818. Some aspects of the City (the huge restaurants especially) he found admirable, although on the whole he thought it compared poorly with Stockholm, and he was much annoyed by the dirty streets and the noisome and even ferocious pigs which prowled them. He drew some engaging watercolors of New York: this one of Broadway and City Hall, with the corner of St. Paul's Chapel at the left and across the street, three doors up, the house of John Jacob Astor. Some of Klin006wstrom's work was later engraved for the book he wrote about his American travels. When this view was engraved, several pigs were added to the traffic on Broadway. Watercolor, 21 1/2 × 27 1/2″. Bequest of Mrs. J. Insley Blair. 52.100.8

121. Baroness Hyde de Neuville, wife of the French ambassador to the United States, painted this watercolor of the corner of Warren and Greenwich streets in the winter of 1809. Sleigh-riding and sledding were an ancient tradition in New York, having been introduced by the Dutch as early as 1652. An English visitor a few winters earlier had found no carriages on the streets of the City: sleighs were used for transportation of people and produce. Since the snow naturally muffled the sound of vehicles, pedestrians were sometimes silently run down. As late as 1908, ordinances were being passed by the City insisting that each sleigh be equipped with bells. Watercolor, 8 × 13 1/2″. Bequest of Mrs. J. Insley Blair. 52.100.6

122. Among the possessions of Major-General Pierre van Cortlandt and his wife was this silver coffee pot initialed PVC made by Hugh Wishart, who worked in New York from about 1784 to 1824. It is accompanied by a bill of sale dated 1809. The Museum of the City of New York also owns a pair of cake baskets made by Wishart for the Van Cortlandts with a bill dated 15 May 1812 showing the charge for the pair as $156.55. Height: 9 3/8″. Bequest of Joseph B. Brenauer. 46.229.22

123. Brooks Brothers opened as clothiers in 1818. One of the store's founders was Edward Sands Brooks. In his home, first at 143 Cherry Street and later at 18 East 23rd Street, stood this rich pier table in the American Empire style made about 1830–35. It is of mahogany with gilt stencil decoration. The front columns are alabaster with gilt carved-wood Corinthian capitals. The back is a mirror. Height: 37 1/2″; width: 42 1/8″. Gift of Rev. William H. Owen, descendant of Brooks. 33.236.3ab

124. A boldly carved standing eagle forms the back splat of a side chair which has been attributed to the workshop of Duncan Phyfe. The eagle, featured on the seal adopted by the Continental Congress in 1782 and the Federal government in 1789, is a frequent motif in the decorative arts of Federal America. The chair, one of eight, belonged to De Witt Clinton. Height: 31 1/4″. Bequest of Mrs. Henry O. Tallmadge. 60.103.36

125. De Witt Clinton owned this fall-front desk, derived from a French form, with mahogany veneers and ormolu mounts, made in New York about 1815–20. The desk may have been the work of the émigré cabinetmaker Charles-Honoré Lannuier. On his arrival in New York in 1803, Lannuier advertised that "he makes all kinds of Furniture . . . in the newest and latest French fashion." Height: 64″. Gift of Mrs. William Keyser. 53.119

126. A New York parlor of the early nineteenth century is recreated in this handsome setting. The portrait by C. C. Ingham is of Sophia Miles Belden at her harp, the very one sitting in the room. George Templeton Strong, her neighbor in Gramercy park, knew Mrs. Belden well. He describes her as "a lively and eccentric old lady, of English birth," who had the strength of mind on her deathbed to dictate how her funeral should be conducted and to name her pallbearers, one of whom was Strong himself. A portrait of her husband, George Belden, hangs over their butler's desk, made by Duncan Phyfe. Bequest of Mrs. Giles Whiting. 71.120.102, 99 & 6

128. About 1825, ladies of New York wore dresses like this one ▶
of copper-colored satin edged with white satin and black velvet.
The popular headdress of the time was the turban. Gift of Mrs.
Arthur K. Peck. 37.348.8

129. Robert and William Nunns, pianoforte makers, produced ▶ ▶
this upright rosewood piano and stool with stenciled decoration
about 1830. The front panel is of pleated gold silk with an ormolu
rosette in the center. The candle brackets at the sides are of
brass. In 1830, a Nunns pianoforte was awarded a prize by the
Mechanics' Institute at their annual show. Height: 62 3/4";
width: 48". Gift of Mrs. Deas Murphy, Mrs. Robert McAllister
Lloyd, and Mrs. Paul Townsend Jones in memory of their
parents, Mr. and Mrs. Robert Lenox Belknap. 36.427.1a–d

127. Duncan Phyfe made this sideboard of the type called
"pedestal-end" for his own house at 193 Fulton Street about
the year 1825. The woods used are mahogany and crotch
mahogany veneer. The mirror beneath the central drawer is
unusual. The sideboard is of very substantial proportions:
51 5/8" high and 74 1/8" long. Gift of Mrs. J. Bertram Howell,
descendant of Duncan Phyfe. 70.86ab

130. Furniture by Duncan Phyfe, the single most important furniture maker in New York's history, dominates this period room in The Museum of the City of New York. At the left of the fireplace is a Phyfe card table with Prince-of-Wales feathers carving; on the right his fine worktable (in which ladies kept their needlework). The portrait is of Henry Post, Jr., by Rembrandt Peale. In the center of the room is a remarkably fine gaming table with backgammon and checkerboards made by the Frenchman Charles-Honoré Lannuier, working in New York from 1803 to 1819. Although much of Lannuier's work is true to his background, this table was made in the Anglo-American style of his competitor Phyfe. As was often the case in nineteenth-century American rooms, many of the decorative accessories are imports, among them the glass chandelier and the Aubusson rug. Phyfe card table, height: 29 1/4″, 34.400.13; worktable, height: 31 1/2″, 34.400.15; portrait, oil on canvas, 30 × 23″, 46.327.1; Lannuier table, height: 29 1/4″, 34.400.1ab. Gifts of Mrs. Harry Horton Benkard. The woodwork was given and installed by Mr. and Mrs. Francis B. Crowninshield.

V: PORT OF ENTRY:
URBAN PROBLEMS ARISE

The inhabitants of New York are the most locomotive people
on the face of the earth.

—JAMES BOARDMAN, 1830

In the nineteenth century New York bore the brunt of one of the greatest mass migrations of all time: Western Europeans emigrating to the United States. Even as early as 1819, Mayor Cadwallader Colden (grandson of the royal lieutenant-governor) reported that in the previous twenty-one months 18,930 foreign immigrants had arrived in New York City, but between 1820 and 1830 the immigration rate of most years was only about 4,000. In 1830, the figure was suddenly nearly 14,000; in 1835, it was 32,715. Five years later it was 60,609 (or a twenty percent addition to the City's population of 300,000 in one year!). In 1845, there were 76,514 immigrants. In 1850, an incredible 212,796 landed at New York. Between 1840 and 1856, over 3,000,000 immigrants entered through the port of New York. It is impossible to say how many of these immigrants remained in New York and its environs, but certainly a majority settled in the City.

The native New Yorkers were absolutely stupefied by these hordes. An entirely new attitude toward immigration arose. In earlier centuries immigration to New York was encouraged by almost everyone; it was to everyone's advantage to have new settlers for the half-inhabited country. The Dutch West India Company, as we have seen, made strenuous efforts to attract new settlers. Various royal governors made spasmodic attempts at colonization in the eighteenth century. Throughout the entire English period there had been English, Scottish, Irish, French, and German Protestants trickling into the City without opposition or

much comment. They were quietly absorbed, and many became quite successful in the first generation; in the second they were an undistinguishable element of the population. Now, taxpayers were asked to welcome a very different kind of immigrant, usually untrained, largely illiterate, demanding of free public services, and, above all, of a different religion.

In the case of the Irish immigrants the religious question immediately emerged and accounted for most of the native American prejudice against them. Many Irishmen had been prominent in New York colonial history, including Lieutenant-Governor Cadwallader Colden, Richard Montgomery, Chancellor Livingston's brother-in-law and the hero of Quebec, and many others, but they were almost invariably Anglo-Irish and Protestants. The Irish arriving in the thirties and forties and thereafter were nearly always Roman Catholic.

The two great New York diaries, Philip Hone's and George Templeton Strong's, were kept in this period and both express the horror felt by the Old Americans toward the newcomers and particularly toward the Irish and their religion. Each writer supported the Native American party, which was anti-Catholic, as did a host of distinguished New Yorkers, both under that name and later as the "Know-Nothings."

The native poor of New York and the taxpayers bitterly resented the fact that immigrants were allowed to apply for relief immediately upon arrival in the City. Some asked shelter at the almshouse the day they arrived! There were ugly rumors that foreign governments were paying their paupers' way to America to get rid of them. In 1844, there were 2,790 inmates in the almshouse, lunatic asylum, and penitentiary, of whom two-thirds (1,881) were foreigners.

There was one class of New Yorkers, however, who did not share in the Nativist feelings; then as now, politicians fell upon the necks of the new arrivals. Here was a huge body of new voters, ignorant, illiterate, grateful for small favors, and, above all, easily manipulated at election day. An endless dynasty of "bosses"' rose whose strength lay in these immigrants and their votes.

There was still no law in New York for the registration of voters. Prisoners held at Blackwell's Island were set free to vote, and recent arrivals, freshly naturalized citizens, trooped to the polls. Hasty naturalizations were the rule. In 1838, George Templeton Strong went to City Hall to see the naturalization process. His diary entry is a fair example of the feelings of many New Yorkers at the time. "It was enough to turn a man's stomach—to make a man abjure republicanism forever—to see the way they were naturalizing this morning at the Hall. Wretched, filthy, bestial-looking Italians and Irish, and creations that looked as if they had risen from the lazarettos of Naples for this especial object; in short, the very scum and dregs of human nature filled the clerk of Common Pleas office so completely that I was almost afraid of being poisoned by going in."

Tammany Hall held most of these new votes. Already well established (it had been organized in 1789), it was marching steadily toward its zenith under Boss Tweed in the 1860s when it held New York in the full splendor of bribery, patronage, and corruption.

In 1821, New York State drew up a new constitution. The conservatives at the constitutional convention were led by Chancellor James Kent, a New Yorker whose *Commentaries on American Law* is still the foremost American institutional legal treatise, the liberals by Martin Van Buren, then beginning his climb in American politics which led to the presidency. Although many changes were made in the state government, the real struggle was over suffrage. The conservatives wanted to maintain the property qualifications for voters, the liberals to abolish them. The liberals won and suffrage was granted to every adult white citizen who could prove a few mild qualifications. In 1826, it was still further extended by giving every white male citizen of the state over twenty-one, a resident of the state for one year and the county for six months, the right to vote.

In 1834, the mayor began to be elected by popular vote. The first chosen was Cornelius Van Wyck Lawrence. His election was ominous because it was marked by serious disturbances during which the militia had to be called out. Lawrence was a supporter of Andrew Jackson, and the election, which lasted for three days, was accompanied by Jacksonian insults, inebriation, and scuffles. There were 35,141 votes cast for mayor, Lawrence winning by only 179. The Common Council, however, was won by the Whigs. Philip Hone (himself mayor from 1826 to 1827) said the election of the Common Council by the Whigs was a "signal triumph of good principles over violence and illegal voting." The Whigs celebrated with a great banquet at Castle Garden and were addressed by Daniel Webster. It was in this election that the Democrats first referred to their opposition as "The Silk Stocking Party," a term still in use for an East Side voting district in New York. This referred to the presence of many old Whigs—who wore the no-longer-fashionable knee breeches and silk stockings of an earlier day—dug out of retirement to vote against the Democrats.

Disturbances and riots, or the verging on riot, became an unhappy accompaniment of New York City elections, indicating the presence in the City of a mob element constantly alarming to the respectable populace. At Five Points, a notorious haunt of the raffish at the junction of Baxter, Worth, and Park streets, in the heart of the Democratic country, there was a serious riot in 1835, between two branches of the Democratic Party, the native versus the Irish, over an attempt to raise an Irish regiment to be called "The O'Connell Guards."

Extreme agitation came in the 1840s over the issue of state support for Roman Catholic schools. Education throughout the colonial period had been in the hands of Protestant religious groups. When a free school of forty-two children opened on 19 May 1806 on Bancker (later Madison) Street near Pearl, it was the beginning of the public school system in New York City. Other public, nonsectarian schools were founded in 1811 by the Free School Society on Henry Street and by the African Free School Society on Cliff Street. The state established its public school system in 1812; the Free School Society of the City of New York was granted a share of the funds, but it was not under the control of the state. Religious societies operating schools also received state funds until 1824, when the Common Council restricted them to only the nonsectarian Free School Society, the Mechanics' Society, the Orphan Asylum Society, and the African Schools. This was thought to settle the issue.

When the rapidly increasing number of Roman Catholics demanded support and were refused, their complaints were carried to the state legislature, and the question became violently partisan. Opponents of aid to Catholic schools founded the "Democratic American Association" which nominated the painter and New York University Professor Samuel F. B. Morse for mayor. When he was defeated, a new "American Protestant Union" was formed with Morse as president. A Catholic ticket was then organized. The question became so important that it was finally resolved by the legislature in 1842, when the state took over the City system and prohibited any aid to parochial schools.

The fight for aid to the Catholic schools was led by Bishop (later first Archbishop) of New York John Joseph Hughes, an aggressive prelate not too particular about his methods, who played an important role in the City's history from 1838 to 1864.

The Native American party scored one victory. In 1844, they elected as mayor James Harper, founder of the publishing firm of Harper & Brothers. George Templeton Strong, who supported Harper, said that the election was the worst blow to befall "the Hibernian race" since the Battle of the Boyne. After visiting Native American headquarters the evening of the election he reported that "not an exile of Erin ventures to show his nose in the neighborhood." Harper's not very successful administration attempted to pass blue laws which were unpopular and largely ignored. It was nearly the last bid of this party; from that time on they were so outnumbered by the forces of Tammany Hall that even if elections had been honest—and they were not—it was virtually impossible for the Native Americans to elect anyone to any office.

The result of all this was that New York was notoriously one of the worst-governed cities in the civilized world. In 1840, with a population over 300,000 and rapidly growing, the organization of city government had not advanced much over that of New Amsterdam. The water supply was poor, fire protection badly handled, the "watch department" (police) ill organized, too small, and inefficient, and the City government wholly unable to prevent riots.

And yet the City grew by leaps and bounds. In 1839, Philip Hone found Wall Street blocked with huge boulders of granite being used in new bank buildings. He wrote: "The spirit of pulling down and building up is abroad. The whole of New York is rebuilt about once in ten years." The incredible expansion of the City brought a housing shortage. All leases expired on the first of May, and year after year that was the universal moving day. The confusion on Moving Day became famous and astonished visitors. George Templeton Strong described Moving Day, 1844: "Fine weather, to the great comfort of the locomotive public. Never knew the city in such a chaotic state. Every other house seems to be disgorging itself into the street; all the sidewalks are lumbered with bureaus and bedsteads to the utter destruction of their character as thoroughfares, and all the space between the sidewalks is occupied by long processions of carts and wagons and vehicles. . . . We certainly haven't advanced as a people beyond the nomadic or migratory stage of civilization. . . . " The unfortunates who found their new abodes still occupied or unfit for habitation gathered in City Hall Park with all their goods and chattels. If they were still there in the evening the City kindly threw open the jail, where they spent the night.

Fires were worse than ever in this burgeoning

city. New Yorkers seem to have regarded them philosophically, much as they now regard traffic jams. Going to watch fires was almost an amusement; George Templeton Strong and his friends responded every time they heard the fire bells and were connoisseurs of conflagrations. The Great Fire of 1835 lived long in the memory of New Yorkers. It was said to have destroyed $30,000,000 worth of property and bankrupted many fire insurance companies.

The "fire department" which fought these blazes was still primitive in the extreme and the system verged on the comic. Each fire-warden was attached to a particular engine which he with his firemen, hose-men, and hook-and-ladder men dragged to the scene of the fire and operated. Citizens had leather buckets, one for each fireplace in the house, which had to be kept in the front hall. When there was a fire, the citizens were formed by the fire-warden into double lines from the engines to the nearest pump and passed water to the engines. These engines became practically anthropomorphized and the object of much polishing and cherishing on the part of their firemen. The fire companies, which were composed of volunteers, were extremely competitive; it was not unknown for two companies to come to blows over which was to have the honor of saving a building—while of course it continued to blaze. The companies were a strong element in the political and social life of the time, and leadership in a fire company could be a means of advancement on both fronts, as it was in the notorious example of Boss Tweed. The Great Fire of 1835 was probably the worst of the era, but there was another especially bad in 1845, and in 1858 the Crystal Palace, a great glass hall used for exhibitions, burned to the ground.

The complaints about the poor policing of the City were numerous and justified; the force was unable to keep order, which was amply shown in the ridiculous Astor Place Riot and on nearly every election day. In point of numbers, however, when New York had 500,000 people and the Watch Department consisted of about 1,800, the City was more heavily policed than it is now. In 1844, the state legislature ordered the formation of a

131. Palmo's Opera House opened in 1844 at 39–41 Chambers Street, between Broadway and Centre, in a building formerly occupied by public baths and The National Academy of Design. This print shows the interior during that period. This was the first theater in New York to sell numbered seats which were retained throughout the evening's entertainment. Until then one bought an undesignated space and defended it against latecomers. As an opera house Palmo's failed, and in 1848 it was converted into a theater. Engraving, 7 1/2" square. The J. Clarence Davies Collection. 29.100.854

132. The Havana Opera's ballet company played at Palmo's ▶ in the summer theatrical season of 1847. Their visit was eagerly anticipated by New Yorkers. The numerous Lehmans listed on the program were one large family of brothers and sisters who danced, sang, acted, and did rope-tricks. Mademoiselle Adelaide, the prettiest of the many sisters, was featured. The Irish farce *Dumb Belle* had been played in New York by many companies since 1838; the role of O'Smirk was a favorite of actors of low comedy. 21 1/2 × 6". Gift of Harry Shaw Newman. 40.160.3112

PALMO'S OPERA HOUSE.

Extraordinary Success
OF THE
FRENCH BALLET
COMPANY.

From the Havana and New Orleans Theatres.

The performance of these

EXTRAORDINARY ARTISTES

Have attracted the most Brilliant and Fashionable Audiences wherever they have appeared —The extraordinary beauty and ease of

MLLE. ADELAIDE,
Thursday Evening, July 22d, 1847.

The Performance will commence with the popular farce of the

DUMB BELLE.

Vivian	Mr Kingsley	O'Smirk	Mr. Flynn
Manvers	Phillips	Eliza	Miss Mary Duff
James	Thompson	Mary	Miss Eliza Mitchell

To be followed by a Grand

DIVERTISEMENT.

Pas de Matelot.......by...........M'lls. Julie and Flora
El Bolero de Cadiz....by.....Mlle. Adelaide and M. Schmidt
Pas Comique.........by.........Mr. W. Thompson

Overture.........by...........The Orchestra

To conclude with the New Ballet Comique, in One Act, entitled, La

Diable Rouge
Or, The Vine Dressers of Como.

Signor Alejo, (Vine proprietor on the Lake of Como,).......Mr. Antoine Lehman
Fransqueto, (peasant of the environs,)......................Mr. Schmidt Lehman
Don Manuel de la Ronda, (Spanish Cabellero on the point of
marriage with Francesqueta,).......................M'lle Caroline Lehman
Don Pasquale, (his friend,)......................Mr. W. Thompson
Francesqueta, (rose of Como,)......................M'lle Matilde Lehman
Alma, (the good Genii)......................M'lle Adelaide Lehman
Diable Rouge' (subject to the power of the good Genii)......Mr. Christian Lehman
Peasants, men, women, Servants, &c.

INCIDENTS, DANCES, &c.

The Lovers interrupted. Arrival of Don Manuel, and interesting arrangement of Signor Alejo.

Dance by Characters.

The Rendezvous. Appearance of the good Genii Scene, &c.

Pas Seul......................**M'lle. Adelaide**

Mysterious aid and entrance of the Diable Rouge, his tricks upon the proprietor.

GRAND FIGHT

The Diable Rouge more than a match for his antagonists. Mishaps of the Cabellero.

Grand Pas de Trois.

M'lle's Adelaide, Mathilda and S. Lehman.

The Contract interrupted by the Diable Rouge. Re-appearance of the good Genii, To conclude with a

GRAND PAS DE DEUX.

By M'lle. Adelaide and Mons. S. Lehman. and Finale by the Characters.

Prices of Admission.

Dress Circle & Parquette................50 Cents.
Second Tier............................25 Cents.
Private Boxes, for 8 Persons..............$5

Doors open at half-past 7, performance to commence at 8 o'clock precisely.

HERALD JOB PRINTING OFFICE, 97 NASSAU-STREET.

Christy's Opera House
Mechanics' Hall, 472 Broadway, above Grand
THE ORIGINAL AND WELL-KNOWN
CHRISTY'S MINSTRELS

Organized in 1842—The Oldest Established Company in the World.
the first to harmonize Negro Melodies, and Originators of the present popular style of Ethiopian Entertainments—whose success in this City during the past FIVE YEARS, is without precedent in the annals of Public Amusement in New York.

PARTICULAR NOTICE—Owing to the great length of the Entertainment, and the peculiar arrangement of the Programme, any REPETITION of the several acts are entirely precludes It is hoped this explanation will be acceptable to the Patrons of Christy's Minstrels.

THE COMPANY
Under the Direction and Management of......... E. P. CHRISTY

Programme for this Evening.
PART I.

Medley Overture	Full Band
Quartette, where is the Spot that we was Born on	Company
The Old Folks at Home	E. P. Christy
Down in the Cane Brake	George Christy
Would I were a Boy Again	E. P. Christy
Katy Dean	E. Pierce
My Sally Dear	N. Gould
Masquerade Waltz, with Street Organ and Automaton Imitations	E. Pierce and G. Christy
Phantom Chorus, or the Darkey's Apparition, from the Opera of "La Sonnambula"	Company
Quick Step, "Crown Diamonds"	Full Band

PART II.
VOYAGE MUSICALE,

Comprising a Grand "Pot Pie" of indescribable Musical Combinations, from a Penny Whistle to a considerable sized tin Horn, Chinese Bells, &c. &c. Particulars left entirely to the imagination of the audience.

Song of the Dance, Burlesque	M. Zorer
Miss Lucy Long	G. Christy
Polka, Burlesque	T. Vaughn and G. Christy
Ethiopian Fling	Lewis Mairs
Violin Solo	J. Donniker
El Bolero Africane	G. Christy and Lewis Mairs
Solo on the Guitar	Gould
Hungarian Warblers	Zorer, Christian, G. Christy & Raynor
Comic Pas de Matelot	L. Mairs & Pierce
Accordeon Solo	C. Keene

PART III.

Representing the peculiar characteristics of the Southern or Plantation Negroes

Banjo Solo	E. Pierce
It will never to give it up so	Pierce and Vaughn
Banjo Trio	G. Christy, Pierce and Vaughn
Plantation Jig	G. Christy
Rail Road Overture	Full Band
Plantation Quartette	Raynor, Upson, Donniker &c
Finale, Down in Carolina, introducing the Holiday Festival Dance	E. Pierce and G. Christy

ADMISSION 25 CENTS.
Doors open at 7.   Commence at 8 o'clock.

Gentlemen UNACCOMPANIED with Ladies, will please observe the FRONT SEATS are RESERVED for the accommodation of Ladies and Children. The propriety of this arrangement it is presumed, will be generally admitted.

The Patrons of Christy's Minstrels are respectfully informed, that the SATURDAY AFTERNOON Concerts are discontinued.

---

133. A record for American theatrical longevity was set by E. P. Christys' Minstrels, who played continuously for more than a decade—beginning at Palmo's Opera House in 1842 and carrying on at Mechanics' Hall, 472 Broadway. Although by no means the first performers to appear in blackface, they were the most popular and delighted audiences from all levels of society. It used to be said that every rural visitor to New York City saw the Christy Minstrels and Barnum's Museum. The Christy Minstrels were succeeded at Mechanics' Hall by the Bryant company, and it was on this stage that the Bryant Minstrels performed for the first time anywhere the greatest of minstrel melodies, "Dixie," which was given as the concluding "walk-around" on 4 April 1859. Note in Part I the take-off on Bellini's *La Sonnambula*. Spoofs of operas were immensely popular; this same season a Donizetti take-off was playing called *Lucy Did Sham Amour*. Playbill, 12 × 6″.
The J. Clarence Davies Collection. 29.100.881

police department with a chief appointed by the mayor. The mayor, the unfortunate James Harper, attempted to uniform the force (which up to then had worn ordinary clothes with badges). The police were furious; they refused to wear "livery." The Board of Aldermen, ignoring the legislature, passed another and different reorganization plan setting up its own force. After an absurd interval of a year, during which New York had *two* police forces competing with each other and at one point battling in front of City Hall, the legislature's plan was approved by the aldermen. It was only in 1853, however, that the police after much persuasion consented to appear in a neat uniform of blue coat with gray trousers and blue cap. Most citizens regarded the force as only slightly improved by this procedure.

One municipal problem was solved. In 1842, the Croton Reservoir, standing on the site of the present New York Public Library, was opened. Since 1798, various plans had been put forth for bringing abundant and pure water to the City, which was so badly in need of it. Nothing much happened until 1832, when the state and city began investigating the possibility of bringing water into the City from the Croton River. A continuous tunnel of masonry was constructed under the direction of Major David B. Douglas, a professor of engineering at West Point, who built $40\frac{1}{2}$ miles between 1837 and 1842. The water reached the receiving reservoir at Yorkville on 27 June of the latter year and the distributing reservoir at Murray Hill on the Fourth of July. On 14 October, President John Tyler and two former presidents of the United States, John Quincy Adams and Martin Van Buren, along with a host of governors, mayors, and other dignitaries officially opened the waterworks with speeches, the singing of an ode, and finally nine cheers by the assembled multitude. The opening of the Croton Reservoir was a major step in the making of a metropolis.

Despite short periods of stagnation such as the Jacksonian depression of 1837, the Panic of 1857, and occasional destructive fires in the business district, the Port of New York continued its astonishing growth.

New York was the port of embarkation for many of the California Gold Rushers of 1848 and 1849 and the center of coastal traffic in the East as well as being the great American port of entry. Its harbor was filled with shipping of incredible variety. A painting by Thomas Thompson in The Museum of the City of New York and the view from Brooklyn by Currier & Ives give a good idea of this variety and of the daily drama of arrival and departure by water. The most important Customs House in the United States was in New York. Barges carried customs officials out to the arriving ships, and the Barge Office is shown in a painting by Regis Gignoux. The present Sub-Treasury Building at 32–34 Wall Street was then used as the Customs House.

New York was home port for some of the greatest sailing ships in the world, for example, the famous *Nightingale* shown in a Currier & Ives print as well as the most celebrated of yachts, the *America*.

Land transportation within the City was changing rapidly. The New York and Harlem Railroad began to operate horse-cars in 1832 between Prince and 14th streets. This line was extended to Yorkville in 1834, to Harlem in 1837. Steam trains were introduced in 1834. A line ran up Sixth Avenue from Barclay Street to Central Park, which was then under construction; another line went up Eighth Avenue from Barclay to 59th; and on the East Side one stretched up Second Avenue from Peck Slip to Harlem.

These transportation facilities made it possible for more citizens to move "uptown." By 1848, some residences had already been built on Union and Madison squares. Fifth Avenue had houses between 14th and 23rd streets, but only a very few were as far north as Murray Hill in the thirties. By 1854, there was considerable settlement up to 37th Street. Nicholas Biddle Kittell's painting of Mr. and Mrs. C. A. Carter gives a good idea of an interior of a well-to-do home of the period. One of the best impressions of the way New Yorkers lived in the 1840s and 1850s can be had from the splendid Brett Doll House in The Museum of the City of New York.

For amusement New Yorkers went to the theater (there were five in 1837 and their number rapidly increased after that), to the opera, saw wild-animal shows, went to the public gardens like Niblo's and Vauxhall where they strolled along flowered walks, bought refreshments, and enjoyed fireworks and musical entertainment. They also heard the celebrated Christy Minstrels as Abraham Lincoln did on his trips to New York, went to horse races and auctions, or visited Castle Garden where distinguished visitors to New York were welcomed, where many concerts were given, and where Jenny Lind made one of the greatest theatrical appearances of all time. For quieter amusement, there were in 1859 twenty-seven libraries and an amazing thirteen daily newspapers.

An invention little noted at its first appearance but soon to change the face of many cities (none more than New York's) was the elevator. The first platform freight elevator was put into use by Hecker and Brother, millers, at 201–3 Cherry Street in 1850. In 1859, Otis Tufts of Boston installed the earliest permanent passenger elevator in New York in the new Fifth Avenue Hotel. It was advertised under the delightful name "vertical screw railway" and was a sensation. The first office building to use an elevator was the Equitable Life Assurance Society at 120 Broadway in 1870; from that time on the sky was truly the limit for future buildings in New York.

134. The earliest of the approximately 100,000 photographs in The Museum of the City of New York is this view of the Battery photographed by Victor Prevost in 1853. His negatives were made on waxed or oiled paper. When Prevost took this photograph the Battery was being enlarged at a cost of $150,000. At the extreme left of the view on the corner of Battery Place and West Street is the Philadelphia Hotel. Two doors away is No. 10 Battery Place, the office of Cornelius Vanderbilt's steamship line. 10 × 13″. Gift of Mrs. J. West Roosevelt. 38.93.1

135. Mary Varick worked this fine sampler between 1820 and 1825 with unexpected motifs in addition to the usual alphabets, digits, and quotations. In the center are the portrait bust of George Washington, the American eagle, the date of Washington's inauguration, and a reference to the cherry tree legend which first appeared in print in 1806. Note at right the direct if unlovely Biblical quotation typical of sampler prose: "As a jewel of gold in a swines snout so is a fair woman which is without discretion." Framed, 19 3/4 × 15″. Bequest of Mrs. J. Insley Blair. 52.100.39

136. Isaac Van Amburgh was the first native-born American lion-tamer. Descended from an early New York Dutch family, his long career of training many kinds of wild animals and performing with them fascinated his contemporaries. Before he organized his own menagerie and aviary he appeared in plays like *The Lion Doomed, or, The Bandit of Benares*, in which two lions were introduced on the stage in "a large and safe den" which Van Amburgh entered to feed them in the presence of the audience. His Zoological Institute with headquarters at 37 Bowery was in existence only during the season 1834–35. This colossal woodblock poster, believed to be the largest early American multiple sheet poster, is one of two known copies. 9 × 6 1/2′. Museum Purchase. 62.121

137. Stephen C. Foster wrote many songs for the Christy Minstrels like "Oh Susannah," shown here in an early sheet-music edition. Although, like Christy and his performers, Foster was white and not a Southerner (both were born in Pennsylvania and died in New York, Foster in Bellevue Hospital), he excelled at "Ethiopian songs" which he sold to Christy at ten dollars a song, five dollars extra if Christy was listed as composer. On this cover are shown E. P. Christy at the top and his brother George in female garb as one of the dancers in the center vignette. At the right the dancer has a heel-and-toe technique which would become modern tap dancing. The famous semicircle of performers which was the hallmark of all minstrel shows has "Bones" at left playing clackers, which were like castanets, and at right "Tambo," the tambourine player. Sheet-music cover, 13 1/4 × 10 1/4″. Gift of William A. Hildebrandt. 40.280.599

HAMILTON

138. A work of art particularly prized by New Yorkers was destroyed in the Great Fire of 1835. Robert Ball Hughes had executed a marble statue of Alexander Hamilton which was unveiled in the Rotunda of the Merchants' Exchange on 28 March 1835. Paid for by a public subscription, it stood fifteen feet high with its pedestal. The fire destroyed it despite valiant attempts at rescue by a party of sailors from the Navy Yard. The *Evening Star* was moved to write: "Among the ruins, not the least to be lamented was the loss of that splendid statue of Hamilton, which towering brightly amidst the sea of flames, that dashed against its crackling base, cast a mournful glance on the terrific scene, and then fell nobly, perishing under the crush of the edifice of which it had been, as it were, the tutelary genius." The loss of the Hughes's *Hamilton* left New York without a public statue. The original model, however, survived. Plaster. Height: 27". Gift of Mrs. Alexander Hamilton and General Pierpont Morgan Hamilton. 71.31.12

139. Disasters, either providential or man-made, inspired Currier & Ives to some of their best efforts. The absurd and tragic Astor Place riot (actually several riots beginning on 7 May 1849) between supporters of the English actor Charles Macready and the American tragedian Edwin Forrest resulted in thirty-one dead and hundreds wounded. Currier & Ives show the events of Thursday, 10 May, when Macready performed *Macbeth* at the Opera House surrounded by 300 police. The attacking mob of "Forresters" had nearly overwhelmed the police when the Seventh Regiment National Guard appeared on the scene and subdued them, but only after vigorous battling. Colored lithograph, 12 1/2 × 8". Gift of Mrs. Henry G. Bartol. 47.27.1

140. It was the North versus the South at the great horse race held at the Union Course on Long Island on 13 May 1845. Thomas Kirkman of Alabama entered his Peytona in the best two out of three four-mile heats against Fashion, owned by Henry K. Toler of New Jersey. Peytona, here shown running ahead, won the $20,000 purse, with times of 7.39 3/4 and 7.45 1/4. This N. Currier lithograph drawn by C. Severin is not only one of the rarest American sporting prints, it is one of the finest. More than two hundred figures of spectators are distinctly represented, and in the center of the course fourteen different stages and carriages are shown, displaying many of the current modes of transportation. Note for example the omnibuses labeled "Broadway," "Bowery," and "Kipp & Brown." Around the time of this print there were 258 regular omnibuses operating in the City. Colored lithograph, 18 × 28 1/2". The Harry T. Peters Collection. 58.300.52

141. Few performing artists have received an ovation to compare with New York's first welcome to the soprano Jenny Lind in the autumn of 1850. The City went wild, with her manager P. T. Barnum skillfully fanning the enthusiasm. This rare Currier & Ives print shows the scene at Castle Garden the night she made her American debut. The auditorium was jammed; tickets went for fantastic prices. Notice that the musicians are standing, which was the custom—except for cellists—until nearly the end of the century. One of the three men standing offstage at left is said to be Barnum. The receipts as indicated amounted to $26,238, then a record-breaking sum. Lind's share was $12,600, all of which she cannily donated to New York charities, making her more popular than ever. The interestingly sad circumstances of her birth (she was illegitimate), her high-mindedness (she refused to sing some operatic roles because the morality of the heroines was shaky), even her ferocious anti-Catholicism (she never sang in France or Italy), endeared her to the typical upper-class American audiences of the times. Her two-year tour was a triumph until she fell out with Barnum; then it was downhill. She never returned. Colored lithograph, 9 × 14″. The J. Clarence Davies Collection. 29.100.1871

142. Three thousand dollars of the proceeds of Jenny Lind's concert were donated by her to the Widow and Orphan's Fund of the local fire companies. In return the firemen gave her this rosewood bookcase made by the Brooks Cabinet Warehouse at 127 Fulton Street, Brooklyn, which contains a specially bound set of the octavo edition of Audubon's *Birds of America*. Height: 72″. Gift of Arthur S. Vernay. 52.272.16

143. Chatham Square was the site of auctions, or "vendues" as they were often called, from the early nineteenth century. As may be seen from the signs (W. N. Seymour's Hardware Store, H. Kipp's Furniture Warehouse) and the chairs, baskets, and crockery about, it was a neighborhood which supplied household necessities to a lower-class clientele. It was also used for horse auctions; in 1810, the Common Council provided rules for the cantering and galloping of horses being exhibited for sale. E. Didier showed this *Auction in Chatham Square* at the National Academy of Design's 1843 exhibition. Oil on canvas, 22 × 27 1/2". Anonymous gift. 51.222.1

144. Louis Kossuth, who had headed a ▶ short-lived Hungarian rebellion against the Hapsburgs, arrived in the United States in 1851 for a triumphal visit. This rather remote hero and his cause were taken up by the Americans with enormous if surprising enthusiasm. In this naive painting by "E. Percel," Kossuth (called "General" by courtesy) in beaver hat and riding the white horse is given full military honors on his landing at the Battery, 6 December 1851. Oil on canvas, 44 × 63 1/2." Gift of Colonel Edgar William and Mrs. Bernice Chrysler Garbisch. 66.2

145. The financial panic of 1837, which led into a depression persisting five or six years, inspired this fine colored lithograph entitled *The Times*, drawn by Edward W. Clay and published in 1837. The view, although fictitious, gives a good impression of the hardships resulting from the government's decision that all public lands must be paid for in specie, with a consequent shortage of money. The setting is New York City, but the buildings labeled are only generalized. The Custom House and the Mechanic's Bank were both on Wall Street. Note the satiric names on some of the signs: "S. Rumbottle Liquor Store"; "Shylock Graspall Licensed Pawnbroker"; "Peter Pillage Attorney at Law." The head in the clouds represents President Andrew Jackson and the balloon designated "Safety Fund" is on fire. Note the idle shipping and across the harbor a very early representation of a locomotive. This lithograph is very rare. 18 7/8 × 12 1/8″. The J. Clarence Davies Collection. 29.100.2355

146. Thomas Thompson, who spent much of his long life (he was seventy-two when this painting was done) portraying New York, was fascinated by its harbor. He was long associated with the National Academy of Design, and its historian Thomas Cummings says he was "distinguished in his department, liberal in his views," meaning in this case that he had supported the Academy by buying $200 worth of its bonds. When The Museum of the City of New

York acquired this *View of New York and Governors Island* in 1956,
it had been in the Thompson family since its execution in 1848,
having been shown to the public only at the one time it was on
exhibit at the National Academy. It gives an excellent depiction of
the busyness of New York harbor, with a fine variety of shipping,
against a background of the City's skyline dominated by church
spires. Oil on canvas, 18 1/2 × 77 1/2". Museum Purchase. 56.33

147. Samuel Waugh's *The Bay and Harbor of New York*, which shows immigrants landing at the Battery, is a huge section of an even-larger panorama painted about 1855. Entitled *Italia*, it depicted a tour through Italy and concluded with arrival in New York harbor. Waugh exhibited it in Brooklyn in 1856–57, and in 1859 at the New York Hope Chapel on the east side of Broadway just below 8th Street. Castle Garden (shown at left), formerly a place of amusement, was opened for the reception of immigrants on 3 August 1855. Bedloe's Island had become too small for the immense numbers who began to arrive in the late 1840s and early 1850s. At this time the Irish still constituted by far the largest percentage of immigrants. In 1860, 105,123 immigrants landed, of whom the Irish accounted for 47,330, the Germans 37,899, and the English (always counted separately from the Irish even though subjects of the same crown) 11,361. No other nationality accounted for more than 2,000. The man in the brown frock coat is the typical anti-Irish caricature of the time; note also the trunk labeled "Pat Murfy for Ameriky" at right. The Chinese junk shown in the harbor actually visited New York in 1847, the first vessel from "the Celestial Empire" to call, and Nathaniel Currier issued a print showing the boat and her measurements. Oil on canvas, 99 1/8 × 198″. Gift of Mrs. Robert M. Littlejohn. 33.169

148. New York was the principal port from which the Gold Rushers left on their months-long voyages to California. This contemporary watercolor by Joseph B. Smith, which is unusually early since gold was only discovered in 1848, shows the *Steamer Hartford Capt LeFevre bound for California. Sailed from New York February 1849.* The departure was from a pier in the East River. Watercolor, 29 × 42″. Bequest of Mrs. J. Insley Blair. 52.100.3

149. This figurehead is from the
ship *Albany*, a 468 ton packet
built at a shipyard on the East
River about 1831. The figure is a
reaper with a sickle in one hand
and sheaves of wheat in the other,
a reference to flour, one of upstate
New York's primary exports
during the colonial period and for
decades afterward. During the
Gold Rush, the *Albany* was one
of the aging ships pulled out of
coastal service to make the trip
to California. She sailed for San
Francisco, 9 January 1849, and
arrived on 7 July of that year.
This figurehead was rescued when
the ship was sold for the last time
in 1863. Height: 78″; width:
24″. Gift of Augustus Van Horne
Ellis. M37.15

150. Fanny Palmer (Frances Flora Bond Palmer) was employed as
an artist by Currier & Ives for more than twenty-five years. She
did many of their finest views, including this *View of New York from
Brooklyn Heights*. She was famous for her ability to sketch rapidly,
and prints like this one show a quick artist's eye. Mrs. Palmer was
the head of a whole tribe of related artists from the Palmer and
Bond families in New York and Brooklyn who were capable
recorders of their time. In this print, note the steamship
"C. Vanderbilt" at left. In 1849, when this print was produced,
Commodore Vanderbilt was nearing the height of his career as
the giant of the steamship business on the East Coast. At one time
more than a thousand boats could be counted in his fleet. Colored
lithograph, 11 5/8 × 17 1/8″. The Gerald Le Vino Collection.
57.100.125

151. The printmaker Nathaniel Currier first achieved popularity with this *Ruins of the Merchant's Exchange After the Destructive Conflagration of December 16 & 17, 1835*. The Great Fire of 1835 started on the night of 16 December in a store at the corner of Merchant (Hanover) and Pearl streets and burned until it had destroyed more than 600 buildings over a seventeen block area east of Broadway and south of Wall Street. The fire's main effect on the City in terms of architectural development was to eliminate finally almost all traces of the old Dutch town which had survived so many other fires. Among the important buildings destroyed was the Merchant's Exchange on Wall Street. Its smoking ruins are shown in this fine colored lithograph drawn by J. H. Bufford and published by Nathaniel Currier. The exchange erected to replace the one burned is now incorporated into the First National City Bank Building at 55 Wall Street. 9 1/2 × 12 1/2″. The Gerald Le Vino Collection. 57.100.42

152. The U.S. Barge Office was this picturesque building on the wooded shore at the southeast corner of Battery Park. From about 1830 to 1880, it served as the dock for the flat-bottomed barges customs officials used to row out to incoming ships for inspection. Regis Gignoux shows it here about 1850. At the extreme left is Castle Garden. Oil on canvas, 21 3/4 × 26 3/4″. Gift of Maurice M. O. Purdy in memory of his wife Alice Jean Purdy. 70.35

153. Mr. and Mrs. Charles Augustus Carter were painted ▶ about 1848, soon after their marriage, and are shown in the parlor of their home, probably 11 Bleecker Street. Carter in 1843 was Assistant Superintendent of New York Hospital. The room in which the young couple are seated is a fashionable interior of the 1840s, with Gothicized furniture, a table in the center around which the ladies of the household would gather with their sewing, and a busy floral carpet laid wall-to-wall. Note the stylish way of hanging paintings, well above eye level. The painting is signed at the lower right with initials only and has been attributed to Nicholas Biddle Kittell. Oil on canvas, 21 1/2 × 23 1/2″. Gift of Mrs. Edward C. Moen. 62.234.12

154. Captain Samuel Chester
Reid was a naval hero of the War
of 1812, who by engaging several
British ships in the Azores and
later scuttling his own vessel
delayed the British on their way
to action at New Orleans, thereby
assisting Andrew Jackson in
winning the Battle of New
Orleans. The grateful citizens of
New York presented Reid with
this rich tea set made by N.
Taylor & Co., working in New
York between 1808 and 1817.
Height of teapot: 10″. Bequest
of Gabrielle di Cesnola
Delcambre, granddaughter of
Capt. Reid. 34.96a–d

155. From the time of the first stirrings of the
Revolution Marinus Willett was in the fray as one of
New York's most radical patriots and a dedicated Son
of Liberty. In the Federal period he was sheriff of New
York City and County and finally, in 1807, mayor.
This silver teapot and sugar urn with his initials were
made by Ephraim Brasher, who worked in New York
from 1766 to 1810. Height of teapot: 7″. Gift of Mrs.
William H. Wheelock. 46.255a–c

156. Philip Hone, who served as mayor of New York for one term ending in 1827, kept (from 1828 to 1851) one of the two great diaries of New York life in the nineteenth century. The other was written by George Templeton Strong and runs from 1835 to 1875. Hone's first home was opposite City Hall Park; his later house on Broadway was on the site now occupied by the Woolworth Building. Among its furnishings was this glass decanter with sulphide medallion initialed PH attributed to the Englishman Apsley Pellatt, about 1835. Height: 10 1/4″. Gift of Mrs. Henry G. Bartol. 50.40.Iab

◀ 157. Much of the charm of China Trade porcelain lies in the slight derangement of American motifs by the Chinese painters. This sugar bowl from a tea set belonging to Nathan Sanford, chancellor of the State of New York, is decorated with the arms of New York State. The supporters have become noticeably oriental, the arms in the shield have been replaced by a sprig of flowers, and the assertive eagle has taken on the lineaments of a songbird. Height: 5″. About 1800–1815. Bequest of Miss Mabel Choate. 59.117.11ab

158. Gershom Mendes Seixas was the ▶ first American-born rabbi of Shearith Israel, the oldest Jewish congregation in New York, where he began his ministry in 1768, serving to his death in 1816. During the Revolution he was responsible for taking the congregation's Torah scrolls and ceremonial objects out of New York to preserve them from the disorders of the times. From 1784 to 1814, he was regent and trustee of Columbia College. This green-glazed earthenware pitcher with his portrait medallion was made by his son, David G. Seixas, at his pottery in Trenton, New Jersey, between 1812 and 1816. Overall height: 9″. Gift of Mrs. Louis J. Reckford. 32.91.2

159. One of the finest surviving early American doll houses was
built by the Rev. Dr. Philip Milledoler Brett between 1838 and
1840. The house was enjoyed by generations of Brett children
before being installed in The Museum of the City of New York in
1961. The construction has several unusual or even unique features:
a garden (where the grandparents are having tea); a latticed
porch; multilighted window sashes with workable shutters; and no
kitchen. The furnishings are on the whole American classical,
though pieces in other styles have been added, including the
Victorian rocking chairs. There are also pieces which were
antiques even when the house was furnished: a miniature Bible and
other books of the eighteenth century and French and English
hallmarked silver of the same period (among them the wine cooler
in the dining room). A portrait of the builder, the Rev. Dr. Brett,
hangs in the central drawing room; in the dining room on the left
wall is a framed Brett coat-of-arms; hanging in the library is an
engraving of Rutgers College, of which one Brett was president.
The overall dimensions of the doll house are height: 38″; width:
81″. Gift of Mrs. John W. G. Tenney and Philip Milledoler Brett
in memory of their parents, Mr. & Mrs. Philip Milledoler Brett.
61.235

VI: THE LAPSE OF LAW AND ORDER:
THE CIVIL WAR
AND THE DAYS OF TWEED

City of wharves and stores! city of tall facades
of marble and iron!
Proud and passionate city! mettlesome, mad,
extravagant city!

—WALT WHITMAN, *City of Ships*

The Civil War was unpopular in New York for most of its entire course, sometimes violently so. The City had close economic ties with the South: New York handled more Southern cotton each year than any other city except New Orleans and Mobile, and the credit economy of the South was heavily in debt to New York. Twice before the outbreak of war the news of a possible secession drove down the stock market. New York businessmen worried that in the event of a Southern secession debts owed by Southerners to New York would be repudiated. And New York liked Southerners; they visited the City often and bought heavily at the City's shops; many great Southern houses had New York–made furniture and fittings. There were hotels in New York that catered especially to Southerners.

If the upper classes felt that way, the enormous foreign-born population could hardly have been expected to show much comprehension of the issues of the war. During the conflict their hostility to it and particular reluctance to serve in the military was constantly seething. Many of them, after all, came to this country to escape military service.

The cause of abolition was not popular in New York; in fact, the City might almost be described as a hotbed of *anti*-abolitionism. In 1850, George Templeton Strong wrote that the abolitionists "deserve to be

scourged and pilloried for sedition or hanged for treason . . . " and that "the designs of Northern Abolitionists are very particularly false, foolish, wicked, and unchristian." The meetings of the abolitionists were always being riotously broken up by mobs although the abolitionists numbered among their leaders New Yorkers as well-connected as John Jay, grandson of the chief justice, who served as counsel for many fugitive Negro slaves.

It took New York a long time to get interested in Abraham Lincoln. When he came to New York on 27 February 1860 to deliver the address that has become famous as "the Cooper Union," neither the Young Men's Republican Union nor the Draper Republican Union Club would sponsor him, so William Cullen Bryant and three other citizens had to sponsor the lecture (for which Lincoln received a fee of $200). Although the *Times* dismissed him as "a lawyer who has some local reputation in Illinois," the speech was enthusiastically received by a distinguished audience, printed, and circulated widely, and a year later Lincoln was in the White House.

In 1860, the population of New York was 813,669. The Bronx, Queens, and Richmond still had only 81,988 people among them, but Brooklyn was a large city with 279,122. Altogether, more than 1,100,000 people lived in what was to become Greater New York.

When the war broke out the mayor was Fernando Wood. He was one of New York's handsomest mayors, intelligent, able, and tricky. The foundation of his considerable personal fortune before entering politics was Gold Rush shipping and real estate in San Francisco and New York. He was a member of Tammany Hall and elected as mayor on a Tammany ticket, serving terms from 1855 to 1858 and 1860 to 1862. He eventually fell out—presumably over a division of the municipal spoils—with his fellow Tammanyites and formed his own political organization which he named "Mozart Hall." Despite this elevating name it was no less corrupt than Tammany. He was elected again in 1860. When Wood first appeared on the civic scene as a mayoral candidate, his reputation was already somewhat shadowed by a business scandal; by the time he left office it was completely besmirched. Nevertheless, he was so persuasive at first that he gained the support of citizens of the most Knickerbocker respectability. Even George Templeton Strong, a hard man to please if ever there was one, was impressed. In 1855, he wrote: "Mayor Wood continues our Civic Hero—inquiring, reforming, redressing, laboring hard with ample result of good. . . . He is the first mayor, for thirty years at least, who has set himself seriously to the work of giving the civic administration a decent appearance of common honesty. He is a very strange phenomenon."

Like many mayors, Wood tackled the problem of street prostitution directly after entering office and attempted to rid Broadway of its nocturnal "strumpetocracy." His campaign was popular but unsuccessful. During the Panic of 1857, he consolidated his position among the mob by addressing crowds in front of City Hall, inflaming them by drawing their attention to the difference between "the rich who produce nothing and have everything and the poor who produce everything and have nothing."

Usually Wood was attuned to the popular temper and amazingly accurate in guessing which way the wind was blowing, but he miscalculated the Civil War, which he thought could not be won by the North and would result in a permanent division in the country. As secession and hostilities approached, his own outspoken sympathies were with the South. His brother Benjamin bought the *Daily News* (which had been founded in 1837) and made it into a pro-Southern organ.

On 7 January 1861, Fernando Wood addressed the Common Council with one of the most extraordinary speeches ever given by a public official in the United States, which took the line that dissolution of the Union was inevitable and that no attempt ought to be made to preserve it by force. He went so far as to assert that New York might then become a separate free city, perhaps the most extreme advocacy of home rule in New York's long history. The message was violently anti-state legislature. Wood, no slouch himself at governmental corruption, had the nerve to point out (which was true) that "the political connection between the people of the city and the state has been used by the latter to our injury. The Legislature, in which the present party majority (the Republicans) has the power, has become the instrument by which we are plundered to enrich their speculators, lobby agents, and abolition politicians. . . . Why may not New York disrupt the bonds which bind her to a corrupt and venal master—to a people and a party that have plundered her revenues, attempt to ruin her commerce, taken away the power of self-government, and destroyed the Confederacy of which she was the proud Empire City?"

The next day the *Herald* (which had been founded in 1835) wrote coolly: "The message is devoted entirely to an elaborate attack upon the powers at Albany and its theory is that as the Federal Union is about to be broken into pieces like so much fragile crockery, it is well to be on hand to pick up the pieces: that the City of New York is rather a valuable fragment, and that we should look out and keep it for ourselves, even if we have to break the State government into bits."

The attack on Fort Sumter brought a quick and noticeable change in the atmosphere: the Northern cause was instantly popular. When news of the bombardment reached the Stock Exchange its members joined in hearty cheers for Major Anderson. Some of the newspapers changed their colors literally overnight: on Monday, 15 April 1861, the *Herald* advocated peace, on Tuesday it urged the prosecution of the war. New

160. Serious historical research has been devoted in recent years to the Draft Riots of July, 1863. Historians now believe that figures of dead and wounded were grossly exaggerated by police and politicians to make themselves look good. One historian dismisses most statistics as "tall tales" and believes that only about 100 persons lost their lives. *Harper's Weekly* published some vivid woodcuts illustrating the terrible events. The Colored Orphan Asylum stood at Fifth Avenue and 43rd Street. Archive

York's Seventh Regiment (militia) was ordered out on the 17th, and the merchants of the City quickly subscribed $6,000 to complete its equipment.

At a mass meeting called by members of the Stock Exchange and the Chamber of Commerce on Saturday, 20th April, more than 100,000 citizens gathered around the statue of Washington in Union Square, the largest mass meeting that had ever been held in New York. Five different speakers' stands were erected, and from these assorted leading citizens addressed sections of the crowd. Six more regiments left for the front in the next few days. Committees were formed, sanitary (hospital) commissions organized, etc. The pro-Southern Fernando Wood was defeated in the mayoral election of December, 1861, and replaced by George Opdyke, a Republican.

Just as New York merchants had feared, the debts of Southerners were repudiated by them to the estimated amount of $200,000,000. Although some firms were bankrupted and there were numerous suspensions, the business of war soon replaced the trade that had been lost.

Patriotic euphoria was soon dispelled. The Union defeat at Bull Run and the failure to take Richmond discouraged New Yorkers and led to the election of Horatio Seymour, a Democrat, as governor of New York State. He opposed the abolition of slavery and apparently did not believe that the war for the Union could be won. Volunteer enlistments in the Union Army fell off; New York State and especially the City were far behind in their requirements of men. In March, 1863, the Conscription Act, ordering compulsory military service, was passed by Congress. Many people, including Governor Seymour, considered this move illegal, and it was highly unpopular with the working class who resented the stipulation that payment of $300 or procurement of a substitute enabled the well-to-do to escape service. The draft was especially unpopular in New York City among the Irish, who seethed with indignation. Trouble was anticipated by government, citizens, and mob when the drawing of names for the draft commenced.

On the morning of Saturday, 11 July 1863, the

lottery for military service began at the enrolling office at 677 Third Avenue (46th Street). There was no difficulty that day. On Monday, however, the drawing had but begun and a few names been called when a furious mob, largely drawn from Lower East Side gangs but including some women and even children, attacked and set fire to the building. In two hours the entire block had been destroyed.

The mob numbered several thousand. To face them there were only about 800 police and a few marines from the Brooklyn Navy Yard. A pitched battle between these forces occurred at 43rd Street and Third Avenue; several marines were killed and others inhumanly beaten. For three days the rioting continued in various parts of the City from Second Avenue westward to the Hudson, as far north as Harlem and as far south as Mulberry Street. Many houses were sacked and burned. Mayor Opdyke's house was attacked and his wife and son chased into the streets. Known abolitionists and Negroes were especially badly treated. The number of dead has never been known exactly, but it is believed that the number of killed and wounded may have reached 1,000. Of these, probably between 400 and 500 were rioters killed by the police and the military. More than fifty buildings, valued at over $1,000,000, were burned and many others damaged.

The behavior of the City government was timid, to put it kindly. On Monday the Board of Aldermen met and proposed to take action but, lacking a quorum, adjourned without doing anything! Some militia men finally were brought in. Governor Seymour, who was in the City but behaved in a manner that left no doubt he remembered that the mob was largely composed of Democratic voters, addressed them gently from the steps of City Hall, referring the question of conscription, which he made clear he personally opposed, to the courts. Bishop Hughes, playing his customary role of dog in the manger, did nothing at all until the last possible moment, when he gently recommended to the rioters that they might be better off at home.

By Thursday, 16 April, peace was restored. The Federal government, also placating the rioters, had suspended the draft in New York and Brooklyn. When it was resumed on 19 August the drawing was held under the guard of no less than 10,000 soldiers. The Common Council, still conciliatory (to say the least) to the mob, asked that the military be removed, and had the nerve to ask that the Federal government compensate the City for damage done during the riots. These cool requests were too much even for Mayor Opdyke, who vetoed both measures.

Business in the City was practically at a standstill for a week. The price of gold plunged and securities trembled. George Templeton Strong in his Wall Street office thought that not surprising "with the city in insurrection, a gunboat at the foot of Wall Street, the Custom-House and Treasury full of soldiers and live shells, and two howitzers in position to rake Nassau Street from Wall to Fulton!"

With amazing resilience business recovered, but the serious effect of the Draft Riots of 1863 is shown by the startling reduction in the population of the City. For the second time in its history—first during the American Revolution—the population of New York actually decreased. Between 1861 and 1865 it went down from 814,254 to 726,385. That loss was quickly made up, however, and by 1870 the population was approaching a million at 942,292.

Population increase and great commercial prosperity did not bring good government in their wake. The mid 1860s and the early 1870s were the time when the municipal government of New York City reached its lowest point of fraud, corruption, bribery, inefficiency, and squalor. "The Tweed Ring" made New York world-famous for its bad government. George Templeton Strong wrote in 1868: "To be a citizen of New York is a disgrace. A domicile on Manhattan Island is a thing to be confessed with apologies and humiliation. The New Yorker belongs to a community worse governed by lower and baser blackguard scum than any city in Western Christendom. . . . "

The actual control of the City was at Albany: the Legislature of New York State ran the City—which meant in effect two centers for corruption rather than one. In 1857, the legislature formed a Board of Supervisors for the County of New York, strictly subordinate to the legislature at Albany since it had no power to tax. This arrangement made it possible for the controlling party at Albany and that at New York to work together for a division of the spoils. The mayors (including as we have seen, Fernando Wood) complained about this, more or less sincerely.

Under Wood, before the Civil War, offices in the city government were almost openly sold. Complaints about this state of affairs were growing until the war diverted the attention of reformers. In the election of 1865, John T. Hoffman, Grand Sachem of Tammany, was elected mayor and then reelected in 1867.

In the election of 1867, 22,779 more votes were cast than in the election of only two years previous. Nearly all of these were newly naturalized citizen votes. Immigrants were being naturalized and enfranchised at a fantastic clip—sometimes 1,000 a day—by three venal judges with Tammany backing: Albert Cardozo, George G. Barnard, and John H. M'Cunn. As a result of their work, in 1865 there were 77,475 naturalized voters, and only 51,500 native American voters.

The judicial trio were in the pocket of William Marcy Tweed, the "Boss." Tweed was born in New York City in 1823, of Scottish parentage, and was a chairmaker like his father (advertisements exist for William M. Tweed, "manufacturer and wholesale dealer in fine gilt and variegated colored chairs" at 325 Pearl Street and 12 Ridge Street). He made wood, cane, rush, willow, and straw seated chairs suitable for hotels, parlors, and public offices, and was quite successful. After he became foreman of the Volunteer Fire Company "Americus," or "Big Six," he knew nothing but politics, of the Tammany variety, and abandoned chairmaking. At the age of twenty-nine he went to Congress as a Democrat but served only one term. During his public career—if an unblushing and unparalleled sequence of frauds on the taxpayers can be referred to by that name—between 1852 and 1870, Tweed was alderman of the seventh ward, commissioner of the public schools(!), supervisor of the county of New York (the link with the state legislature), and commissioner of public works. In addition, he was a state senator. Some of these positions overlapped but no mind, his most important job was chairman of the Tammany General Committee and later "Grand Sachem" of Tammany. As head of that organization he had his vote-getters in each ward and election district. As a City official he found that other City workers had a tendency to vote along lines recommended by the power that had installed them. He was not slow to take advantage of the pleasing discovery that the city payroll is a place to raise up righteous voters, and the City of New York had never had so many workers—or rather employees.

In 1870, Tweed consolidated his position by having the state legislature give the City a new charter tailored to his specifications. Tweed bribes to legislators to insure this result are said to have amounted to $1,000,000. The new charter placed entire financial control of the City in the hands of four men: the mayor, the comptroller, the chairman of the department of public works, and the chairman of the department of parks. These positions were naturally all held by Tweed men, namely A. Oakey Hall, the mayor; Richard B. Connolly, the comptroller; Peter B. Sweeny, chairman of parks; Tweed himself was chairman of public works. This was the "Tweed Ring," and the Boss's power was complete. George Templeton Strong, always a sure reflection of the solid citizen, wrote in discouragement: "The body politic of this city and county, judges, aldermen, councilmen, supervisors, and so on, our whole local government, is so diseased and so corrupt and so far gone that we can no longer count on any recuperative, restorative action of its vital forces."

Mayor A. Oakey Hall, "Elegant Oakey," who was in office (one can hardly say he "served") from 1868 to 1872, was a handsome rascal who put up a tony front for the Tweed Ring. He was a man of unquestioned talents (a capable lawyer, an experienced newspaperman, author of a number of books, a playwright, and on the stage himself in one of his plays), all of which were at the disposal of the "Boss."

The Ring had various ways to steal, but the most frequently used and the most effective in its simplicity was a system of "kick-backs." Contractors for City work merely padded their bills and sent them to the City, where they were authorized by the board of four, and paid, the difference between the genuine and the padded bill being split among members of the Ring. The building of the new County Court House was said to represent the theft of $8,000,000. As the thievery grew more and more notorious (for there was hardly any secrecy about it) an indignation meeting was held at the Cooper Institute in April, 1871. When told of this meeting and the determination of the citizens to put a halt to the plundering, Tweed only made his celebrated reply, "Well, what are you going to do about it?"

It was later than the "Boss" thought. A leak from within the Ring had given newspapermen sufficient precise information about the system to enable the *New-York Times* to begin publishing a series of articles on 8 July 1871 detailing the peculations of the previous decade. Great credit belongs to George Jones, proprietor of the *Times*, and Louis J. Jennings, editor, who along with Thomas Nast of *Harper's Weekly* (who drew a series of biting cartoons of Tweed and his activities) were directly responsible for the downfall of the brigands.

A few days after the *Times* started its series, Tammany Hall went too far. The previous year a procession of Orangemen celebrating the Battle of the Boyne had been attacked by a mob of Irish Catholics. The police had made no effort to protect the marchers and there were no punishments for the assaults. As 12 July 1871 approached, Connolly and Sweeny of the Ring, who were Irish Catholics, ordered Mayor Hall to forbid the Orangemen to march, which he did. This was bringing the politics of the Old World to the New with a vengeance, and nothing since the Draft Riots so shocked and united the respectable people of New York. It was too much even for Governor John T. Hoffman, although he was Tammany himself and a former mayor under the Tiger's aegis. He ordered the parade to go forth and dispatched militia to protect it. The Protestants were attacked by Irish Catholics, as expected, between 25th and 26th streets on Eighth Avenue. The militia fired and were in turn attacked by the mob. More than fifty persons were killed and many more wounded.

The vindication of basic American principles by so unlikely a champion as Governor Hoffman showed the way the wind was blowing. In the election of November, 1871, Republicans carried the state, securing a good majority in the legislature, although it appears that some were actually Tammany wolves in Republican sheepskins and under the influence of Tweed. Tweed himself was elected state senator. Even so, he could not stop reform. He was indicted for felony, tried, and sent to prison after two trials. He escaped within the year and made his way to Spain, but was found, extradited, and brought back to serve his sentence. He died in the Ludlow Street Jail (a debtors' prison) in 1878.

"Elegant Oakey" served out his term as mayor. He also was indicted and tried, but handled his own defense so brilliantly that the jury disagreed and he was freed. He emigrated to London, where he represented the New York *Herald*. Connolly and Sweeny also took up residence in Europe. Of the notorious trio of judges, Barnard and M'Cunn were impeached and removed from office; Cardozo resigned to escape the same fate. Very little of the stolen money was ever recovered. There has never been any agreement on how much that amounted to, but estimates range between $30,000,000 and $200,000,000.

The reformers who had overthrown Tweed now cast about for a mayor of unimpeachable integrity to succeed A. Oakey Hall. They found a civic antique named William F. Havemeyer. He was seventy years old, and decades before he had served as mayor for two terms, 1845–46 and 1848–49. He was elected again in 1873, but died the following year of apoplexy in his office at City Hall. George Templeton Strong said: "He was a rather dense but worthy old citizen, obstinate but without force to save himself from being made a catspaw by political scallywags. . . . "

What one has to admire is the strength and resilience of Tammany Hall. After all the scandals and exposure, the utter disgust of decent citizens, the international fame of New York's misgovernment, the Tiger bounced back. Securely based on ward-heeling votes, voting frauds, bribery, and in many cases more or less open connections with the leaders of business in the City, Tammany was soon winning elections again. It should not be overlooked that Tammany's base was by no means entirely immigrant and lower class. In return for valuable commercial privileges, a shameful number of New York's leading citizens supported the Hall *and* the Ring. Water grants, for instance, were a great source of scandal during the Tweed administration. The grants, which enabled the owner to construct profitable piers and storage facilities along the East River, were received at ridiculously low prices by some of "the best people," a Rhinelander, a Goelet, an Astor, and a Delano among others. Some of these grants had to be rescinded by public demand in 1882, but others remained valid and extremely profitable. In return, Tweed received outright commendation. In 1871, for instance, just as the horrendous disclosures were about to be made, a special committee of prominent citizens headed by John Jacob Astor II examined the books of Comptroller Connolly, pronounced them flawless, and complimented Connolly on his exemplary honesty!

During Mayor Havemeyer's brief regime the Panic of 1873 burst on the U.S. economy with shattering force. Rumblings had previously been felt—in 1872, there were 4,000 business failures in the country—but few were prepared for the crash of banking houses which began in New York in September of 1873. The usual concomitants of financial panic followed: President Grant hurried to New York for consultations; bankers conferred; the Stock Exchange closed for ten days. But no stabilizing measures succeeded. A majority of American railroads (which had been heavily overinvested) went into bankruptcy. By 1875, there were half a million unemployed. The depression lasted about six years. Even in 1876–77, there were more than 18,000 business failures. New York, the country's financial center, was especially stricken. Not until 1879 did commerce and industry revive; then prosperity came back with astonishing quickness. The decade 1880–90 was one of general prosperity, and in New York "the Gilded Age."

The 1860s and 70s were a strange era. In the midst of misgovernance and financial upset, the City somehow survived and expanded. An editorial in the *Evening Post* stated accurately that "New York is the most inconveniently arranged commercial city in the world. Its wharfs are badly built, unsafe, and without shelter, its streets are badly paved, dirty, and necessarily over-

161. Thomas Nast, the German-born artist who is probably the most influential political cartoonist ever to have worked in the U.S., satirized himself in this pen-and-ink drawing. The features of "Boss" Tweed are transformed into those of the Tammany Tiger. Gift of Cyril Nast. 43.239.2

crowded . . . its railroad depots have no proper relation to the shipping or to the warehouses . . . its laborers are badly lodged and in every way disaccommodated. . . ." Andrew Dickson White compared New York to Constantinople, in the nineteenth century the least flattering comparison he could possibly make since Turkey was synonymous with backwardness and governmental ills.

Yet New York's population grew from 942,292 in 1870 to 1,164,673 in 1880, and as if to prove that strength grows out of adversity many of the greatest institutions of the City were born at this time: the American Museum of Natural History in 1869, The Metropolitan Museum of Art in 1870, and the Lenox Library in 1877. New York was linked with Europe in 1866 by the laying of the great Atlantic Cable. But the chief achievement of the era was the building of Central Park.

The skeptical George Templeton Strong checked on the progress of Central Park in 1859. He found it full of "Celts, caravans of dirt carts, derricks, steam engines" at work but thought it judiciously laid out. He hoped the "hideous" State Arsenal, "an eyesore that no landscape gardening can alleviate," would soon be destroyed by accidental fire. The Arsenal has survived; it still broods over the Central Park Zoo and is now headquarters of the Parks Department of the City of New York. Strong concluded that the park would "be a lovely place in A.D. 1900."

By 1871, however, even Strong was converted. One evening in July of that year he strolled uptown from his home at Gramercy Park, "entered the Park at 72nd Street and explored a new and lovely region in and around the Ramble. The Park is a priceless acquisition. Thank God for it. . . ."

The Commissioners of the Central Park also adopted a plan for the improvement of the west side of New York from 55th to 155th streets and laid out Riverside Park and Morningside Park. At the same time Olmsted and Vaux were laying out Prospect Park in Brooklyn, which they thought superior to their work on Central Park.

The effect of these parks, especially Central Park, on the life of the City was immense. For the rich,

driving in Central Park in the afternoon became a necessity, and skating on the frozen ponds was diverting. The John Bachmann view, *Central Park— Summer, Looking South, New York, 1865,* gives a good idea of the intense use of the park, which has never slackened from that day to this. The park brought people uptown and led directly to the extension of dwellings and businesses toward the villages of Yorkville and finally Harlem. The steady northward growth of the City was accelerated.

The new houses uptown—reached by horse omnibus from offices around Wall Street—were becoming increasingly elaborate as prosperity returned, but they were still far from the exuberance of the Gilded Age. Their furnishings were in the style now called "Victorian."

Victorian furniture made in New York is nearly always associated with the name of John Henry Belter, of 522 Broadway and later 722 Broadway. A great consumer of rosewood (the preeminent material of Victorian furniture), he was a leader in the process of laminating—gluing thin layers of rosewood together, pressing and steaming them—and energetic carving. At his factory on Third Avenue near 76th Street he manufactured sets of rosewood furniture for parlor and bedroom between 1844 and 1863. His products are the very drop and essence of "Victorian," and The Museum of the City of New York contains an outstanding collection of his products. Another furniture-maker working in the same taste was Leon Marcotte. The richest sort of object of the era would be typified by his Lenox armchair in The Museum's collection. Even doll house furniture was made in this style.

If the New Yorker of today could shop in the New York of just about a hundred years ago, he would find many familiar names. A number of the present-day stores were already active then or even middle-aged. Department stores were led by Arnold Constable (founded 1825), the oldest, and Lord and Taylor (founded 1826), and Bloomingdale's which opened in 1872. Groceries could be bought at the Great Atlantic and Pacific Tea Company (1859). Brooks Brothers had been supplying the gentlemen of New York since 1818. Furniture could be bought at W. and J. Sloane (1843), liquor and wines at Austin, Nichols (1855), books at Brentano's (1853), a piano at Steinway & Sons (1853), music for it at Schirmer's (1861), toys at F. A. O. Schwarz (1862), and candy at Loft's (1860). Most of the banks New Yorkers use today were already long established (although they have undergone a remarkable amount of amalgamation and name-changing): in addition to the oldest, The Bank of New York (1784), there were the (Chase) Manhattan (1799), the Manufacturers Trust (1812), the Chemical (1824), the Hanover (1851), the National City (1812), and the oldest savings bank, The Bank for Savings (1819).

RIOTERS CHASING NEGRO WOMEN AND CHILDREN THROUGH VACANT LOTS IN LEXINGTON AVENUE.

162. About 350 draft rioters have been identified from contemporary records. Before the riots nearly all had employment and very few had a police record. While most were laborers or factory workers, among the rioters were a dentist and an actor. One was a professor at Columbia! *Harper's Weekly* shows a scene of violence on then partially settled Lexington Avenue. Archive

163. This is the playbill of the first performance of *The Black Crook*, given at Niblo's Garden on 12 September 1866. A run of sixteen months established it as one of the greatest hits of the century. An extravaganza with music and 100 girls (mostly members of a stranded French ballet troupe), it is usually considered the progenitor of the American musical comedy. 9 1/4 × 5 3/4″. Anonymous gift. 42.471

164. The great Atlantic telegraph cable was laid twice by a company organized by Cyrus Field and other prominent New Yorkers. The first message was sent—from President Buchanan to Queen Victoria—in 1858, but the cable later broke, and it was not until after the conclusion of the Civil War that Field was able to use the steamship *Great Eastern* to lay it again, a job completed in 1866. This silver fruit dish, made by Gorham, commemorates the 1866 success and was part of a large set presented to Field by George Peabody, the Anglo-American banker and philanthropist. It is inscribed "George Peabody to Cyrus W. Field in testimony and commemoration of an act of very high commercial integrity and honor, New York 24 Nov. 1866." Tazza height: 16 3/4". Gift of Newcomb Carlton. 34.346.2

165. With almost unlimited swag at his command the "Boss" spread it around lavishly with a house on Fifth Avenue, a yacht, and—the great extravagance of the day—fine horses. This is Tweed's cane, on which is found his usual ornament: the Tammany Tiger. It was a present to Tweed in 1869. Wood, gold handle, length: 34". Gift of Colonel and Mrs. LeRoy Barton. 49.66.2

166. The members of the Board of Aldermen of New York for the two years 1850 and 1851 presented their president Morgan Morgans with this handsome silver goblet made by William Forbes for Ball, Tompkins & Black. The aldermen were in the habit of treating themselves well, and civic irritation over their extravagance and outright peculation reached a climax in 1853, when 500 leading citizens assembled at the Stuyvesant Institute to hear Peter Cooper and other influential men denounce the board and its operations. Reform was still far away; William Marcy Tweed served his first term as alderman in 1851–52. Height: 9". Gift of Frank D. Morgans. 54.97.1c

167–168. The work of John Henry Belter, New York's foremost furniture-maker of the Victorian era, is well represented in The Museum of the City of New York. This center table of carved laminated rosewood, made between 1856 and 1861, is part of a set made for Mr. and Mrs. Carl Vietor. Laminated rosewood was made by glueing together layers of thin rosewood which could be steamed into desired shapes. The end product was highly suitable for carving, as is obvious from this piece in the "rococo revival" style. The top is of mottled gray and pink marble. The label, which is found on the underside of a leg, shows Belter's "warehouse" (actually the retail store) at 552 Broadway. His factory was at Third Avenue and 76th Street. Height: 28 1/4''; diameter of top: 38 1/4''. Gift of Mr. and Mrs. Ernest Gunther Vietor. 38.53.8ab

169. Soon after the Civil War, Central Park became the setting for fashionable walking, riding, and driving. Every afternoon between four and five the famous carriage parade took place along the East Drive from 59th Street and Fifth Avenue to the Mall. Equipages of many types, conservative or high-style, were on display to the pedestrian spectators who lined the drive. In the Currier & Ives print *Fashionable "Turn-Outs" in Central Park*, Thomas Worth shows eight outfits, each different. Note at the upper left the phaeton with two ladies, one driving, and a groom perched behind. This was a new kind of vehicle in America. Ladies sometimes drove them, as here, but that was considered quite daring. Riding in the park, formerly much frowned upon for ladies, was becoming acceptable, with grooms in attendance of course. Colored lithograph, 18 3/4 × 28 3/4″. The J. Clarence Davies Collection. 29.100.2480

170. Driving trotters along Harlem Lane, or "Speedway" as it was later called, was one of the most popular—and expensive—sports of rich New Yorkers of the seventies and eighties. Harlem Lane, now called St. Nicholas Avenue, was entered from the uptown end of Central Park. It ran up to 168th Street. Along the way were bars and inns from which the fast horses could be watched by spectators. It was an equine age, and enormous sums were spent on fine animals and spiffy turnouts. This painting by Henry C. Bispham, dated 1878, shows E. Depew Slater driving his team on Harlem Lane. Oil on canvas, 26 × 42″. Gift of Joseph C. Bullock in memory of Edna Devereux Bullock, granddaughter of E. Depew Slater. 62.29

171. This toy model of the Broadway and Fifth Avenue horse omnibus is from about 1860. It serves as the device of the Friends of the Toy Collection of The Museum of the City of New York. 7 × 14″. Gift of Ives Washburn. 39.482a–c

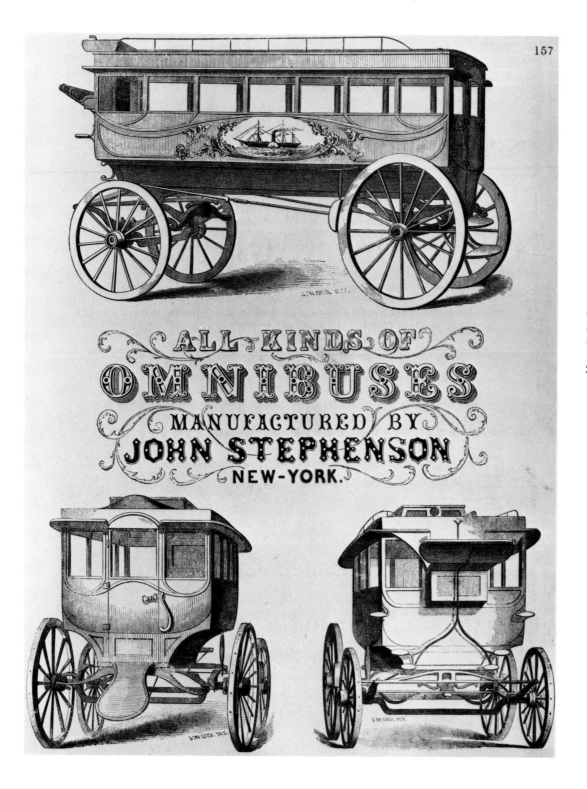

157

ALL KINDS OF
OMNIBUSES
MANUFACTURED BY
JOHN STEPHENSON
NEW-YORK.

172. John Stephenson was the pioneer builder of street-railway cars. He created the very first street-railway car in 1832 for the New York and Harlem Railroad Company, which opened for public travel between Prince and 14th streets on 26 November 1832. When this advertisement was distributed Stephenson had his factory on 27th Street near Fourth Avenue. 8 1/2 × 10 3/4″. Gift of Luke Vincent Lockwood. 31.26.101

173. Brooklyn's Volunteer Fire Department Hose Company No. 5 was organized on the Fourth of July 1853. Like most companies in the New York area it took a catch name, in this case "Frontier." This is their hose carriage, which usually was drawn by men rather than horses. Gouache drawing, 38 × 30 1/2". Gift of the Brooklyn Volunteer Firemen's Association. 34.419.4

174. Horse-cars served as one of the principal modes of transportation in the City for a long, long time. Horse-cars did not disappear from the streets of Manhattan until almost the time of World War I. Each car was drawn by two horses and carried twenty-five or thirty passengers. This horse-car, No. 76 of the Broadway line, is an example of the first type of "fan box" car used in New York and dates from 1855. Length: 151"; width: 88 1/2". Gift of the Second Avenue Railroad Corporation. 32.514

175. The many companies of volunteer firemen were supplied with their treasured engines by Abraham Vanness, who issued this print to advertise his firm at 151 Essex Street, where he was in business from 1846 to 1853. Colored lithograph by George G. Gratacap, 12 × 17″. The J. Clarence Davies Collection. 29.100.2544

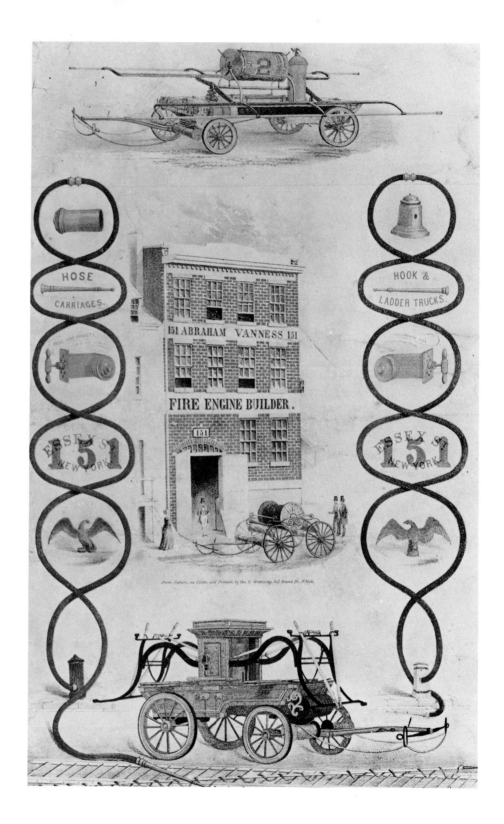

176–177. William Marcy Tweed, who became famous as "Boss Tweed," was the son of a respectable chair-maker of Scottish descent and was born at 24 Cherry Street in a neighborhood which then housed a number of furniture shops. Nothing in his background indicated that he would become New York's most notorious politician and his name a synonym for swindle. The first step in his political career was to organize a volunteer fire company. The companies were then very active in politics. Tweed's was called "The Americus Fire Engine Company No. 6"; it became celebrated as "Big Six." Its symbol was the tiger—to become famous in story and song under Tweed and his Tammany Hall successors. This is the "Americus Six" fire engine built in 1851 by James Smith. The size of the engine justifies its name, and there is some indication that it was rather unmanageable; in 1855, it ran over and injured two members of the company who were fighting a fire at Lord and Taylor's. The engine was quartered at the Americus firehouse, No. 6 Henry Street, a brownstone noted for its luxurious quarters. Gift of Veteran Volunteer Firemen's Association. 31.229. (Detail) The snarling Tammany Tiger is found painted on the front panel of "Big Six."

178. The clipper yacht *America* was sponsored by a group of U.S. yachtsmen and built to their specifications (incorporating many then-new features of ship design) to enter the Royal Yacht Squadron's race around the Isle of Wight, 22 August 1851. The *America*, against all expectations, won, and the trophy awarded on this occasion remains famous as "The *America*'s Cup." It has never been lost in subsequent challenges and is still to be found at the New York Yacht Club. This Currier & Ives print shows the yacht at the time of her victory. She later served as a Confederate blockade-runner and finally as a U.S. naval school ship. Colored lithograph, 8 × 12 1/2". Gift of Miss Grace M. Mayer. 57.78

179. Prospective passengers for California learned about ships' departures from "clipper ship cards," which were issued by American shipping firms beginning with the Gold Rush and continuing for about a decade. The cards were usually about four by six inches, printed in several colors, and often showed a picture of the vessel as well as pier numbers, departure times, and made boasts about speed records. They were urged upon passersby at the piers and steamship offices. At least 700 different cards are known to have been issued, but they are now exceedingly scarce. All of these advertise clippers for San Francisco and all but one were issued in New York City. Note the concentration of steamship offices in a small area of Pearl and Wall streets. Gift of Edward D. Thurston, Jr. 46.62

180. The clipper ship *Nightingale* was named after "The Swedish Nightingale," Jenny Lind, and it inspired one of Currier & Ives's finest marine prints: *Clipper Ship "Nightingale" Getting Under Weigh off the Battery New York* (1854). The artist James E. Buttersworth shows the ship bound for Australia on the first direct service between New York and that continent as she sails out of the harbor with Castle Garden in the background. The Castle Garden reference is especially appropriate since it was there Jenny Lind made her American debut. The *Nightingale* had a strange career. Built as a luxury passenger ship for 250, she went around the world, was converted into a warship during the Civil War (serving in the blockade of Southern ports), underwent a mutiny in the Falkland Islands in 1871, and in 1876 was bought by Norwegians for the lumber trade. Finally she was abandoned at sea in 1895. Colored lithograph, 16 1/2 × 24″. The Harry T. Peters Collection. 57.300.25

181. Fort Lafayette stood on the Brooklyn side of the Narrows near where
the Verrazano Bridge now has one of its towers. During the Civil War
it served as a prison for captured Confederate troops. Thomas Hicks
painted the fort at that time (1861), and it was destroyed by fire in 1868.
Oil on canvas, 9 1/4 × 17″. Gift of Mr. and Mrs. Ferdinand H. Davis.
72.175.1

182. Many were the plans in the last three decades of the nineteenth century to relieve the intolerable and ever-increasing traffic congestion of lower Manhattan. One of the most intelligently developed plans is displayed in this remarkable lithograph called *Proposed Arcade Railway. Under Broadway. View near Wall Street*, issued in 1870. Melville C. Smith, whose name is printed at the lower right, was the chief promoter of the Arcade Railway, which was actually authorized four times by the New York State Legislature but vetoed four times by various governors including Grover Cleveland. None of the railway was ever built, and it was not until 1900 that construction began on the first subway. Colored lithograph, 24 × 17 1/2″. The J. Clarence Davies Collection. 29.100.2400

183. Society gathered in the wide corridor at the Waldorf-Astoria known as "Peacock Alley" because fashionable attire was paraded there. Steinway & Sons delivered this upright piano to the hotel on 23 December 1899. Made of ebonized wood with panels of red tortoise shell inlaid with brass, it is in the Louis XIV style called "Boulle." The piano was used in "Peacock Alley" until the old hotel closed in 1929. "Peacock Alley" survives as one of the bars in the present Waldorf-Astoria on Park Avenue between 49th and 50th streets. Height: 55 3/8"; width: 62". Gift of Miss Sarah H. McLean. 66.32a–e

184. "American Renaissance" is the name given to furniture in the elaborate style of this table made during the 1870s. Carving, gilding, inlay of various woods, and mother-of-pearl stars were used over an ebonized mahogany frame. The table is part of a parlor suite of settee, table, and six chairs which by family tradition is believed to have been awarded a prize at the Philadelphia Centennial Exposition in 1876. Mr. and Mrs. James Lancaster Morgan of 7 Pierrepont Street, Brooklyn, owned this suite. Their elaborate house was photographed inside and out several times during the 1880s and 90s. The resulting photographs, collected in The Museum of the City of New York, are an unusually complete record of a well-to-do New York family's life-style toward the end of the nineteenth century. This table, laden with doilies and vases, may be seen in one of the photographs. Height: 30 1/8"; width: 54". Gift of John Hall Morgan and Lancaster Morgan. 27.118.2

185. The real-estate wealth of James Lenox, founded on a farm of thirty acres left by his father in 1840, and including most of what is now the seventies between Fifth Avenue and the East River, enabled him to collect rare books and manuscripts on a scale hitherto unknown in America. Diffident to a degree, for many years nearly a recluse, "he staked out his own course, hoed his own row, paddled his own canoe," as a friend wrote. Between 1845 and 1869, he gradually filled his huge house at 53 Fifth Avenue with literary treasures, room by room, stacked to the ceilings. When a room was filled, it was locked, and the collector often bought duplicates rather than search for a book he knew he had. His immense accumulation, known as "The Lenox Library," became one of the foundations of the New York Public Library in 1895. This armchair of ebonized rosewood veneer with inlay of lighter woods and mother-of-pearl may have been made in New York in the seventies, and is decorated on the back with the coat-of-arms and crest of James Lenox. Height: 39"; width: 27". Gift of Mrs. Franklin B. Dwight and W. Phoenix Belknap, Jr. 47.217

186. The Richard K. Haight family lived at the southeast corner of Fifth Avenue and 15th Street when they sat for their portrait about 1849. Their house was described as a palazzo and was thought to be one of the most elegantly fitted up in the City, as is apparent in the portrait. The Haights traveled extensively: Mrs. Haight published the letters she wrote in 1836 and 1837 from Europe, Turkey, Egypt, and Syria. Many souvenirs of their travels, including statuary and Greek vases, are shown in the drawing room. Attributed to Nicolino Calyo. Gouache on paper, 20 × 15″. Bequest of Elizabeth Cushing Iselin. 74.97.2

VII: UNEMBARRASSED RICHES: NEW YORK IN THE AGE OF GOLD

There's millions in it!

—MARK TWAIN, *The Gilded Age*

Three great public celebrations, the most important since the opening of the Erie Canal, marked the decade of the 1880s in New York: the inauguration of the Brooklyn Bridge in 1883, the unveiling of the Statue of Liberty in 1886, and the centenary of the inauguration of George Washington in 1889. The Brooklyn Bridge was the future: it led the way toward expansion of the City. The Statue of Liberty was the present: it recognized the greatest single phenomenon in the history of nineteenth-century New York: immigration. The Washington Centennial looked back to the glorious days when the new nation centered in New York.

The construction of the Brooklyn Bridge occupied nearly a generation—from 1870 to 1883. It commenced, surprisingly, under the benevolent grasp of Boss Tweed. Tweed pushed through approval by the legislature of the bridge bond issue, in return a block of stock in the bridge company was reserved for him. The plan for linking the cities of New York and Brooklyn already had a considerable history. William C. Kingsley had drawn up plans and estimates and raised $5,000,000 for the project, and the "New York Bridge Company" was incorporated in 1867. John A. Roebling was appointed engineer. He was injured on the site and died before work commenced on the Brooklyn Tower in January of 1870. His son, Washington A. Roebling, succeeded him, but fell seriously ill in 1872 and directed much of the last decade of work from his home in Brooklyn, using a telescope focused on the construction. On 24 May 1883,

the bridge was dedicated by President Chester A. Arthur, Grover Cleveland, then governor of New York State, and Franklin Edson, then mayor. At the time of the ceremony Brooklyn was only about one-half the size of New York, but it was a considerable city. Its 600,000 people made it third largest in the United States after New York and Chicago. The linking of the cities of New York and Brooklyn by the bridge was an obvious step in their rapidly approaching union.

The unveiling of the Statue of Liberty commemorated the end of an immigration—the so-called "Old Immigration," primarily of Northern Europeans, which had slowed down considerably. The year the statue was unveiled there were "only" 300,000 immigrants to the United States. Their number ran around 500,000 a year through the remaining eighties, and some years in the nineties fell below a quarter of a million. Most people thought the era of immigration over and the period of assimilation well commenced. But suddenly in 1900, the annual numbers began to swell again. In 1903 and 1904, there were 800,000 newcomers a year; in 1905, more than a million. In 1907, the greatest number of all time was recorded: 1,285,349. This "New Immigration" was primarily from Southern and Eastern Europe. All the problems suffered by New York in the 1840s and 1850s returned in force to a City still unprepared.

The centennial of Washington's inauguration was staged with great style. The architect Stanford White built a temporary plaster arch at Washington Square (later replaced by a permanent one in marble) at the foot of Fifth Avenue, red, white, and blue banners were draped everywhere, President Harrison spoke, there was a marine parade in the harbor which reenacted Washington's celebrated arrival in the City in 1789, and the whole was concluded with a grand ball at the new Metropolitan Opera House.

"Society" played a large role at the Washington Centennial Ball and a much larger role in New York life generally than it does now. The soberest newspapers ran yards of copy on society's houses, fortunes, amusements, parties, and scandals. Through the public prints all classes knew the "stars" of society the way they would later know the stars of stage and screen. The various Mrs. Astors, Mrs. Vanderbilts, Mrs. Belmonts and their daughters who became duchesses were known by every newspaper reader. Crowds gathered outside the great houses on party nights to stare at the guests, their garb, and their carriages. The opening of the Seventh Regiment Armory was a prime social event. A series of great balls, of which the first major one was the Prince of Wales's ball in 1860, attracted incredible attention and space in the dailies. Two of the greatest of these entertainments were the Vanderbilt ball of 1883 and Mrs. Astor's ball of 1 February 1892, on which occasion her major-domo and publicist Ward McAllister gave the press his curious and celebrated list known as "The Four Hundred." The list, which as it turned out contained only 263 names, or perhaps 300, depending on which newspaper you read, had been talked of for years as being the number and names of guests which Mrs. Astor's ballroom could comfortably hold. An incredible amount of interest was generated by this list, which was heavy on Astors, Vanderbilts, and their allies by marriage but also included a few Knickerbockers like the Van Rensselaers and colonial gentry like the Livingstons, who were represented on the list with more family members than any other clan except the Cuttings.

Fifth Avenue was the shrine and mecca of society and of the legions which followed its activities. The migration of the rich from downtown in colonial days steadily northward culminated in the great houses of Fifth Avenue built mainly between 42nd and 72nd streets (earlier they centered around 34th, later spread on up to around 80th, and finally reached the 90s) in the 1880s and 90s. These are forever associated with the names of the Astor and Vanderbilt families and their kin, but in fact upper Fifth Avenue attracted both old rich and new, and like "The Four Hundred" was never really closed to newcomers. Rich men came from out of town to show what could be done on Fifth Avenue. Standard Oil millionaires (Flagler, Bostwick, Rockefeller, Harkness) were thick on the ground, as were copper kings (W. A. Clark), traction kings (Thomas Fortune Ryan), and sugar kings (H. O. Havemeyer). There was a sprinkling of old families (the Roosevelts) and of Jewish families (Schiffs and Lewisohns).

By 1891, only a few Knickerbockers dwelt in comfortable but gloomy splendor at the lower end of Fifth Avenue, the six blocks between Washington Square and 13th Street. At 34th Street the new Waldorf-Astoria Hotel was rising on the site of former Astor mansions. At 40th Street and Fifth, now becoming commercial, was the oldest of the Vanderbilt houses, occupied by Frederick W. Vanderbilt. At 47th was Jay Gould's house, at 48th Robert Goelet's, and at 49th Ogden Goelet's. Between 51st and 52nd were two more Vanderbilt houses. At the northwest corner of 52nd and Fifth was William K. Vanderbilt's mansion, and Mrs. (Vanderbilt) Webb and Mrs. (Vanderbilt) Twombly lived between St. Thomas's Church and 54th. Also at 54th were the Standard Oil magnates, William Rockefeller and Henry M. Flagler. Cornelius Vanderbilt was on the northwest corner of 57th, and on the downtown corner opposite was William C. Whitney. Across the street from him was Collis P. Huntington. The mixture of comparatively old money and brand new is evident. What the house builders had in common was money and a desire to spend it where it made the most show.

Many, if not most, of the original Fifth Avenuers had begun in poverty. Their homes were the American Dream, oddly Europeanized. Many of the houses were of French inspiration: Henri II and Diane de Poitiers would have been at ease in most of them. All seemed determined to avoid *any* Americanisms in architecture and decoration. The interiors might be in almost any taste, or any mixture of tastes. The "Moorish" room caught the fancy of the rich in the 1890s, and furnishings were splendid.

After houses and parties, society's favorite extravagance was horseflesh. The horse and its sports, racing, driving trotters, coaching, played an enormous part in society's expenditure, both in money and time. Yachting, so expensive that it was not the sport of everyone, not even all millionaires, was popular in one section of society.

The favorite cultural enthusiasm of society was the opera, and much ritual and importance were attached to the Metropolitan Opera (which opened in 1883) and its boxes. The New York Philharmonic, the Oratorio Society (founded 1873), and smaller groups had their dedicated listeners.

Generally speaking, the theater did not attract the same attention, but it was beloved by the middle and lower classes. Union Square was the center of the theatrical district, but "the rialto" was slowly moving uptown along with residences and some kinds of business. Edwin Booth had built his new theater in 1869 at 23rd Street and Sixth Avenue; Augustin Daly owned the Fifth Avenue Theatre at 24th; in 1882, theaters reached 40th Street with the building of the Casino. Harrigan and Hart played in many theaters but often at the Park on Broadway at 35th. They held a place in the hearts of lower-middle-class New Yorkers for decades; they were the essence of Irish-American comedy. Many of their sets were designed by Charles Witham, the most famous set designer of his day, who also worked for Edwin Booth and others. In an era of famous roles and players who still have a permanent place in the history of the American theater, one of the most famous creations was Joseph Jefferson's Rip Van Winkle. Madison Square Garden, not a theater but presenting a variety of entertainment, opened in 1890.

At a time when social life and the theater were vigorous, business was good, and the City was growing rapidly again (from 1,164,673 in 1880 to 1,441,216 in 1890), its government was deplorable, and the progress

187. The poet Emma Lazarus, descendant of an old New York Jewish family and long active in Jewish philanthropy in the City, wrote her famous sonnet to the Statue of Liberty, "The New Colossus," for the benefit of the American campaign to raise funds for the base of the statue. It was first read at the National Academy of Design, 3 December 1883, and twenty years later was inscribed in bronze on the pedestal. Manuscript, 10 × 6 1/2″. Gift of George S. Hellman. 36.319

of the City was thwarted at every turn by dishonest politicans and their minions in the ranks of city government, above all, the police force. The state legislature began a whole series of investigations into the municipal government, or misgovernment, of the City of New York which discovered corruption beneath every stone. A special committee appointed by the legislature and chaired by Theodore Roosevelt "to investigate the local government of the city and county of New York" made its report in March of 1884. It found the condition of the entire government "absolutely appalling." The county clerk netted $250,000 a year on the fee system, most of which he turned over to "the political organization which supported him" (i.e., Tammany Hall). The surrogate's office seemed to be run "simply for the purpose of blackmail on those unable to defend themselves." The Parks Department came in for special criticism: it had four members, only one of whom, the president, received a salary. For some time past, each member had of course wanted to be president: in elections, each voted for himself. To release the stalemate, the presidency rotated among the four, each drawing the lavish salary for a few months. The investigating committee remarked that "a more undignified squabble for the spoils of office has rarely been seen."

The *Tribune* added to the committee's report: "The government of groggeries has gone too far. The majority of our aldermen have risen to their positions from behind the bars of corner dramshops, and few of them know as much of the city charter as they do of the composition of cocktails."

A most fruitful source of aldermanic corruption was the granting of franchises to build street railways. These franchises were enormously profitable and worth large-scale bribery from investors to secure them. Several great fortunes were derived from the building of traction systems in New York, notably William C. Whitney's and Thomas Fortune Ryan's. The transit system of the City needed work so badly that, as the *Post* said, "The upper part of the City is made almost useless to persons engaged in any daily business of any kind." Innumerable propositions for better transportation had been put forth, including Melville

C. Smith's curious "Arcade Railway," but most were built experimentally for a short distance or not at all.

In 1886, a horrendous scandal arose in connection with the affairs of the Broadway Surface Railroad Company. This company operated cable cars over a two-mile line from Bowling Green to Union Square. When an investigative committee looked into the franchise of this company, it discovered that certain aldermen had profited enormously from its grant. These aldermen were known to New Yorkers as "The Boodle Board." Several of them turned state's evidence, others fled to Canada or elsewhere to escape indictment, but some were convicted and sentenced to hard labor. The Broadway Surface Line went on, however, and returned immense profits to its owners.

Elevated railroad lines had been built on both sides of the Island by the 1880s. On the West Side they opened up a vast area for settlement which provided relief from population pressure in other parts of the Island. In 1886, a commentator wrote: "The west side of New York presents just now a scene of building activity such as was never before witnessed in that section, and which gives promise of the speedy disappearance of all the shanties in the neighborhood and the rapid population of this long neglected part of New York. . . ."

The railroads were changing the appearance of the City's streets. The great Blizzard of 1888 changed it also, and not just temporarily. The streets had been cluttered with telegraph poles and electric wires (Thomas A. Edison's dynamos at 257 Pearl Street had begun to light the Nassau-Pearl-Wall Street section in 1882). So many people and so much property were injured by the falling of these impedimenta during the blizzard, that after the snow was cleaned up an all-out effort was made to eliminate above-ground poles and place wires beneath the surface. A department of the municipal government charmingly called the "Bureau of Incumbrances" removed 20,377 poles in the next few years and 29,802 *miles* of wire, much improving the safety and attractiveness of the City's streets.

The City was firmly under the Tiger's paw in 1892, and the sachems paid little attention to outcries of the reformers who sprang up, sounded off for a while, and

188. The heavy East Coast snowfall of 11–14 March 1888—averaging twenty-two inches in the New York City area—has become celebrated as "The Blizzard of '88." New Street, looking toward Wall Street, shows the snow's effect on the myriad strands of telegraph, telephone, and electric wire crisscrossing the City on poles. Partly as a result of damage during the blizzard, the wires were laid underground over the next few years. Photographer unknown. Archive

then disappeared. The Reverend Charles H. Parkhurst did not disappear. In 1892, he began his accusations against Tammany Hall by denouncing its City officials for corruption and accusing the police of not only countenancing vice but actually protecting it. Parkhurst was minister of the Madison Avenue Presbyterian Church and president of the Society for the Prevention of Crime. He preached a series of vigorous sermons in which he castigated City officialdom in the most intemperate terms. He failed, however, to substantiate his charges before a grand jury, which rebuked him for sensationalism. Then in disguise he personally visited brothels and illegal bars and saw policemen going in and out on the best of terms with madams and publicans. Early in 1894, the state legislature appointed a committee commonly known as the Lexow Committee (after its president, State Senator Clarence Lexow) to investigate the police department of New York City. The investigation called public attention to a truly frightful system of bribes, kick-backs, and shake-downs in the department said to amount to $7,000,000 annually. Sixty-seven policemen were indicted; none ever served any time.

Reform was in the air. For the election of 1894, a "Committee of Seventy" was formed to work for the defeat of Tammany in the municipal offices. It included Abram S. Hewitt, J. P. Morgan, Anson Phelps Stokes, William Travers Jerome, and others. Support by the Republicans, the State Democracy, the Anti-Tammany Democracy, the German-American Reform Union, and dozens of other reform organizations led to the overthrow of Tammany—temporarily. William L. Strong was elected mayor. To the Board of Police Commissioners he appointed Theodore Roosevelt.

Roosevelt is the only president of the United States actually to have been born in New York City (at 28 East 20th Street, now a museum). He served a term in the state assembly and ran for mayor in the election of 1886, an odd three-way affair in which the Republican Roosevelt was pitted against the Democrat Abram S. Hewitt and Henry George, the "single-tax" philosopher who was supported by many workingmen. Hewitt won. As police commissioner Roosevelt was honest and made some worthwhile changes in the humbled but uncontrite department. He was given great power by the mayor, and its effect on a mind essentially immature was unsettling. Apparently playing Haroun-al-Raschid, Roosevelt used to sally forth at night from Police Headquarters dressed in a cape and black silk sash with fringe to his knees to catch unwary cops snoozing on the job or consorting with whores and saloonkeepers. The public was amused for only a short time. Roosevelt's enforcement of blue laws was capricious and highly annoying to the citizens, and soon the newspapers were calling for his dismissal. Mayor Strong was equally disenchanted, and in 1897 Roosevelt left. He was never much of a hero to his fellow New Yorkers.

Strong was a good mayor, but having been elected on a reform ticket he was lacking in party affiliation and consequently in strength. He was a setup for defeat in the election of 1897. The movement toward consolidation of the City of New York with its nearer neighbors was proceeding, and it was known that the victor in the election of 1897 would be the first mayor of Greater New York. The reform movement nominated the distinguished former mayor of Brooklyn and president of Columbia University Seth Low, the Republicans Benjamin F. Tracy, Tammany Robert A. van Wyck, and the "Jeffersonian Democrats" the single-taxer Henry George, who died in the midst of the campaign and was succeeded in the candidacy by his son Henry George, Jr. The anti-Tammany vote was so split that the Tiger easily won, and to Van Wyck, who was entirely under the thumb of Tammany boss Richard Croker, went the honor of being first mayor of Greater New York City.

189. The New York *Mirror* newspaper issued this lithograph of *Union Square in Midsummer* as a supplement to its regular edition of 12 August 1882. The newspaper's offices are shown next to the Union Square Hotel. Union Square was then headquarters for New York's many actors as well as theatrical costumers, piano suppliers, and others catering to that profession, as indicated by the many shop signs. Around the edges of the print are portraits not only of celebrated performers of the time but also theatrical entrepreneurs. Among the actors and actresses are Edwin Booth, Modjeska, Mrs. Langtry, Lotta (Crabtree), Fay Templeton, and Minnie Maddern (Fiske). The view is taken looking along 14th Street; the central block is that formerly occupied by S. Klein's Department Store. Lithograph printed in color, 17 1/2 × 26″. Gift of Morris Ranger in memory of his brother George Ranger. 31.224.15

190. William Waldorf Astor built the Waldorf Hotel on the northwest corner of Fifth Avenue and 33rd Street on a site formerly occupied by his own huge house. The hotel was thirteen stories tall and had 530 rooms and 350 private baths. It opened on 14 March 1893. Shortly afterward, William's cousin John Jacob Astor IV, who lived across a garden from him, tore down *his* house and outdid his cousin by putting up a seventeen-story hotel called the Astoria. It was connected with the Waldorf, and the combined establishment, which was the largest hotel in the world (1,000 rooms, 765 private baths), opened its doors on 1 November 1897. The architectural style was "German Renaissance," recalling the Astor family's original nationality. The artist Hughson Hawley here shows the hotel as it appeared about the time of its opening. It was demolished, beginning on 1 October 1929, and with incredible speed the Empire State Building was erected on its site and dedicated 1 May 1931. Watercolor, 58 × 63″. Gift of John I. Downey. 45.40.1

191. *The* Mrs. Astor lived in the first house on the right at the corner of Fifth Avenue and
65th Street. Herself the descendant of a prominent New York family (she was born
Caroline Webster Schermerhorn), in 1853 she married William Backhouse Astor, Jr., one of
the richest men in America, although not head of the Astor family. Having quickly
established her social position despite various female rivals, mainly from her husband's
family, she reigned imperturbably for fifty years as the queen of American society. Richard
Morris Hunt built her this French chateau in 1893. All the way up Fifth Avenue to 72nd
Street lived Mills, Whitneys, Gerrys, Belmonts, and other famous New York families. Mrs.
Astor died in 1908; her house, like most Fifth Avenue mansions, did not long survive her.
The site is now occupied by Temple Emanu-El. Photograph by Byron.

192. Jacob A. Riis, a Danish immigrant, horrified the public with his revelations of slum life in New York in a series of vivid and moving books, including *How the Other Half Lives* (1890) and *The Children of the Poor* (1892). Especially heartrending was his account of "the Street Arabs," as the homeless children of New York were known. "Street Arabs in sleeping quarters" from *How the Other Half Lives* shows three waifs in a corner on Mulberry Street. Fortunate Arabs were taken in at night to the Newsboys' Lodging House at the intersection of Duane, William, and New Chambers streets. A moving spirit there was Horatio Alger, gathering background for his extraordinarily successful novels. Riis's work effected massive reforms in housing. The Jacob A. Riis Collection.

193. The photographic record of the European immigration into New York during the 1890s is unusually complete. These scenes give remarkable glimpses into life in the foreign neighborhoods of New York toward the end of the nineteenth century. Bohemian cigarmakers at work in a tenement room. The Jacob A. Riis Collection.

194. Pushcart market on Hester Street, about 1890. The Byron Collection.

195. This view in front of the Plaza Hotel captures one of the most elegant panoramas to be found in the City at the turn of the century. The two buildings on the east side of Fifth Avenue between 59th and 58th streets are the Savoy Hotel, opened in 1894, and the recently erected Balkenhayn apartment house. Both were demolished in 1926 to make room for the Savoy-Plaza Hotel, in turn torn down in 1967 so that the General Motors Building could be erected. On the next block is an impressive group of five houses (architecturally designed to resemble a single structure) built in the 1860s by Mrs. Mary Mason Jones. The house at the south corner was occupied by Mrs. Jones until her death in 1891. This lady has a small niche in literary history since she appears in Edith Wharton's great New York novel *The Age of Innocence*. Her so-called "Marble Row" was not fully demolished until 1929. The building on the right, opposite "Marble Row," is the Cornelius Vanderbilt mansion, inspired by the Château de Blois, built in 1880 and enlarged in 1893. Photograph by Byron.

196. Byron made this view of City Hall looking northeast from the Park Row Building in 1899. 12 3/4 × 10 1/4". The Byron Collection. 7864

197. Beginning in 1736 as an infirmary located where City Hall now stands, Bellevue Hospital in 1816 formally opened its new establishment on the site of the Belle Vue Farm on the East River at 26th Street. Horse-drawn ambulances were first kept "at the ready" at Bellevue Hospital as early as 1869, and by 1892 there were nine in service, answering 4,858 calls that year. The 1895 vehicle shown here with hard rubber tires must have been less than salubrious for an injured patient as the horse trotted along the stone streets. Photograph by Byron. Byron 2911/735

198. A fashion was set around 1900 for giving dinners in unusual surroundings. By general agreement the most unusual was the "horseback dinner" given on 28 March 1903 by C. K. G. Billings. The heir of a Chicago gas company fortune, he was mad for horses, and in the present Fort Tryon Park at 196th Street and Fort Washington Road he constructed a stable for his racehorses costing $200,000. He celebrated its opening by inviting thirty-six horsey friends to dinner in the grand ballroom of Sherry's (then society's favorite restaurant), on the southwest corner of Fifth Avenue and 44th Street. Each guest was supplied with a horse—not a high-strung Billings thoroughbred but a patient riding-academy steed—whose saddle carried a dining tray. Champagne was supplied in saddle bags with a rubber tube for imbibing. Waiters dressed as grooms. At the conclusion of the human repast, which astonished even contemporaries, the mounts were supplied with oats. Photograph by Byron.

199. The great Hudson-Fulton Celebration, which commemorated the voyage of ▶ Henry Hudson in 1609 and Robert Fulton's steamboat trip up the Hudson in 1807, was held in New York in late 1909. Replicas of the *Half-Moon* and the *Clermont* were built, and a mammoth naval parade sailed up the Hudson led by those ships and followed by warships from England, Germany, France, Italy, and many other countries. These and 800 other vessels were anchored in the Hudson between 42nd Street and Spuyten Duyvil. This is the menu cover of the dinner given to honor guests of the Hudson-Fulton Celebration Commission held at the Hotel Astor, 29 September 1909. 10 1/8 × 8 1/2". Gift of Mrs. C. F. Buechner. 38.389.2

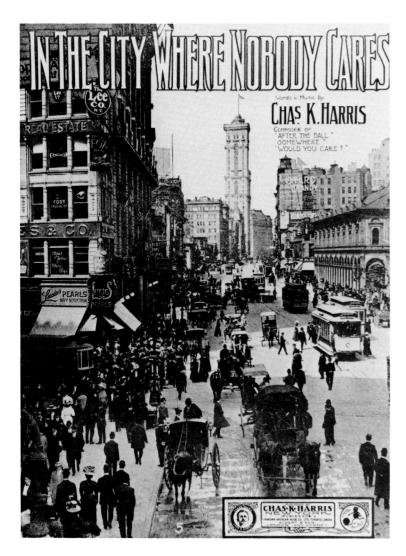

200. "In the City Where Nobody Cares" was one of the many hit songs of Charles K. Harris, who began his career in Milwaukee supplying vaudeville performers with songs "written to order." In 1892, his "After the Ball" was inserted into a musical called *A Trip to Chinatown;* the sheet music for it sold five million copies, and it was one of the greatest hits of the era. Harris moved to New York, where he became one of the kings of Tin Pan Alley (28th Street) and wrote hit after hit. The cover for this sheet music (1908) shows Broadway, looking north from below 34th Street. 14 × 11″. Gift of Malcolm Newton Stone. 39.449.3

201. Advertising by means of musical jingles is by no means an invention of the twentieth century. A hundred years ago enterprising manufacturers and merchants combined with music publishers to issue a long series of songs in which commercial products from baby jumpers to rat poison were extolled. The covers of the sheet music, of which this is a fine example, generally show either the product in use or the place where it is manufactured. Ernst Reinking wrote this "Aniline Polka-Mazurka" in 1869 to honor the Aniline and Chemical Works of Messrs. Rumpff & Lutz, whose busy factory is shown on the cover. Emphasizing smoke pouring from the factory's chimneys would not likely occur today, but at the time smoke was obviously regarded as an impressive sign of industrial enterprise. Notice the price of seven and one-half cents. Lithographed music cover, 12 × 8 3/4″. The J. Clarence Davies Collection. 29.100.1151

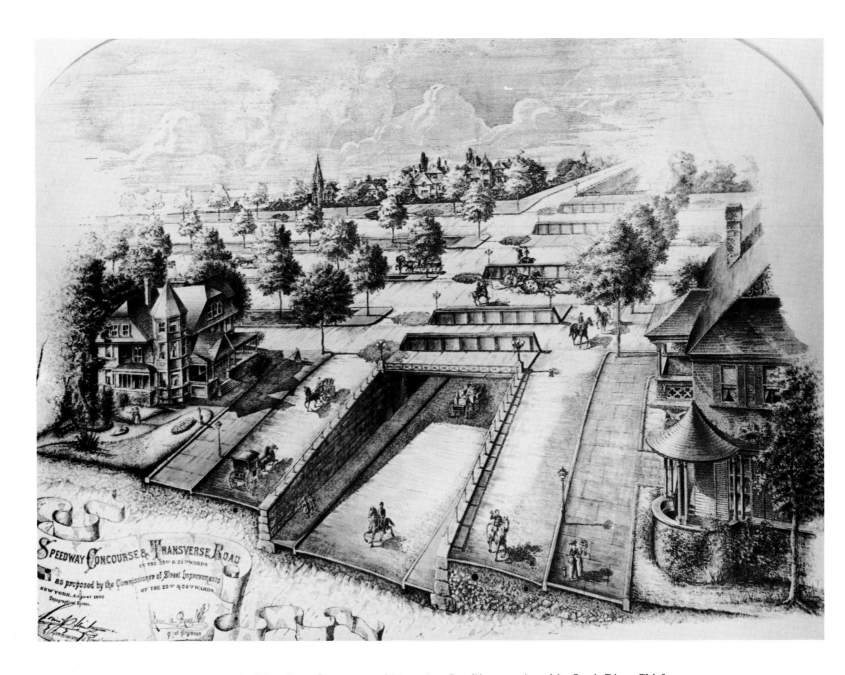

202. The "Speedway Concourse and Transverse Road" was projected by Louis Risse, Chief Engineer of the Board of Public Improvements, in this print dated August, 1892. This original design called for a central roadway between bicycle paths and pedestrian walks and was meant to link Manhattan and the large parks of the Bronx such as Van Cortlandt. Although the design was changed in construction, the Grand Concourse became one of the chief thoroughfares of the Bronx. Colored wood engraving, 12 3/8 × 16 1/4".
The J. Clarence Davies Collection. 29.100.3482

203. In addition to their vast output of views, sporting scenes, animals, sentimentals, portraits, and so on, Currier & Ives produced advertisements, song-sheets, and comics such as this *A Beautiful Pair* of 1871. The attraction for buyers here is not only the pun; the print was intriguingly naughty in a day of long skirts when anything to do with a lady's "lower extremities" (i.e., ankles) was indelicate. Colored lithograph, 8 × 12 5/8″. The Harry T. Peters Collection. 56.300.1438

204. At the celebrated Vanderbilt ball on 6 March 1883, Miss Sarah Cooper Hewitt appeared in this fancy dress costume copied by Worth from Sarah Bernhardt's costume as Roxanne. The robe is of bright blue satin brocaded in red roses, the skirt of pale pink satin and white striped silk voile, and the turban of gold net. With the costume were worn maroon velvet shoes embroidered with gold thread, chamois gloves embroidered with gold and colored stones, and a belt containing two daggers. Miss Hewitt was also armed with a full-length sword as shown. Gift of The Cooper Union Museum. 62.59.1a–p

205. The Seventh Regiment built its new armory on Park Avenue between 66th and 67th streets over a two-year period, 1877–79. When the building was completed, a fair was held to raise money to furnish the fortresslike structure. President Rutherford Hayes opened the fair on 17 November 1879, and it ran until 6 December. These dolls represent a party of four dressed and assembled for the fair. Although the dolls are French in origin, the elaborate ball gowns are from a New York dressmaker, and the officers' uniforms were made by Brooks Brothers, who also made the Seventh Regiment's uniforms. Heights: 18 and 24″. Gift of Mrs. William E. Quimby. 41.410.1–4

206. The popular Victorian rococo style is reflected in this set of doll house furniture of the 1850s. It is composed of pressed tin and upholstered in flock. The suite, which even includes the etagère beloved of Victorian householders, descended in the Quackenbush family whose home was on Murray Hill, Manhattan. Scale: one inch to the foot. Gift of Mrs. A. B. Anderson. 71.159a–n

207. The officers and employees of the Delaware, Lackawanna, and Western Railroad Company presented a tea set with this tray in eighteen carat gold to their president Samuel Sloan to commemorate his thirty years as president of the company on Christmas Day, 1897. Sloan was an Irishman from County Down who until middle age was in the import business in New York. At the age of fifty he became active in railroads and made the D. L. & W. into a major line by such feats as changing the gauge of the entire road with a traffic stoppage of only twenty-four hours. Before his death at the age of ninety he had served as actual president of no less than seventeen different companies and corporations. This tray, which measures 28 1/2 × 18 1/2", was made by Tiffany & Co. Bequest of Mrs. Katharine Colt Sloan, daughter-in-law of Samuel Sloan. 51.301.ad

208. The first major section of New York's subway was finished in 1904. To commemorate completion of one stage of a new transportation system for the City, the Rapid Transit Railroad Commissioners for the City of New York presented this silver tray by Tiffany & Co. to August Belmont II, who was president of the Rapid Transit Subway Construction Co. A map of the railroad is engraved in the center of the tray. Medallions, one of them a portrait, the others showing construction sites, form a border linked by laurel leaves. The shovel handles at either end of the tray are engraved with the New York City arms and embellished with picks. 21 1/8 × 37 3/4″. Gift of August Belmont, grandson of August Belmont II. 68.109a

210. Mayor Robert A. Van Wyck used this silver spade to break the earth at the excavation for New York's first subway in 1900. The initial section was built from City Hall Park north to Grand Central Station. Van Wyck was a native New Yorker, a graduate of Columbia Law School, a descendant of the Dutch settlers, and served as first president of the Holland Society. He was also a Tammany Hall politician and involved in more than one unpleasant scandal during his administration, including the admission that he owned $500,000 worth of stock in the so-called "Ice Trust," whose aim was to keep the price of ice high during the summer months. Length: 36 1/4″. Gift of Mrs. William Van Wyck. 54.373

209. The history of yachting in the waters off New York goes back to the Dutch, who used to race up and down the Hudson. The New York Yacht Club met for the first time on 30 July 1844. Later in the century two of its most active members were the brothers Robert and Ogden Goelet. Heirs to the mammoth Goelet real-estate holdings, they were well able to support this most expensive of sports. Between 1882 and 1897, Ogden Goelet offered two racing prizes each year, one for sloops and the other for schooners. This extraordinary bowl made by Tiffany & Co. was won by *Titania*, C. Oliver Iselin's sloop, in 1889. Height: 12″; diameter: 17″. Gift of Mrs. C. Oliver Iselin. M39.1.1

212. The Yiddish theater in New York came into its own in the late 1890s, especially after the arrival from Russia, in 1891, of Jacob Gordin, the most important Yiddish playwright. Together with Jacob Adler, an outstanding actor, Gordin changed the course of Yiddish theater from vaudeville and farce to serious drama. During his short career in America (he died in 1909) Gordin staged the dramas of Sudermann, Ibsen, Gorky, and other contemporary playwrights. This bust of Gordin was made by Julius Butensky. Height: 28". Gift of Mrs. Boris Volynsky. 65.71

211. Richard Wagner's Hungarian student, secretary, and assistant, Anton Seidl, came to New York in 1885, to conduct at the Metropolitan Opera. In the years between 1886 and 1889, he had the extraordinary distinction of conducting the American premieres of *Aïda, L'Africaine, Götterdämmerung, Das Rheingold, Tristan und Isolde,* and on 4 January 1886, *Die Meistersinger.* That event is commemorated in this three-handled silver loving cup inscribed on the base, "Anton Seidl from his New York admirers, Feb. 25th 1887," and decorated with three scenes from opera. The cup was made by the Gorham Manufacturing Company. In 1891, Seidl became conductor of the New York Philharmonic and was on the podium for the world premiere of Dvořák's Symphony No. 9, *From the New World,* composed when Dvořák was living at 327 East 17th Street. Height: 11 1/2". Gift of Mrs. Anton Seidl. 32.400.1

213. Alice Gwynne Vanderbilt, wife of the financier Cornelius Vanderbilt II, whom she married in 1867, presided over the immense "Breakers" in Newport. She wore this pale green velvet evening dress trimmed with pearls about 1900. It was made by White, Howard & Co. of New York and Chicago and bears their label. Gift of Countess Lâszló Széchényi, Mrs. Vanderbilt's daughter. 51.284.2ab

214. The ball given at the Academy of Music on 12 October 1860 in honor of the visiting Prince of Wales (later Edward VII of Great Britain) was considered "the greatest ball ever given in the City of New York" and a landmark in its social history. More than 4,000 people jammed the ballroom and supper room. The dresses of the ladies were naturally their best efforts. Mrs. James Colles (née Mary Josephine Blachly) wore this lavender ciselé uncut velvet gown. Gift of Miss Harriet Colles, daughter of the wearer. 31.20.1b–c

215. Mrs. Jay Gould wore this dinner dress about 1885. It is made of lavender satin with lace trimming; the skirt has a pink satin front with tiers of lace and flowers scattered down the front. The dressmaker was M. A. Connelly of 7 East 16th Street, New York. Gift of Finley Johnson Shepard. 39.212.9

216. Frederic-Auguste Bartholdi changed the sculptural elements in the Statue of Liberty several times before it was was finally completed in 1884. In this terra-cotta bozzetto the figure holds a broken chain in the left hand instead of the final arrangement of a folded arm holding a tablet inscribed July 4, 1776. Height: 21″. Given in memory of James Patrick Silo by his wife Estelle Cameron Silo. 33.386

217. More than one million New Yorkers and visitors are ▶ said to have watched the unveiling of the Statue of Liberty on 28 October 1886. Despite a dank sky and rain that fell at intervals throughout the day, unparalleled enthusiasm greeted "the most famous statue in the world." When President Grover Cleveland officially accepted the gift from the people of France on behalf of the people of the United States, steamers blew their horns, tugs whistled, cannon roared, and bells chimed all over the City. Edward Moran, taking an optimistic view of the actual weather conditions, conveys the color and undiminished excitement of the occasion in his *The Unveiling of the Statue of Liberty Enlightening the World*. Oil on canvas, 39 1/2 × 49 1/2″. The J. Clarence Davies Collection. 37.100.260

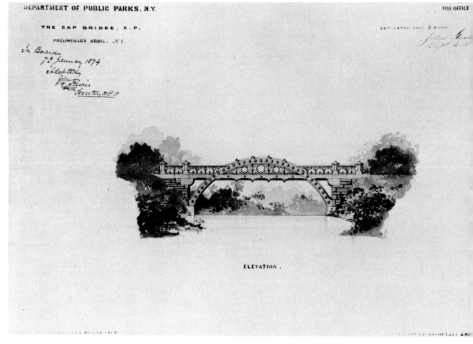

219. Bridges played an important role in the "picturesque" landscaping of Central Park proposed by Olmsted and Vaux. Each bridge was individually designed by Calvert Vaux. This is "The Gapstow Bridge" in a preliminary study, with a manuscript note at left showing it was approved by the Board of Commissioners for Central Park on 7 January 1874. Watercolor, 13 7/8 × 20 1/2". Deposited by the Department of Parks. L845.9

218. "The Board of Commissioners of the Central Park" was established in 1857. In 1858, the board offered prizes for the best proposals for developing and constructing a huge city park above 59th Street. Thirty-nine plans were submitted. The best was pronounced to be that named the "Greensward Plan" by its anonymous authors, Frederick Law Olmsted and Calvert Vaux. The original Olmsted and Vaux competition drawings consisted of 11 × 13 1/2" layouts tinted with watercolors, and a number of existing and corresponding proposed views. This is view No. 5, with map, photograph of the terrain looking southwest across the lake from Vista Rock, and an oval watercolor of the "effect proposed." Laying out the Park according to the Greensward Plan began about 1 June 1858. Deposited by the Department of Parks. L845.1e

220. Despite the scars made by a century of misplaced civic
benefactions, Central Park still maintains its original noble
proportions and, so far as its place in the life of the City is
concerned, has changed but little in that century. This bird's-eye
view of *Central Park—Summer, Looking South, New York, 1865*, was
drawn by John Bachmann and lithographed by Julius Bien. The
original planting designed by Olmsted and Vaux is shown in detail
with its incomparable blending of the formal and the natural.
Bethesda Fountain, the Terrace, and the Mall are seen much as
they are today. A number of balloon ascensions were made in New
York about this time, and there were even plans, which failed to
come off, for floating a balloon from New York across the Atlantic.
Colored lithograph, 11 3/4 × 17 5/8". The J. Clarence Davies
Collection. 29.100.1944

221. This watercolor shows "the effect proposed" in the Greensward Plan, with luxuriant planting such as Olmsted and Vaux wanted.

222. Skating on the City's frozen ponds is one of New York's most durable sports. At least as early as 1652, the Dutch were enjoying it every winter. A rink was opened in the new Central Park in 1859, and the *Times* reported that it was "quite a fashionable resort for skaters . . . many hundreds are enjoying the exercise daily." Johann Mongles Culverhouse, an emigrant from Rotterdam to New York about 1849 and painter of many winter sports, did this *Skating Scene, 1865, Central Park*. The view is from the east looking west near the 72nd Street entrance of the Park; the building at left where skaters are warming themselves is near the Terrace. Oil on canvas, 20 × 35″. The J. Clarence Davies Collection. 29.100.1301

223. Among dealers in fine horses Hiram Woodruff was preeminent at mid-century. This painting by Johannes Oertel shows the Woodruff Stables on Jerome Avenue in 1861. Woodruff sold horses to Commodore Vanderbilt, August Belmont, Jay Gould, the theatrical producer Lester Wallack, Ogden Mills, and other connoisseurs of horseflesh at prices which sometimes rose to $30,000. Jerome Avenue was a boulevard planned to give access to the racetrack built by the American Jockey Club in Westchester County. Stables and inns catering to lovers of horses and horse sports were spotted along its route. Oil on canvas, 24 1/4 × 40″. Gift of Harris Fahnestock. 34.340

224. The iron and glass Crystal Palace, which had opened in 1853 as one of the world's first "fireproof" buildings, burned to the ground on the night of Tuesday, 5 October 1858. It had served as the site of a world's fair and as a showcase for American products placed there by no less than 3,960 exhibitors. All of these exhibits, together with numerous fine art objects on display, were destroyed, but there was no loss of life. Currier & Ives pictured the disaster in one of their finest and most dramatic fire prints. Colored lithograph, 16 7/8 × 25 3/8″. The Harry T. Peters Collection. 56.300.85

225. The great houses of Fifth Avenue were below 59th Street until after the Civil War, and for a good many years after that the distant upper stretches of the avenue were covered with shantytowns. Squatters were not permitted in Central Park, but shanties could be thrown up in the unbuilt area which surrounded the park. Dirty and malarious, the shanties gradually overwhelmed the neat country estates which had dotted the area earlier in the century. This depressing scene exactly suited the gloomy talents of the New York artist Ralph Blakelock, who painted this oil of *Fifth Avenue at 89th Street in 1868.* Oil on canvas, 15 7/8 × 23 3/4″. Gift of Archer M. Huntington. 32.333

227. Work in progress on Brooklyn Bridge is shown in this ▶ photograph by G. W. Pach dated 25 October 1878, which includes a footbridge, anchor bars, and a finished strand of cable ready to lower into position. 13 1/4 × 9 1/2″. Gift of Shirley C. Burden. 57.15.16

226. A bridge to link Manhattan and Brooklyn was proposed as early as 1802, and the idea was revived at intervals for more than half a century. In 1867, the New York Bridge Co. was incorporated, John A. Roebling was appointed chief engineer, and plans were drawn. The first caisson was sunk on 19 March 1870, but construction was to occupy thirteen years, and the bridge was not formally opened until 24 May 1883. This is the Brooklyn wooden caisson before its launching on 19 March 1870. Photographer unknown. 9 × 15 1/4″. Gift of Shirley C. Burden. 57.15.1

228. The New York stone tower is shown here completed to the height of the roadway in September, 1873. Photographer unknown. 13 × 16 1/2″. Gift of Shirley C. Burden. 57.15.11

229. The Brooklyn Bridge was formally opened to the public on 24 May 1883. This bird's-eye view of the bridge from New York, looking northeast, shows the grand display of fireworks on opening night. A week later there was a tragedy when panic among pedestrians resulted in the death of twelve persons and injuries to many others. Colored lithograph, 24 × 15″. The J. Clarence Davies Collection. 29.100.1752

231. The Winter Garden Theatre at Broadway and Bond Street was giving the most lavishly staged plays in America under the management of Edwin Booth when it was totally destroyed by fire, 23 March 1867. Booth almost immediately began to plan a new theater carrying his own name and under his management. It was built on the southeast corner of 23rd Street and Sixth Avenue and opened with *Romeo and Juliet* on 3 February 1869. Here the artist Charles W. Witham shows the new theater with the stage set for the first act of that play. Until the theater failed financially in 1874, Booth and a distinguished company performed Shakespearean and other plays to great acclaim. Watercolor, 21 × 15". William Seymour Collection. 39.134.15

230. The Panic of 1857, the worst depression in twenty years, inspired James H. Cafferty and Charles G. Rosenberg, two New York painters, to produce this remarkable picture they precisely entitled *Wall Street, half past two o'clock, October 13, 1857*. The painting shows Wall Street looking west from about William Street toward Trinity Church. The numerous figures in front are all portraits of financiers of the time; once there was a key to their identification but it has been lost. The short man at the curb on the extreme right is believed to be Commodore Vanderbilt. Oil on canvas, 50 × 39 1/2". Gift of the Hon. Irwin Untermyer. 40.54

232. The Philharmonic Society of New York (now the New York
Philharmonic) gave its first concert at the Apollo Rooms, 412 Broadway,
on 7 December 1842. It is the oldest permanent orchestra in the
English-speaking world, and there are only two orchestras anywhere that
are older, Leipzig and the Paris Conservatoire. Chamber music groups
were slower to develop, but later in the nineteenth century, especially
after the great German immigration had brought many trained
musicians to this country, groups such as the "New York Philharmonic
Club" shown in this print entered the musical life of the City. The print
is undated but was issued between 1889 and 1902, when the lithographers
H. A. Thomas & Wylie operated on West 24th Street. 19 × 26 1/2".
Gift of Miss Kate Halk in memory of Mr. and Mrs. Felix Arnold.
40.120.7

233. *Hamlet* has been performed in New York since at least 1761, when
William Hallam played the title role at David Douglass's theater on
Nassau Street. Edwin Booth established a record when he played the
prince for one hundred nights in the season November, 1864–March,
1865. Nearly thirty years later he chose the role for his final appearance
on the stage, 28 March 1891. Harry A. Ogden, then only fifteen years
old, made this pencil sketch of Booth's production in 1871. Ogden was
for many years on the staff of the Strobridge Lithographing Company
and was responsible for the many color plates in the monumental
Collection of Uniforms of the U. S. Army, 1775–1906. The costume worn by
Booth in 1871 is in The Museum of the City of New York. 7 1/2 × 4 1/2".
Gift of Harry A. Ogden. 32.290.3

234. The Metropolitan Opera first presented Richard Strauss's *Salome* on the night of 22 January 1907; Olive Fremstad sang the title role. The critics were outraged, but not so much by the advanced dissonances of the music as by the writhings of the heroine and the skimpiness of her costume. A storm unparalleled in the history of American operatic performances broke over the unfortunate management of the opera house. The piece was jerked out of repertory and not heard again at the Metropolitan for twenty-seven years. Oddly enough, only two years later Oscar Hammerstein presented *Salome* at his Manhattan Opera House without any protests being made. Salome was sung by Mary Garden to great acclaim. She is shown here with Charles Dalmores, who sang Herod, in a photograph by Percy C. Byron. Museum Purchase. 41.420.689

235. *Rip Van Winkle* was one of the greatest popular successes in the ▶ history of the American theater, and it was played for thirty-eight years by Joseph Jefferson. When he died in 1905, at the age of seventy-five, Jefferson had been an actor for seventy-one of those years. Son and grandson of distinguished actors, he made his debut at the age of four in the company of Thomas "Daddy" Rice, then first performing the blackface number called "Jim Crow" which was to make him America's first great minstrel. Jefferson went on to play many roles including Asa Trenchard in *Our American Cousin* and Bob Acres in *The Rivals*, but it was his performance as Rip Van Winkle that made him the country's most beloved actor for decades. Washington Irving's story also served as the libretto for the first "American" grand opera, written by G. F. Bristow in 1855. This portrait of the actor in his celebrated role was painted by Nicholas R. Brewer in 1901. Oil on canvas, 90 × 72". Gift of Mrs. J. D. Adams. 34.251.1

236. George P. A. Healy was the leading society portrait painter of the 1860s; he was the John Singer Sargent of his day. His portrait of Mrs. August Belmont (née Caroline Slidell Perry) was done about 1860. Member of one of America's most distinguished naval families (she was the daughter of Matthew C. Perry and niece of Oliver Hazard Perry), she married, in 1849, August Belmont, the banker, who had first come to this country to represent the Rothschilds. Their house on the northeast corner of 18th Street and Fifth Avenue was notable for its luxury even in the Gilded Age. Oil on canvas, 65 × 52″. Gift of August Belmont IV, grandson of Mrs. Belmont. 51.317

237. Michele Gordigiani, a visiting Italian artist, painted *Cornelia Ward Hall and Her Children* about 1880. The painting gives an excellent idea of the interior of a well-to-do New York home of the period; the lush upholstery, the Japanese screen, the potted palms are typical. The father of the family, John H. Hall, was a banker. In 1880, the family lived at 551 West 57th Street; afterward their home was at 559 Fifth Avenue. Oil on canvas, 53 1/2 × 68 1/2″. Bequest of Mrs. Martha Hall Barrett, who is shown as the little girl on the sofa. 61.155.1

238. An English-born artist, William Monk, did this pencil drawing of the financial district in 1912. It is Wall Street looking west from William Street. 21 7/8 × 15 1/4″. The J. Clarence Davies Collection. 29.100.2108

VIII: GREATER NEW YORK

It'll be a great place if they ever finish it.

—ATTRIBUTED TO O. HENRY

Important New Yorkers had urged the consolidation of New York City, that is, Manhattan Island, with Brooklyn and the nearby areas in New York State for years. Andrew H. Green, one of the City's most influential citizens throughout much of the nineteenth century, directed the attention of his colleagues on the Board of Commissioners of Central Park to this important subject in 1868, urging that New York, Kings County, part of Queens, Richmond, and part of Westchester County come under "one common municipal government." In 1874, three towns in Westchester did decide to cast their lot with New York City. They were Kingsbridge, Morrisania, and West Farms. This area, which included between 30,000 and 40,000 people, was long known as the "Annexed District."

Years later, in 1890, Green presented a memorial on the subject of consolidation to the New York State Legislature, saying "the counter is one between the retreating forces of the tribal system and the coming forces of the cooperative system, between barbaric tradition and educated aspiration," a statement strong enough to show how deeply Green felt on the subject. Railroads, ferries, bridges, transportation links of all kinds were bringing the settled areas closer together. The year of this memorial the state legislature passed an act creating a commission headed by Green to study the proposal, and in 1894 the question finally came to a vote by the area's inhabitants.

The results of the vote were interesting. In New York (Manhattan and the Annexed District) the vote was 96,938 for consolidation, 59,959 against; in Queens,

7,712 for, 4,741 against; in Richmond, 5,531 for, 1,505 against; in Mount Vernon, 873 for, 1,603 against; in Eastchester 374 for, 260 against; in Westchester, 620 for, 621 against (!); in Pelham, 261 for, 153 against. In Brooklyn, by far the largest of the candidates for annexation, the vote was very close: 64,774 for, 64,467 against. The Brooklyn vote was protested and the consolidation bill defeated in the Legislature. All that New York gained in the election were the little towns in the eastern half of lower Westchester—Throgs Neck, Unionport, Olinville, Williamsbridge, Wakefield, Eastchester, and part of Pelham—an addition of about 17,000 people.

Tammany was greatly in favor of consolidation (more offices to fill with patronage, more franchises), and now Tammany Boss Richard Croker really went to work, uniting with the upstate Republican Boss Thomas C. Platt. This powerful combination was bound to have its way. Senator Clarence Lexow, who seemed fated to lend his name to important commissions, now headed a legislative committee on annexation. The consolidation bill with Democratic and Republican support passed in 1896. A new charter was drawn up, and the mayor of Brooklyn approved it; William L. Strong, then mayor of New York, vetoed it on the grounds of hasty compilation and serious defects in some of the legislative arrangements. Strong was right, and it was not long before changes had to be made in the wording of the charter. At the time, however, the legislature overrode the veto and Greater New York was born on 1 January 1898.

"The City of New York," for that has been its

239. Rooms decorated in the vaguely Near Eastern taste referred to as "Moorish" or
"Moresque" or "Turkish" were a rage among the rich in the 1880s and 90s. The house of
John D. Rockefeller, Sr., at 4 West 55th Street had a Moorish sitting room, now in The
Brooklyn Museum. This is Rockefeller's bedroom from the house, which has been installed
in The Museum of the City of New York. "Moorish" influence may be seen in the tufted
upholstery with fringe and the chandelier. Rockefeller purchased the house in 1884 from
Arabella Worsham, later Mrs. Collis P. Huntington. Gift of John D. Rockefeller, Jr.

240. The townhouse at 32 Park Avenue was originally built by gilded America's favorite architect, Richard Morris Hunt, in his French manner but on a lesser scale than he used for the great Vanderbilt houses on Fifth Avenue. In 1905–6, the house was completely remodeled by the firm of Little and O'Connor for Mr. and Mrs. Harry Harkness Flagler of the Standard Oil family. The interior was redecorated by one of New York's foremost designers, Willard Parker Little. This is part of the drawing room, which is a superb example of the rather advanced decorative taste of turn-of-the-century New York. Rich Americans still thought they had to live in imitations of European grandeur. The Flagler drawing room shows this at every turn. It is, to begin with, adapted from the Sala dello Zodiaco in the Ducal Palace at Mantua, Italy. The ceiling is copied from an ecclesiastical building in Venice. The painted doors and overmantel painting were done by an American, Bryson Burroughs, but they are clearly in the style made internationally popular by the Frenchman Puvis de Chavannes. The use of framed antique embroideries on either side of the mantelpiece is very characteristic of the taste of the time. The room is a gift of Harry Harkness Flagler, 1949. The dresses were worn about 1905 by Caroline Cruikshank Timpson, aunt of the donor's husband. Gift of Mrs. Russell Cruikshank. 62.78.1ab, 2ab

corporate name since the charter, comprised: "all municipal corporations and parts of such corporations other than counties within the counties of Kings and Richmond, Long Island City, the towns of Newtown, Flushing, Jamaica, and that part of Hempstead in Queens County west of a line drawn from Flushing between Rockaway Beach and Shelter Island to the Ocean." The new city had 359 square miles and there were now 3,437,202 New Yorkers. New York was the second largest city in the world, passing Paris; only London, with more than 4,000,000 inhabitants, was larger.

Many towns founded on Long Island in the seventeenth century, notably Flushing, Flatbush, Jamaica, Gravesend, and Brooklyn itself finally became part of New York City. In 1900, two years after consolidation, the decennial census showed the population of the City distributed like this:

Manhattan	1,850,093
Brooklyn	1,166,582
Bronx	200,507
Queens	152,999
Richmond	67,021

The next census—in 1910—showed a loss for Brooklyn of about 30,000 people, but the Bronx doubled its population, and Queens almost did the same. Manhattan in 1910 reached its all-time high in population: there were 2,331,542 people jammed into its twenty-two square miles. It was one of the most densely populated places on the face of the globe.

The government of this vast City was under a charter which was both cumbersome and hastily contrived. In 1901, when a reform party brought in Seth Low as mayor, a new charter was drawn up which lasted until 1938. "Boroughs" were organized: Manhattan; the Annexed District became the Bronx (from the local river); Queens was made up of Long Island City, Newtown, Flushing, Jamaica, and the Rockaways; Staten Island became the borough of Richmond; and Brooklyn. The mayor was elected for four years, and there were five elected borough presidents.

The first problem to which the government of the new City had to address itself was intracity transportation. New Yorkers were getting about in horse-drawn vehicles, on elevated railways, and by surface trains (steam, cable, or electric). At the end of the century there were still no underground railroads, and the automobile was used by only a few rich or flashy citizens.

In 1899, electric cars began running on the Third Avenue surface line between 65th Street and Harlem Bridge. Electrically operated cars superseded cable traction, which had been introduced about a decade before. By 1903, the surface and elevated railroads in New York City annually carried more paying passengers each year than all the steam railroads of North and South America combined!

No matter what improvements were made on the elevated and surface lines, however, it was clear that it would soon be necessary to carry at least some of New York's immense traffic underground. In 1894, the voters approved the construction of a rapid transit line. There was great discussion over the ownership of the underground lines: should they be public or private? After the customary wrangling and maneuvering, the City hired private companies to construct the lines, which the municipality then leased back to them for operation. Naturally, such a system demanded great integrity in the granting of such franchises, which, alas, was not present.

The formal breaking of ground for the rapid transit system took place on 24 March 1900 at City Hall Park. By 1904, the subways were in operation over a long stretch from City Hall to 145th Street under the control of the Interborough Rapid Transit Company, the "IRT." Eighty-four miles of subway were constructed at a cost of $56,000,000 in this initial work. City Hall Park was soon connected with Battery Park, and in 1908 the line from Bowling Green to Borough Hall, Brooklyn, was opened.

The roar of subterranean construction was soon an almost permanent feature of City life. In 1913, new lines were commenced by two companies working on a City franchise for their construction and operation. One

THE POSITION OF POLICE IN$PECTOR

I'M HERE WITH ME CAN

DULL CARE

POLITICAL SCREEN FOR DISTRICT LEADERS

GRAFT

$

VELVET GRAFT

NOTHING TO "DO" BUT— EVERYBODY

241. The great political cartoonist Thomas Nast—he invented both the Democratic donkey and the Republican elephant—who had helped topple the Tweed Ring, died in 1902. His son carried on the tradition of political cartooning. In this pen-and-ink drawing of 1907 he criticizes the corrupt police and district leaders during the McClellan administration. Note the "S" that has become a dollar sign and the Irish phrasing of the politician. 20 × 16". Gift of Eric H. Marks in memory of Marcus M. Marks, President of the Borough of Manhattan, 1913–19. 47.242.4

of these lines was the IRT and the other the Brooklyn Rapid Transit (later called Brooklyn-Manhattan Transit, the "BMT"). By 1918, the "shuttle" connected Grand Central Station and Times Square, and most of the features of today's subways were in use although there was to be continuing construction.

While this building was in progress, most of the street railways of the City had been combined by William C. Whitney, Thomas Fortune Ryan, and others into the giant Metropolitan Street Railway Company, the stock of which was watered on an almost unprecedented scale. The total capitalization was run up to $260,838,000, of which about $236,000,000 was unloaded on the public. There were investigations by commissions and grand juries in 1901, 1903, 1907, etc., and although a grand jury handed in a presentment in which they said "that the physical and financial destruction of these properties was due in no inconsiderable degree to dishonest and probably

criminal acts," there was no prosecution. The Metropolitan Street Railway Company scandal stood out even among the various odorous financial manipulations of the time, and the result of the skillful plundering of the company was that by the end of 1907 the entire street railway system of New York was being operated under receivership.

New bridges were built early in the century over the East River, Harlem River, and the Spuyten Duyvil Creek. The Pennsylvania Railroad built its great Roman station between 1906 and 1910 on Seventh Avenue between 31st and 33rd streets. The New York Central opened Grand Central Station in 1913.

Despite these improvements in public transportation, traffic congestion on New York streets, already a problem for a century, was worse than ever, and now automobiles in fair numbers were beginning to aggravate the problem. In 1898, the *Times* noted "that automobiles have almost ceased to be regarded as

242. The Washington Square area began to be used as a park and military parade ground in the 1820s. The first New York University building, on the east side of the square, went up in 1837. The present Washington Square Park design dates only from the 1880s, however, and the famous arch only from 1892. Paul Cornoyer, who painted this *Washington Square, 1900*, was noted for his oils of the City in snow or rain. This view is looking northeast. 32 × 26″. Gift of Mrs. Farrow Harrow. 49.299

243. The American Post-Impressionist Childe Hassam was born in Boston, studied in Paris, and painted the American landscape from the New England coast to the Pacific Northwest, but New York City inspired some of his finest work, and his studio was for many years at 130 West 57th Street. Like Cornoyer and many other artists he liked to paint New York in the snow or rain. This is called *Rain Storm, Union Square, 1890*. Oil on canvas, 28 × 36″. Gift of Miss Mary Whitney Bangs. 69.121.1

244. Childe Hassam also painted this *Winter Afternoon in New York* in 1900. Oil on canvas, 19 × 23″. Bequest of Mrs. Giles Whiting. 71.120.107

curiosities and the embarrassment of the passengers caused by many staring eyes, is gradually wearing off." The first automobile parade took place in 1899, from the Waldorf-Astoria to Claremont (at 116th Street) and back. The first automobile road-race in America was held 14 April 1900, between Springfield and Babylon, Long Island, a distance of fifty miles. The fastest car was a Riker electric, driven by Mr. Riker, which made it in 2 hours, $3\frac{1}{2}$ minutes. But, in 1899, automobiles were forbidden in Central Park because they "might frighten horses and otherwise be a disfigurement or annoyance." The first traffic regulations were put into effect in 1900 at certain hours of the day, and in the next few years traffic policemen were organized, against a considerable body of public opinion which thought traffic regulations an infringement of personal liberty. Automobiles called for more roads of course, and roads were planned for the increasing traffic, such as the Concourse in the Bronx, first projected in 1892.

The building of Pennsylvania Station revived the neighborhood around it. Herald Square became a center of middle-class shopping at the junction of Broadway, Sixth Avenue, and 34th Street. Macy's opened its Broadway building in 1901. There was construction everywhere, and the buildings were taller and taller. In 1902, the Flatiron Building was erected. It took its name from its location on the "flatiron" formed by Fifth Avenue, Broadway, and 23rd Street. The Metropolitan Life Insurance Company put up its headquarters building on Madison Avenue and 24th Street in 1908. At 700 feet in height it was the tallest office building in the world.

The new building of the New York Stock Exchange opened in 1903, and it is still in use. Just four years later, in the midst of all this booming construction in New York, the Panic of 1907 cast a shadow. A decline of prices in the spring of 1907 was followed by the failure of the Knickerbocker Trust Co. in New York on 22 October, which triggered a stock market panic. Bank failures spread across the country during the autumn, and it seemed that a disaster like that of 1837 was only a step ahead. Late in the year, however, the U.S. Treasury and the firm of J. P. Morgan & Co.

each lent the banks of New York $25,000,000 and staved off more failures.

During the early years of the century John Pierpont Morgan stood at the head of American finance. After 1873, when he broke the monopoly of Jay Cooke in handling government bonds, he gradually became the most prominent figure in money management. Morgan reorganized inefficient and wasteful railroads. In 1895, he was able to halt the flow of gold from the U.S. Treasury. In 1901, he organized the United States Steel Corporation. In financial crises he was the man to whom the entire financial world turned; no one has ever had quite the same authority although many have been much richer. Often ruthless and dictatorial in the extreme (he cared nothing for public opinion), J. P. Morgan stood for stability and order in financial affairs. Born in Hartford, Connecticut, where the Morgans had long been settled, he first worked for his father in London, then was associated with Drexel & Morgan in the U.S. He traveled much throughout his life, and was in Rome when he died. He was, however, a New Yorker for most of his life, and often active—usually behind the scenes—in City affairs. He was president of The Metropolitan Museum of Art and the most important donor to it. The head of all American collectors of the fine arts, Morgan left his great library to be administered as a public institution of New York City.

Other new cultural institutions were springing up everywhere in New York; the old ones were building new homes. In 1892, the cornerstone of America's largest religious edifice, the Cathedral Church of St. John the Divine, was laid on the site bounded by Morningside Drive, Amsterdam Avenue, and 110th and 113th streets. In the same neighborhood Columbia University began construction of its new campus in the 1890s, and farther north at 138th Street and Convent Avenue the College of the City of New York bought land and began *its* new campus.

New York was already noted for its glitter—speaking literally: it consumed four times the amount of electricity London used, although London was larger, and far more than any other city in the world of any size. By 1906, 3,000 electric signs were counted, with 100,000 lights. In an enthusiastic article that year the *Tribune* proclaimed that "the most remarkable single tract of night illumination in the world lies in Broadway, from 34th Street up to 46th Street. In this district alone current for nearly 40,000 globes in use for illuminated signs is furnished."

Broadway was already called "The Great White Way," which had been the title of a novel published in 1901 by Albert Bigelow Paine. The first theater in what is now the theater district was the Belasco (later Republic) on 42nd Street west of Broadway, which opened on 30 September 1902. The building of theaters was explosive: within a few years the west forties were full of them. In 1901, New York had more legitimate theaters than any other city in the world—forty-one. Paris had twenty-four, London thirty-nine. This figure for New York does not include vaudeville houses, burlesque shows, the Yiddish theater, and many other more or less permanent theatrical attractions. By 1903, on Broadway, about a quarter of the productions were "musical comedies," a relatively new term for what was previously called by a variety of names: "spectacular fantasy," "a burlesque revue," " a comic opera," etc. The characteristic American form, one of the country's most important contributions to world theater, had been slowly emerging since *The Black Crook* of 1866, but it was still several decades from full splendor. The first of the great revues later called *The Ziegfeld Follies* came on in 1907.

The three-hundredth anniversary of the visit of Henry Hudson, the true beginning of the history of the City, was celebrated in 1909 and combined with the centennial of Robert Fulton's Hudson River packet into a colossal New York celebration. From all over the world came warships and merchant vessels; anchoring in the Hudson, a line of ships extended from 42nd Street to the Spuyten Duyvil. Escorted by another great fleet which had assembled in Lower New York Bay, replicas of the *Half-Moon* and the *Clermont* sailed up the Hudson between the Manhattan shore and the line of anchored vessels. They were saluted by cannon all the way to 110th Street, where there were various ceremonies at a reviewing stand, including the gift of 2,100 cherry trees from the Japanese residents of the City to be planted along Riverside Drive. The day concluded with illuminations and a glorious display of fireworks over the Hudson.

The festivities continued for days: the cornerstone was laid for a Hudson memorial on Spuyten Duyvil Hill at 227th Street (although the statue of the discoverer was not mounted on the 100-foot column until 1938); there was a banquet at the Hotel Astor; New York University unveiled a plaque honoring the seven educators who had taught school in New Amsterdam; there was a great reception at the Metropolitan Opera House; a military parade; a naval parade; and, most exciting of all, Wilbur Wright brought his aeroplane to New York and executed a daring flight from Governor's Island to Grant's Tomb and back, the first aeroplane flight over Manhattan Island.

The mayor of New York fortunate enough to be in office at the time of the Hudson-Fulton celebration was George B. McClellan, Jr., son of the Civil War hero. Like many of his predecessors of prominent or ancient lineage, McClellan was Tammany Hall; nevertheless, he was often not very obedient to its dictates. A mayor of fair accomplishment he always carried the stigma of the sachems and the wigwam, but he does have the distinction of having recorded his years in office in probably the best book of memoirs written by a mayor of New York, *The Gentleman and the Tiger*, which was posthumously published. His great rival for the mayoralty was William Randolph Hearst.

In 1895, the rich, young Hearst from California had bought the New York *Morning Journal*. Having found in the underpopulated West insufficient challenge for the expansion of his ego, he arrived in New York and plunged into the affairs of the City. Although always associated with California and famous for his home there at San Simeon, Hearst in fact spent much of his life in New York City at his apartment on Riverside Drive. With almost unlimited funds, stemming from his mining properties, he hired an extraordinarily talented group of newspapermen to work on the

245. Working conditions in the numerous small garment industry firms were known to be appalling at the turn of the century, but there were few reforms until the disastrous fire at Triangle Waist Company on 25 March 1911 brought the problem to public attention. Triangle was at 22 Washington Place, at Greene Street, east of Washington Square, occupying the three top floors of a ten-story loft building. One hundred and forty-seven people, nearly all women workers, were burned to death. The owners of Triangle were indicted and tried, but, to great public indignation, were acquitted. The fire did lead, however, to major reforms in the building code. Victor Joseph Gatto was an eyewitness and painted this scene from memory. Oil on canvas, 28 × 19″. Gift of Mrs. Henry L. Moses. 54.75

Journal, which he also made into an afternoon newspaper. A Democrat, he supported William Jennings Bryan in the election of 1896, later opposed U.S. entry into World War I, was for many years violently anti-English (later turning coat on that issue), fought with Theodore Roosevelt, and once editorially recognized political assassination as a legitimate tool of change! In 1896, the circulation of the *Journal* had become enormous: one day that year 1,506,000 copies were printed, a record in journalism. Entering into politics, Hearst won two terms (1903–7) as U.S. Representative from New York City, and served surprisingly quietly. In 1905, as the candidate of the "Municipal Ownership League" (the "ownership" was of the subways), he ran for mayor against McClellan, the incumbent, and William M. Ivins, the Republican. He lost by only 3,000 votes to McClellan, loudly demanded a recount, and for years his newspapers kept up the steady complaint that Hearst had been robbed of the election. In the midst of this uproar he ran for office again—for governor of New York State—and was defeated by Charles Evans Hughes. Nothing daunted, he *again* ran for mayor—on the "Civic Alliance" ticket—in the election of 1909, and was soundly trounced. He is of course most famous for his screaming "yellow" journalism, which was largely responsible for getting the U.S. into war with Spain in 1898. Although repeatedly defeated for public office, Hearst through his newspapers and his immense real estate holdings—around Columbus Circle he owned many blocks—was a potent force for a long time in New York.

Mayor McClellan was succeeded in office by the man he refers to in his memoirs as "the strange and eccentric Judge Gaynor." William J. Gaynor was perhaps New York's most unusual mayor. Like McClellan he was supported by Tammany Hall, but was even less inclined than McClellan to do anything for it after he got in office. It used to be said that the Tammany sachem Charles F. Murphy emerged from Gaynor's office at City Hall with a longer face each time he went for a visit. Gaynor had been an unusual candidate for Tammany to back in the first place. He

was of Irish—and English!—descent, but a fallen-away Catholic, divorced and remarried. He served as a judge in the Second Judicial District Supreme Court of the State of New York (Kings County, Queens, part of Westchester), where he made a great reputation for his fairness, his irritability, his impatience with ill-prepared attorneys, and his wit. When he was sitting in Brooklyn, newspapers sent reporters to cover all his trials, and they seldom came back to Manhattan without some examples of his wit:

To an attorney who wanted a change of venue from Kings County to New York, Gaynor said: "I never grant such a motion. The Bridge is the same whichever end you start from."

Of one law he said: "This ordinance is a fair sample of too much law and government, like many others enacted in Brooklyn, one of which is that no householder shall allow his chimney to take fire."

He was extremely learned in the law (he once wrote an article for a law journal on the legal aspects of the arrest of Jesus Christ; he decided it was illegal) and astonishingly well-read. He used to quote Cervantes and Epictetus to the stunned malefactors of Kings County, and in writing a decision on a dog-bite case managed to quote Lord Byron and Motley's *Rise of the Dutch Republic*. He had an extraordinary respect, almost a worship, for the Anglo-Saxon Law, for the rights of the individual, and a profound dislike for interfering and do-gooding zealots. His attachment to our ancient liberties, it must be admitted, was sometimes exaggerated. He violently opposed and secured injunctions against the traffic regulations put in during McClellan's regime on the grounds that they curtailed the constitutional liberty of the individual.

After he was elected to the New York mayoralty, he continued to live in Brooklyn and walked across the Brooklyn Bridge to his office at City Hall (three and a half miles) every day, rain or shine. He had promised personally to answer all letters received in the mayor's office, and did his best. His biographer, Lately Thomas, quotes hundreds of these, for Gaynor's writing talent was as good as his speaking style. To a woman who had written to complain of street orators, he replied: "Free

CHARACTERS.

MINNIE		Soprano
JACK RANCE	Sheriff	Baritone
DICK JOHNSON (RAMERREZ)		Tenor
NICK	Bar tender at the "Polka"	Tenor
ASHBY	Agent of the Wells Fargo Transport Co.	Bass
SONORA		Baritone
TRIN		Tenor
SID		Baritone
HANDSOME	Miners	Baritone
HARRY		Tenor
JOE		Tenor
HAPPY		Baritone
LARKENS		Bass
BILLY JACKRABBIT	An Indian redskin	Bass
WOWKLE	Billy's squaw	Mezzo
JAKE WALLACE	A travelling camp-minstrel	Baritone
JOSÉ CASTRO	A greaser, from Ramerrez's gang	Bass
A POSTILION		Tenor
MEN OF THE CAMP		

At the foot of the Cloudy Mountains in California.

A Mining Camp in the days of the gold fever.
1849-1850.

246. Giacomo Puccini's opera with an American setting, or at least what the composer thought was an American setting, opened at the Metropolitan Opera on 10 December 1910. *The Girl of the Golden West* was based on a hit play of the 1905–6 season written by David Belasco. This program is autographed by the composer, playwright, conductor (Toscanini), impresario (G. Gatti-Casazza), and the singers, including Enrico Caruso and Emmy Destinn. 11 × 16″. Gift of Mrs. Richard S. Emmet. 68.4

speech is best. Let them say what they like. If they say something good, it will have wings. If they say something worthless, it will fall for lack of wings."

He also promised to see as many constituents as possible at City Hall and did interview hundreds. Although in many ways cantankerous, he became immensely popular with New Yorkers. His accessibility may have been his undoing. About to sail for Europe, Gaynor was shot on board ship by a disgruntled City employee. He did not die, but the bullet lodged in his throat and could not be removed. He could speak only in a croak, but carried on as mayor for three years. He died suddenly on board ship en route to Europe in 1913. His funeral procession was said to have brought out a larger crowd of mourners than any since Lincoln's.

The New York of Mayors McClellan and Gaynor is chronicled in the greatest detail in The Museum of the City of New York's Byron Collection of Photographs. Joseph Byron opened his New York

photography studio in 1888. At the age of fourteen his son Percy sold his first photograph: of the dedication of the temporary Grant's Tomb in 1893. The Byron Studio closed its books in 1942, and in that year Percy C. Byron presented "a good part of the labor of two lifetimes" to the museum, a collection of over 15,000 prints. This collection is weighted in the period 1890 to 1910, for which it is an unbelievably rich documentation on the City, covering street scenes, interiors, hospitals, schools, ships, sports, business firms, social events, theater, etc. A lavish selection of illustrations from that period was included by Grace M. Mayer in her book *Once Upon a City* (Macmillan, 1958).

Byron was the photographer of the City of the early nineteen hundreds; its poet was O. Henry (William Sydney Porter). It was he who coined the phrase "Bagdad on the Subway," and it is to him that perhaps the most famous quotation about New York is attributed, the one at the head of this chapter. In "The Four Million," in *Cabbages and Kings*, O. Henry gave an incomparable picture of life in the City, particularly among the middle and lower classes. He had a great affinity for the raffish life; he was New York's Guy de Maupassant. Yet it is not often realized that O. Henry was forty years old before he ever saw New York and that he lived there only eight years (1902–10). Once arrived in the City, however, he became obsessed with it and rarely left. He lived in many parts of town, but for the longest period on Irving Place, and from that headquarters he prowled the City, hearing stories which he later transformed into fiction. It was only with the greatest reluctance that he left New York, even for a visit to his native North Carolina.

After one such visit he wrote to a friend: "There was too much scenery and fresh air. What I need is a steam-heated flat and no ventilation or exercise."

Another friend recalls O. Henry stalking the railroad station at Port Washington on a forced trip to Long Island, muttering: "The thing I like most about this place is the railroad that runs out of it toward Manhattan."

And finally, for the New Yorker, all his stories and the anecdotes about him turn on his often repeated statement: "There's more poetry in a block of New York than in twenty daisied lanes!"

247. Longacre Square was renamed Times Square after the New York *Times* built its tower there in 1904. The newspaper moved into its new home the last day of that year with a display of fireworks at midnight, inaugurating the still-live New York tradition of spending New Year's Eve in Times Square. Just a few months earlier the Astor Hotel opened on Broadway between 44th and 45th streets. Long one of New York's most cherished institutions, the major hotel of the theater district, it was demolished in 1967 to make way for an office building. In 1914 Byron photographed an automobile show (still a rare occasion) in the grand ballroom of the hotel.

248. The attempted assassination of Mayor Gaynor on shipboard, 9 August 1910, was photographed by William H. Warnecke of the New York *World*. 15 × 18 3/4″. Gift of Cornelius F. O'Connor. 43.119

249. Mayor Walker was good for ceremonial ▶ occasions even while being investigated. Here, surrounded by politicians, he tosses out the first ball at the season's opener between the Philadelphia Nationals and the New York Giants at the Polo Grounds on 12 April 1932 (the Phillies won). Less than six months later, September, 1932, Walker had to resign his office. Archive

250. Alfred E. Smith was born on Oliver Street in Manhattan in 1873. Using the Democratic Party's New York City organization as a base, he rose to sheriff, president of the Board of Aldermen, and finally governor of the State of New York for four terms, but was defeated when he ran for president of the U.S. in 1928. He became president of the firm that managed the Empire State Building. The derby was his trademark. Length: 12 3/4″. Gift of the family of Governor Alfred E. Smith. 45.117.33

251. George M. Cohan wrote World War I's most famous American song on the morning the United States entered the war (6 April 1917) at his home in Great Neck, Long Island. This fair copy is in his hand and signed by him. 8 1/2 × 11″. Gift of George M. Cohan. 35.366

252. Big receptions for visiting heroes are among the most active New York traditions. An important twentieth-century reception complete with ticker-tape parade (tickers began spewing out tape on Wall Street in 1867), mayoral speechifying, and a banquet is recalled in this dinner menu. General Pershing, arriving victorious from Europe after the First World War, was feted at the Waldorf-Astoria on 10 September 1919. 14 × 10 1/4″. Anonymous gift. 70.154.1a

253. World War I called forth the talents of many artists to design posters for recruiting offices, Liberty Bond drives, Red Cross, etc. Many of the posters were extremely well drawn and lithographed. The most famous American poster was by New York artist James Montgomery Flagg: *I Want You for U.S. Army.* 39 3/4 × 29 1/2″. Gift of John W. Campbell. 43.40.160

254. New York women, including little girls (note left side of long table), rallied to the cause during World War I. Here they roll bandages surrounded by patriotic posters. In true New York fashion the ladies are organized along political lines: they are the Patriotic Service League of the 19th Congressional District. Photograph by Wurts. 8 × 10″. Wurts Collection.

255. Few artists have caught New York and
New Yorkers with such observation and
sympathy as Reginald Marsh. *No. 6—Bowery*
of 1944 is the Bowery after it had become the
haunt of alcoholism and poverty. Depicted is
the corner of Doyers Street. Hendrik Doyer
bought the Bowery property in 1793 and cut
it up into lots, at the same time laying out an
intersecting street that he named for himself.
His profession, by historical irony, was
distiller. Chinese ink drawing with touches
of watercolor, 34 × 47″. Gift of Reginald
Marsh. 53.107.2

IX: EVERY STREET A BOULEVARD: NEW YORK IN THE TWENTIES

New York is the nation's thyroid gland.

—CHRISTOPHER MORLEY

When the Woolworth Building was completed in 1913, it was—at 792 feet—"the highest building the world." It retained that distinction for almost twenty years and still stands at 233 Broadway. When the Woolworth was built, it was assumed that there would be few competitors, but the building of skyscrapers ever higher has abated only temporarily during wars and depressions.

The New York on which the Woolworth Building looked down had 5,620,048 inhabitants. The order of the boroughs in population was:

Manhattan	2,284,103
Brooklyn	2,018,356
Bronx	732,016
Queens	469,042
Richmond	116,531

During the first years of the twenties the population began rapidly to rearrange itself. Manhattan in five years, 1920–25, lost more than 300,000 people. Brooklyn had a dramatic rise of nearly 200,000, becoming the most populous borough, a distinction it still maintains, and the other boroughs gained sharply.

The outward movement of population from Manhattan came from several causes. The uncomfortable density of the first few years of the century had strained every facility of the City and made people anxious to move to less crowded surrounding areas. The construction of ever-more office buildings cut down on the Island's living space. And moving out of Manhattan became a symbol of the success of recent immigrants. The Brooklyn Bridge was called "The Jewish Passover" because of the many Jews that had left Manhattan for Brooklyn. Now both the Bronx and Brooklyn attracted the middle class, the *new* middle class.

The election which followed the death of Mayor Gaynor in 1913 brought John Purroy Mitchel into office. He had been serving as president of the Board of Aldermen. He won fifty-seven percent of the vote. Nominally a Democrat, Mitchel was elected, like so many of New York's best mayors, on a fusion ticket. He *was* one of the best: his four-year administration created a legend of efficient government for a city long battered by politicians. A tall, handsome, and athletic Irish-American, he was born in New York, at Fordham in the Bronx, and was educated at St. John's College and Columbia Law School. Mitchel was only thirty-five when elected to the highest office, the youngest mayor New York has ever had. He believed in the novel idea of government by experts and was in a position to carry out that ideal: he surrounded himself with distinguished citizens—Willard Straight, Henry L. Stimson, George Wickersham, Jacob Schiff. He appointed the first woman commissioner in New York City's history: Katharine Bement Davis, in charge of the Correction Department. The police, always the key department in New York municipal government, were run honestly by Commissioner Arthur Woods, who broke up criminal gangs, improved prison management, and brought down the crime rate to one of its lowest points in modern times. Theodore Roosevelt called Mitchel's administration "as nearly an ideal administration . . . as I have seen in my lifetime."

Unfortunately, like Gaynor, Mitchel had some serious faults which acted to his detriment in public life. He was forthright to a degree, "tactless," his enemies said, loved high society, and was too much seen in the company of Vanderbilts to maintain his popularity with average citizens. He appointed some socialites to office, including a Vanderbilt, Cornelius III. The fact that these socialites were at least as well qualified as the average Tammany-appointed officeholder of the past did not seem to count with the voters. World War I raged in Europe and was approaching the United States, and Mitchel indulged in some surprisingly unsophisticated flag-waving: his "patriotic" public statements were sometimes outrageous aspersions. He sneered at the popular State Senator Robert F. Wagner as pro-German, and later made the same charge against his opponent in the mayoral election, John F. Hylan, called "Red Mike" (not in the Marxian sense; he had red hair). In that election in 1917, John Purroy Mitchel received only twenty-four percent of the vote. Enlisting in the army, he was killed in a training camp air accident in Louisiana in 1918.

Mitchel was considered a Manhattan mayor, and although he was himself a Catholic had come out strongly against City aid to Catholic charities, thus offending a large section of the City's population. To oppose him Tammany, struggling to get back on its feet, or rather regain its patronage, put up John F. Hylan, a Catholic, who was billed as the people's candidate from Brooklyn (he was a judge there), as opposed to Manhattan's Mitchel, friend of Vanderbilts. He was supported by the Tammany boss Charles Murphy and the newspapers of William Randolph Hearst, who loathed Mitchel.

Although uninspired and uninteresting, Hylan was not the worst mayor New York has had. There were no scandals in his first term despite his close relationship with Tammany; in 1921, he was reelected with the fabulous plurality of 400,000.

During Hylan's administration the United States entered World War I. New York became America's

256. John Singer Sargent did this charcoal drawing of the monologist Ruth Draper in her role as "The Scotch Immigrant." A New Yorker, Ruth Draper made her debut in London in World War I and played continuously in Europe and America until her death during an engagement in New York in 1956. Her repertoire consisted of thirty-seven sketches in which there were fifty-eight characters—comic, tragic, lovable, or ridiculous. This drawing was often reproduced in her programs and publicity pieces. 25 × 20″. Bequest of Ruth Draper. 57.144.2

great port, first for sending military supplies to Europe, then men and supplies. More than 1,500,000 men left New York by sea for the battlefields of the continent. And of course New York was the headquarters of propaganda and the place where George M. Cohan wrote one of the war's great songs. Other than to stretch a steel net across the Narrows to keep out German U-boats, to hunt down German spies in the City, and to launch some truly barbarous attacks on New York's numerous German-Americans, the City did not feel the war directly any more than did other American cities. It did, however, feel with terrible force the great influenza epidemic of 1918; more than 12,500 New Yorkers died of "the flu."

After the conclusion of the war there was an inevitable reaction, part of which led to stricter laws regarding immigration into the United States. New York was more affected than any other city in the U.S. by the changes in the immigration laws during the 1920s, which finally slowed down and regulated the flow of new arrivals from Europe. In 1921, the first "Quota Law" came into effect, followed by the New Law in 1924, which limited immigration in any year to two percent of the population groups shown in the Census of 1890. In 1929, still another law with an even more complicated quota system went into effect. It was not until 1930 that the effect of these laws was actually felt. In 1921, there were still 805,228 alien immigrants admitted, and throughout the 1920s the annual figure was over half a million on several occasions. But in 1931 it was 97,139, which meant that European immigration had virtually ceased. Not until 1946, with the Displaced Persons Acts, did it again rise to more than 100,000.

Whole neighborhoods in the City were diminished by these changes; the pattern of one member of a family coming first and sending for his relatives when able was largely broken. There was considerable internal American immigration, however, mainly of Negroes from the South into Harlem. In 1910, there were only 90,000 Negroes in New York, representing less than two percent of the population. Before the end of the 1920s they numbered 327,000, or about seven percent of the population, living mainly in Harlem.

The leadership of the so-called "New Tammany Hall" was now composed of Alfred E. Smith, a New Yorker who was Governor of the State, and Robert F. Wagner, State Senator in New York and later U.S. Senator. They dropped Hylan—to his fury—and replaced him with James J. Walker, who was elected in 1925 and began to serve in 1926.

If ever a man was made for his age, it was James J. Walker. After his troubles began (when he was under investigation by the commission headed by Judge Samuel Seabury), the newspapers, who liked him—he was good-natured and provided reporters with unfailing lighthearted copy—compared Walker, the first generation Irish-American, with Seabury, who was an Old American and a descendant of one of America's most famous families of theologians and lawyers, to the disadvantage of Seabury, who had a frosty personality and cared nothing for popularity. The truth was that Walker, although indeed a first-generation American, was hardly underprivileged. His father was a prosperous lumber dealer and was four times alderman from the Ninth Ward (part of Greenwich Village), a state assemblyman, and Commissioner of Public Buildings in New York. A Tammany stalwart, he was in a position to push his son into politics with the best of all recommendations—the backing of Tammany Hall. Walker was born in New York, at 110 Leroy Street (between Hudson and Greenwich in the West Village). He had an engaging manner, thin good looks, the gift of gab, and a love of politics. Although he did not go to college, he did attend law school and become a lawyer, but he seldom practiced. For sixteen years he served in the New York State Assembly with unswerving devotion to Tammany. He was the author (in 1908) of the hit song *Will You Love Me in December As You Do in May?* and had an unflagging interest in night clubs, the theater, chorines, clothes (he sometimes changed complete outfits three times a day), a good time, and plenty of pocket money. His wit was famous; judging from preserved examples, it was really wisecracking, a very different thing. Those were pretty much his qualifications for becoming mayor of the greatest city in America. Once in office, he gave the voters what

257. The cartoonist Rea Irvin did this original drawing of "Eustace Tilley" from which the first cover of the *New Yorker* magazine evolved in 1925; his sketch is repeated on a *New Yorker* in February of each year. Irvin also drew the "department" headings for the magazine; those for the "Talk of the Town" and "Theatre" sections are still in use after more than fifty years. 2 × 3". Gift of Rea Irvin. 67.100.73

258. New York welcomed Charles A. ▶ Lindbergh, returning from Paris to receive the $25,000 prize for his nonstop Atlantic flight at a breakfast at the Hotel Brevoort, 17 June 1927. 7 1/2 × 5". Anonymous gift. 70.154.2

BREAKFAST IN HONOUR OF
CAPTAIN CHARLES A. LINDBERGH
on the presentation of the
RAYMOND ORTEIG 25,000 DOLLAR PRIZE
New York to Paris non-stop flight
FRIDAY, JUNE 17, 1927
HOTEL BREVOORT
NEW YORK

they apparently had elected him for—a good time. His term was during Prohibition, and there was a great current against what was considered "Victorianism." Prohibition was difficult to enforce in the rest of the country; in New York it was impossible. Those bootlegging, speakeasy, happy-go-lucky but also irresponsible and crime-ridden times were right for a mayor who believed in taking just as good care of his friends as they did of him.

People constantly spoke of Jimmy Walker in terms of the theater; he was associated with Broadway as was no other mayor, and what a time it was for the American theater! Today's New Yorkers are accustomed to their City having the reputation as world capital of the theater, but that was not actually true until fairly recent times. The theater in other U.S. cities and on the road was much stronger in 1900 than it is today. But by the 1920s, New York was undisputed capital. The number of shows increased each season until in 1927 the all-time high of 268 attractions appeared on Broadway. Generally speaking, runs were not nearly so long then as they became in the fifties and sixties, but there were some prodigies even then: Frank Bacon starred in *Lightnin'*, a sort of updated *Rip Van Winkle*, which made a record of 1,291 performances between 1918 and 1921; *Abie's Irish Rose* opened in 1922 and had a run of 2,327 performances even though the critics had by no means loved it.

During those glorious years a galaxy of performers perhaps unequaled in history appeared on Broadway. During 1921, for example, the industrious theater-goer could have seen all these stars: Katharine Cornell, Joseph Schildkraut, Eva Le Gallienne, John Drew, Mrs. Leslie Carter, Minnie Maddern Fiske, George Arliss, Otis Skinner, Ina Claire, Marjorie Rambeau, E. H. Sothern, Julia Marlowe, Lionel, Ethel, and John Barrymore, Violet Kemble Cooper, Dennis King, Billie Burke, Alfred Lunt, Lynne Fontanne, Tallulah Bankhead, Helen Hayes, Laura Hope Crews, Laurette Taylor, Doris Keane, Ed Wynn, Al Jolson, Fred and Adele Astaire, Fannie Brice, Ted Lewis, and W. C. Fields. In one season!

During the twenties the great nineteenth-century houses of Fifth Avenue were rapidly being replaced by the most luxurious apartment houses in the City, and Fifth Avenue above 59th Street remained, as it does today, the City's prime residential area. Lower Park Avenue had begun to develop early in the century with fine townhouses, and Sutton Place, formerly a run-down end of 57th Street near the East River, became fashionable in the twenties. A typical new luxury hotel, the Ritz Tower, also on 57th Street, was built in 1925 on the northeast corner of Park Avenue. A good idea of the most advanced interior decoration of the time can be had from the famous Stettheimer Doll House, one of the ornaments of The Museum of the City of New York.

In 1929, the Chrysler Building, 1,046 feet in height, was completed, its altitude far surpassing that of the Woolworth Building. But of course the giant of them all was the Empire State Building. Planned during the optimistic twenties, it was started in 1929 and completed—to a height of 1,250 feet—during the dreary year 1931.

In the 1920s, New York definitely overcame London as the financial capital of the world. Wall Street was more than ever the center of the world's money. The great New York banks, particularly the National City and the Guaranty Trust, extended their branches all over the world, and loans were floated on a scale hitherto unknown.

From all over the world and from all over the United States money poured into Wall Street. *Too* much money. Even in the mid-twenties wise men were concerned about the ever-increasing financial speculation. Money stayed on Wall Street in the form of stock investments rather than returning to labor-employing projects.

Jimmy Walker presided over the City of New York during the whole demented era of the late twenties. The mayor was a great one to welcome people; during his regime were many of the great ticker tape parades of New York's history, including the famous celebration of the arrival from Europe of the aviator Charles Lindbergh.

The stock market crashed in October, 1929. One

259. Maurice Schwartz's Yiddish Art Theatre at Second Avenue and 12th Street produced *American Hassidim* in 1928. Schwartz is the center figure in the photograph. 41 1/2 × 27 1/2″. Gift of Zvee Scooler. 70.77.12

week later Jimmy Walker ran for reelection. New Yorkers were apparently satisfied with their Broadway mayor; they had no way of knowing that the merry days of the twenties and of Jimmy Walker were coming to an end. Walker was easily reelected, trouncing Fiorello H. La Guardia, who had the Republican nomination. La Guardia had been in Congress and was supported by many august New Yorkers, including Ogden L. Mills, Colonel Theodore Roosevelt, Secretary of State Stimson, and the President of Columbia University Nicholas Murray Butler. La Guardia rode hard on the issue of corruption: "The present administration," he said, "is the most wasteful and extravagant in the history of New York, and the slimy trail of waste, recklessness and corruption is unparalleled since the days of Boss Tweed." He accused Walker of dawdling away his time "on Broadway." But the results were:

Jimmy Walker	865,000
Fiorello La Guardia	368,000
Norman Thomas (Socialist)	175,000

Upstate they were not amused by Walker. The Republicans in the legislature decided on another of the innumerable investigations they loved to pursue in the City. Very foxily, they chose a member of Walker's own party—for Judge Samuel Seabury was also a Democrat—to head the investigation. The hearings began in the City in 1930 with an investigation of the magistrates courts. Even the anxious Republicans were astounded at what Seabury uncovered. In 1931 a special committee was set up to investigate the entire government of the City of New York. "Borrowings," it found, from the City's funds were routine on the part of favored appointees. Tammany was in control. The income of Judge George W. Olvaney, leader in Tammany, was said to have amounted to $2,000,000 in four and a half years. The investigators got closer and closer to the mayor. His secretary fled to Mexico. Walker brazened it out and went on the stand the last week of May, 1932. Seabury's questionings revealed Walker for what he was—shallow, irresponsible, and derelict in his duty to the City to the point of criminality. Franklin Roosevelt, Democratic governor of the State of New York, summoned Walker to Albany for an interview. That was the end. It is not known what Roosevelt said, but Walker resigned on the first of September, 1932, and departed for Europe.

Walker was succeeded by the President of the Board of Aldermen, Joseph V. McKee, an unusual Tammany politician who had earned an LLD at Fordham and taught there, and he had been a correspondent for both the *Times* and the *Tribune* newspapers. He served the short remainder of Walker's term but was deserted by Tammany at the special election of 1932. The Hall backed John Patrick O'Brien, who was elected to serve for a little over a year at Tammany's behest. McKee received more than 200,000 write-in votes cast by outraged New Yorkers.

The next regular election was held on 7 November 1933. Tammany put up O'Brien, the "Recovery Party" backed McKee, and Fiorello H. La Guardia ran on the Republican-Fusion ticket. The results were:

La Guardia	858,551
McKee	604,405
O'Brien	586,100

On election night a quarter of a million New Yorkers gathered in Times Square to watch the *Times'* moving electric news sign report the election returns. Over and over they sang La Guardia's theme song, *Who's Afraid of the Big Bad Wolf?* The Age of La Guardia had begun.

260. *Day and Night*, a Yiddish drama in three acts, was produced at the Unser Theatre in the Bronx in 1925. The author was S. Ansky (who also wrote *The Dybbuk*), the music by Lazar Weiner, and the sets and costumes by Boris Aronson. 42 × 28″. Bella Bellarina Collection, gift of Henry Rubinlicht. 69.132

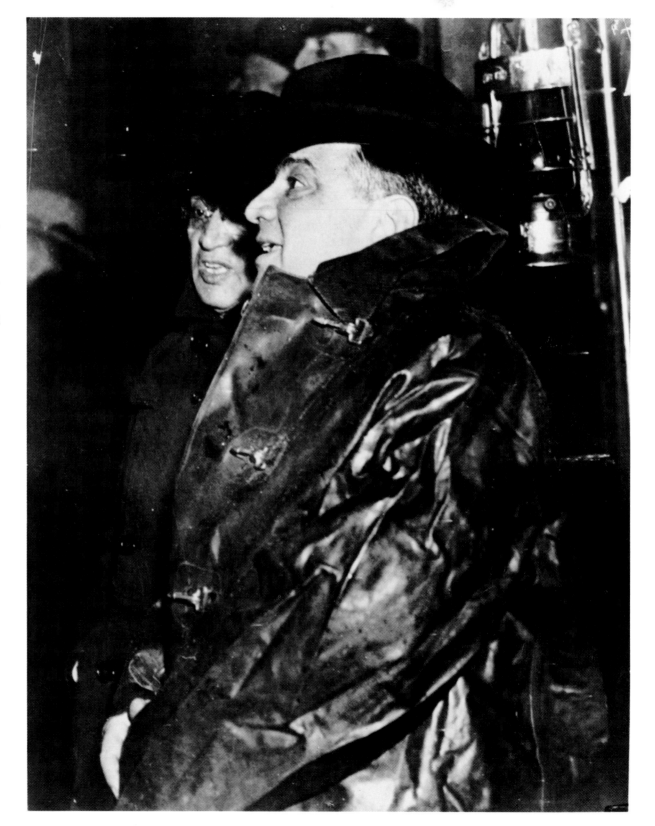

261. Any big fire in the City was sure to draw the tireless Mayor La Guardia as a spectator. Here he watches a blaze at Hudson and Hubert streets on the Lower West Side in December, 1936. 7 × 9″. Gift of The Fire Bell Club of New York, Inc. 43.16.6

X: THE AGE OF LA GUARDIA

Nobody wants me but the people.

—FIORELLO H. LA GUARDIA

If there is a hero of the history of modern New York City, it is surely Fiorello La Guardia, the beloved "Little Flower," whose spirit is still invoked by New Yorkers. La Guardia could not have been invented, and only New York could have produced him. That one man summed up not only in his thinking but in his very person the best in what New York City has always stood for: religious toleration, a liberal view of social problems, a concern for culture, and a craving for improvement. He was a native New Yorker, born at 7 Varick Street in Greenwich Village, 11 December 1882, yet he always called Prescott, Arizona, his home town, a place about as far as one can get from New York City and remain in the continental United States, and he wore an enormous Western Stetson as his trademark. He was the son of an Italian emigrant who became a Protestant, was bandmaster in the United States Army, and served during the Spanish-American War. Achille La Guardia was stationed in Prescott during Fiorello's boyhood. Fiorello's mother was Jewish. His first wife was a Catholic, his second a Lutheran. He himself was a lifelong Episcopalian and was buried from the Cathedral Church of St. John the Divine. He served as American consular agent at Fiume (then in Hungary and a major departure point for Hungarian emigrants to America), as an interpreter at Ellis Island (he knew half a dozen languages), and studied nights to become a lawyer at New York University Law School. At other periods in his early life he worked for the Society for the Prevention of Cruelty to Animals and as a stenographer at Abercrombie and Fitch. From 1917 to 1921 and again from 1923 to 1933, he was a Republican

congressman from New York City, representing East Harlem and surrounding neighborhoods. During World War I La Guardia was a combat flyer and left the service a major.

Although a Republican and frequently elected to public office on that ticket, La Guardia's relations with the party leaders were often uncomfortable. During his congressional stint he opposed Prohibition, immigration quotas, and other pet legislation of the G.O.P. He was mentioned as a mayoral candidate as early as 1921, but failed to receive his party's backing. He later made up with the Republicans and had their support during his successful campaign in 1932.

La Guardia was opinionated, convinced he was right, intolerant of opposition, and possessed of a temper as terrible as Peter Stuyvesant's or William J. Gaynor's. He hated crooks. His first act as mayor is said to have been a call for the arrest of crime leader "Lucky" Luciano, and although ordinarily a great supporter of civil liberties he was not particularly concerned with the rights of persistent and insolent wrongdoers. He and his police commissioner Lewis J. Valentine, who was a capable career policeman disliked by Tammany, made the New York City Police Department into one of the best municipal police forces in the world. He selected Robert Moses as his parks commissioner, and although Moses never ceased to be controversial, even sometimes having terrific shouting matches with La Guardia, new parks, a new airport, and bridges were built, beaches developed, and innumerable other amenities made the City more pleasant.

La Guardia was good at getting rid of local

criminals but not quite so good as the special prosecutor appointed by the governor of New York State in 1935. That was Thomas E. Dewey, a Manhattan lawyer educated at Columbia Law School who established an extraordinary record of not only indicting criminals, especially members of organized crime, but of getting them convicted and put in prison. Between them, La Guardia and Dewey made New York a much safer place to live.

As a public "character" La Guardia was without equal. He kept polished bones in his desk in City Hall which he presented to his appointees when they made a "boner." Like other New Yorkers for three hundred years, he loved to go to fires and adored racing through the City streets with the engines. He conducted concerts. During a newspaper strike he read comic strips to the children of the City over the radio with his ad lib comments. He had style.

La Guardia was one of the busiest men in the world. He took over a city whose people struggled with the great national Depression, a city practically bankrupt and without a recent tradition of good and efficient government. New York was the headquarters of the disaster as it had been of the boom. Thirty billion dollars of paper holdings in the stock market had vanished along Wall Street. Banks had failed, businesses had gone into bankruptcy, and millions of savings accounts had melted away. The Depression was entering its fourth year when La Guardia came into office. The year of his election, 1932, twenty-five percent of the workers in the City of New York were unemployed. Shantytowns of unemployed had sprung up even in Central Park. The political situation was one of seething discontent. In 1930, more than 100,000 Communists and their sympathizers had held a great meeting in Union Square ending in a riot with the police in which more than 100 people were injured.

La Guardia plunged into these problems. He was on good terms with Franklin Roosevelt despite the difference in their political affiliation. Federal aid for the City was granted on an immense scale. Between 1933 and 1939 more than a billion Federal dollars were expended in New York in the form of relief; in 1936,

nearly twenty percent of the population was on some form of welfare. A sales tax, imposed only reluctantly by La Guardia, raised additional sums.

There was considerable construction in New York, even in the worst years of financial misfortune, due mainly to the Federal monies directed into the City. Many projects begun earlier were continued and provided some employment. The great Triborough Bridge system linking the Bronx and Queens with Manhattan by bridge and nineteen miles of accesses and ramps was built between 1929 and 1936. The George Washington Bridge across the Hudson was built in 1931. Some private construction also was maintained. In the dismal year of 1931, John D. Rockefeller, Jr., and his Rockefeller Center, Inc., began construction of the office-building complex bearing that name which has been called "The Acropolis of America." Leases were bought up on nearly all the buildings between Fifth and Sixth avenues from 48th to 51st streets. The land under them, seventeen acres, was owned by Columbia University. It was leased by Rockefeller Center until the year 2015. Fourteen tall buildings were erected flanking a seventy-story, 850-foot central monolith. Construction lasted for nearly a decade, until 1940, and the cost of almost 10,000,000 square feet of rentable space was over $100,000,000. Major additions were made to Rockefeller Center in 1947.

La Guardia's persistence brought about the completion of the 12 miles of track for the Eighth Avenue subway, which had been commenced in 1925 but never finished. The Sixth Avenue subway was begun in 1936 and finished during La Guardia's second term in 1941. After years of negotiation, the three subway systems of New York, all built and owned by the City but two of them, the BMT and the IRT, operated by private companies, were finally amalgamated into the largest subway system in the world. A New York municipal airport, later named for the mayor, was opened in 1939 with a ceremony attended by the amazing number of 325,000 spectators. *All* the statistics of La Guardia's regime were amazing: more than 5,000 acres were added to the park system of the City, in which 66,000 trees and more than a million shrubs were planted; thirty-three miles of parkway were built; more than 130 acres of swampland, mainly in Queens, were drained and made into usable land; and so on.

Even the unhappy thirties could not still Broadway. Although the number of productions never equaled the twenties, the theater continued lively. It was to a large extent dominated by musicals. George Gershwin, Rodgers and Hart, Irving Berlin, Cole Porter, Oscar Hammerstein II, Jerome Kern, and others were all writing musicals. Nearly 200 shows were produced between 1930 and 1939.

In 1936, La Guardia came up for reelection. He ran on the Republican-Fusion ticket but could not have won except for the votes of the American Labor Party, of which there were a remarkable 482,000. He was the first reform mayor of the City of New York to succeed himself. Others like William R. Grace in the nineteenth century and Seth Low in the twentieth had managed to hang on for only one term; La Guardia, ninety-ninth mayor of the City, was to be in office for three terms and serve the City longer than any mayor since the years 1789 to 1801, when Richard Varick had held office.

The year 1939 was the 150th anniversary of the inauguration of George Washington in New York, and the City decided to mark the anniversary with a World's Fair. It turned out to be the greatest World's Fair ever held. During its two seasons more than 45,000,000 people came to Flushing Meadow, where on a former city dump Robert Moses and his assistants created "The World of Tomorrow." The two main landmarks of the Fair, the "Trylon" and "Perisphere," are still unforgotten symbols of one of the greatest and most attractive celebrations in New York's history. Stylistically, most of the great edifices erected—at a total cost of more than $150,000,000—were not actually futuristic; in retrospect we see that they were an incomparable summation of the creative styles of the decade that was ending.

During the second season of the fair, 1940, the census was taken again, revealing this distribution of the City's 7,454,995 people:

Brooklyn	2,698,285
Manhattan	1,889,924
Bronx	1,394,711
Queens	1,297,634
Richmond	174,441

Manhattan had reversed its decline in population; Queens had had startling growth; that of the Bronx was nearly as extraordinary; Brooklyn was slowing down; Richmond remained largely bucolic.

The housing of this population was changing in very interesting ways. For half a century New York had already been essentially a city of apartment buildings, mostly separate entities regardless of how close they were jammed together. Now the concept of the "village" of apartment dwellings began to gain currency and to affect finally multiple-unit construction throughout the United States. The first great demonstration of the planned apartment "village," and in some ways still the most successful, was Parkchester, which was built in the East Bronx in an area bounded by East Tremont Avenue, Purdy Street, McGraw Avenue, and White Plains Road. The sponsor was the Metropolitan Life Insurance Company, now entering the housing field, and the work was done between 1938 and 1942. On an area of which half was reserved for landscaping or playgrounds, more than 12,000 apartments were constructed with offices, stores—including the first branch of Macy's—and places of entertainment at intervals. Now in some cases occupied by the third generation of tenants, it is regarded as a classic of urban planning.

One of La Guardia's pet projects was publicly sponsored housing, and New York was the first city to enter this field. La Guardia had the satisfaction of seeing the completion of the "First Houses" at Avenue A and East 3rd Street, the very center of the historic home of new immigrants on the Lower East Side of Manhattan, in 1936.

The mayoral election of 1941 saw La Guardia running against the Democratic candidate William O'Dwyer. La Guardia won, but only by 132,000 votes. His ticket was the Republican-American Labor-City

262. In a New York hard-hit by the Depression, squatters built shacks in Central Park.
Like such settlements in other parts of the country the huts were called "Hoovervilles."
Early 1930s photograph by Nat Norman. Gift of the photographer. Archive

263. Berenice Abbott's collection of photographs *Changing New York* (1939) recorded New York life during the bleak Depression years. Henry Street, looking west from Market Street, was photographed 29 November 1935. The three skyscrapers are the Transportation, Woolworth, and Municipal buildings. The famous Henry Street Settlement was established in 1893 by Lillian Wald. Archive

Fusion again and he was endorsed—to the fury of Democratic faithfuls—by President Franklin D. Roosevelt. Despite this remarkably broad support, the small victory showed that the people of New York might be wearying of La Guardia and his endless bustle and enthusiasm.

A month after the election, World War II reached the United States. La Guardia commuted between New York and Washington, where he was director of the office of Civilian Defense. For his own City he organized civil defense. New York was blacked out, air-raid drills were practiced, and rescue squads and emergency medical units were organized. Throughout the war La Guardia's frenetic pace kept up. The City was the departure port for millions of U.S. military and, as in World War I, the financial headquarters and the propaganda mill. More importantly, the famous "Manhattan Project," based on nuclear experiments by Enrico Fermi, John R. Dunning, and others at Columbia University, led to the development of the atomic bomb.

The year 1945 saw the end of the war, and the end of La Guardia's third term. He decided not to stand for reelection, but he could not say farewell to politics. He threw his support, still considerable, behind something called the "No-deal Party," which nominated for mayor the president of the City Council, Newbold Morris. Morris was a direct descendant of the distinguished colonial New York family, lords of the Manor of Morrisania. He was a close friend of La Guardia—they were jocularly known as "The Little Flower and the Mayflower." Despite the La Guardia endorsement, Morris made a poor showing against the Democratic candidate William O'Dwyer, who was supported by Tammany Hall and the American Labor Party. O'Dwyer won by more than 700,000 votes, the greatest plurality in the history of New York City mayoral elections.

La Guardia was made director-general of the United Nations Relief and Rehabilitation Administration, but he was already ill with cancer and died on 20 September 1947 at the age of sixty-four. At 8:06 on the morning of that day the New York City Fire Department sounded its traditional "five bell" alarm repeated four times to mark the passing of New York's greatest mayor.

264. Plans were made for the Empire State Building during the optimistic 1920s, but it was actually completed in 1931, one of the worst Depression years. The offices were a long time filling up with tenants. The very top of the building was originally intended as a mooring mast for dirigibles (then regarded as the coming form of air transport), but it was never used for that. Lewis W. Hine made this photograph of the 1250-foot-high building under construction. Gift of the Empire State Building. Archive

265. "El" station interior, Sixth and Ninth Avenue Lines, downtown side, Columbus Avenue and 72nd Street, was photographed on 6 February 1936. Columbus Avenue was formerly called Ninth; the "El" had been built along it in 1878, and there had been little change in nearly sixty years, but the line was shortly to be torn down. Photograph by Berenice Abbott. Archive

266. More than 10,000 crowded into the new Madison Square Garden, which extended from 26th to 27th streets, Madison to Fourth Avenue, on the night of 16 June 1890 to hear the orchestra of Johann Strauss and to inaugurate the new building. The site had formerly been occupied by the New Haven Railroad Station, Barnum's Museum, and an earlier Garden. The new edifice, designed by McKim, Mead & White, is shown here about 1895, in a watercolor by W. Louis Sonntag, Jr. The tower was surmounted by Augustus St. Gaudens's statue *Diana*. It was on the Roof (i.e., nightclub) of the Garden that Harry K. Thaw murdered the architect Stanford White. But this Garden, which was demolished in 1925, was the scene of many other notable events including, in 1900, the first automobile show ever held in America. There were sixty-six manufacturers represented, and their automobiles were shown in motion on wooden tracks. The site is occupied today by the New York Life Insurance Co. St. Gaudens's *Diana* was rescued from the demolition and is now in the Philadelphia Museum of Art. Watercolor, 24 × 17 1/2". Gift of Mrs. Frederick A. Moore. 49.14

267. The Eighteenth Amendment to the Constitution (1919) mandated nationwide prohibition of intoxicants. In New York, as in other cities, "speakeasies" sprang up immediately to provide illegal liquor and were the subject of much folklore. "Speako de Luxe" was Barney Gallant's place at 19 Washington Square North, portrayed in the last year of Prohibition, 1933, by Joseph Webster Golinkin. Lithograph, 22 1/2 × 17 3/4″. Gift of James M. Holzman. 57.176.3

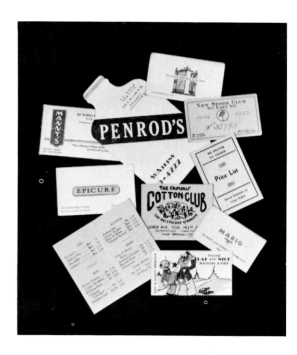

268. To get into "speaks" one had to be known to the management or present a card. These cards are mostly from the days of Prohibition, when enforcement was more or less a joke. The Stork Club's is dated. Others can be dated after 1930 by the telephone numbers, for in that year most telephones in New York changed from four digit numbers (and the exchange) to five digits. The first dial office had been created in 1922 for the PEnnsylvania exchange. The system for the City was ninety-five percent dial by 1946. Several former speakeasies still exist, including the 21 Club.

270. The first of the productions later called *The Ziegfeld Follies* opened at the Jardin de Paris on 8 July 1907 under the title *The Ziegfeld Musical Revue. Follies of 1907*. Florenz Ziegfeld also produced such landmark musicals as *Rio Rita* (1927) and *Show Boat* the same year. After his death in 1932, his widow, Billie Burke, the figure on this poster from the *Follies* of 1934, continued to produce the annual show. 40 × 90″. Archive

269. The market for sheet music was enormous in the first third of the century. In 1907, there were forty-two songs which sold over 1,000,000 copies; some of these even exceeded 5,000,000 sales. A selection of songs published between 1898 and 1931 about New York City or with a New York setting is shown. George M. Cohan introduced his rollicking "Give My Regards to Broadway" in *Little Johnny Jones* of 1904. The figure on the sheet music of "Rose of Washington Square" is Fanny Brice, who sang it in the Ziegfeld *Midnight Frolic of 1920* staged in the roofgarden of the New Amsterdam Theatre on 42nd Street west of Broadway (still standing). Cole Porter's *The New Yorkers* of 1931 introduced two of the liveliest songs the composer wrote about his adopted city: "I Happen to Like New York" and "Take Me Back to Manhattan."

271. George C. Tilyou, principal developer of the vast amusement area called "Coney Island," opened Steeplechase Park in 1897. It took its name from an ingenious device, a mechanical race course, installed near the beach and shown here at right center. The roller coaster, perennial favorite of the crowds at Coney Island, was first operated there in 1884, at another park. An employee of Steeplechase, probably Leo McKay, painted this unsigned aerial view of the Park about 1898. Oil on canvas, 51 × 80″. Gift of Mrs. George C. Tilyou. 54.167

272. The Bowery lost its rural character in the nineteenth century as the City gradually encompassed the old farms which lined Bowery Road. It became for nineteenth-century New York a place for shopping and entertainment (often disreputable) for the humbler citizens. It gained then the raffish reputation which has made it a synonym for the urban down-and-out. *The Bowery at Night*, *1895*, by W. Louis Sonntag, Jr., has it crowded with shoppers and pleasure-seekers and incidentally shows the principal means of transport for New Yorkers just prior to the building of the subways and the coming of the automobile. Watercolor, 13 × 18″. Gift of Mrs. William B. Miles. 32.275.2

273. Edward Harrigan's play *The Leather Patch* had its first performance at the Park Theatre, Broadway and 35th Street, on 15 February 1886. It was a typical Harrigan comedy of low life laid in the notorious "Five Points," the juncture of Baxter, Worth, and Park streets and roughest neighborhood in New York. The plot involved a pair of pants into which money had been sewn under a leather patch. Watercolor, 10 × 14″. Gift of William Seymour. 39.134.3

274. *Mourning Becomes Electra*, Eugene O'Neill's American adaptation of the Orestes-Electra legend, opened on Broadway in 1931, starring Alla Nazimova and Alice Brady. The sets were designed by Robert Edmond Jones, one of the American theater's outstanding designers. This is the setting for the Mannon House in Part I of the play. 24 × 30″. Gift of Robert Edmond Jones. 45.75.2

275. Louis Gruenberg's opera *The Emperor Jones*, based on a play by Eugene O'Neill, had its world premiere at a 2 P.M. matinee at the Metropolitan Opera House on 7 January 1933. Performed ten times during that season and the following, it has never been revived at the Metropolitan, although heard a few times in other opera houses. Watercolor rendering of scene design by Jo Mielziner, 35 × 21″. Gift of Jo Mielziner. 39.452

276. Donald Oenslager designed this Central Park setting for one of the acts of Rodgers and Hart's *I'd Rather Be Right*, which opened 2 November 1937 and ran for 289 performances. George M. Cohan played President Franklin D. Roosevelt. Set model, 8 × 14″. Gift of Donald Oenslager. 62.126.4

277. *Ah, Wilderness!* was one of Eugene O'Neill's most commercially successful plays. It opened in 1933, starring George M. Cohan, and was produced by The Theatre Guild. The Museum of the City of New York owns the manuscript of *Ah, Wilderness!*, with the note in O'Neill's handwriting: "This is the original script and the only one in longhand. Eugene O'Neill." This page, also in O'Neill's hand, shows scene plans for Scenes III and VI. In addition, the museum owns a typescript with the notation by O'Neill: "typed copy of 1st draft with cuts and revisions. More cutting and condensing was done later during rehearsals to shorten the playing time." 8 1/2 × 11". Gift of Mrs. Eugene O'Neill. 42.150.1b

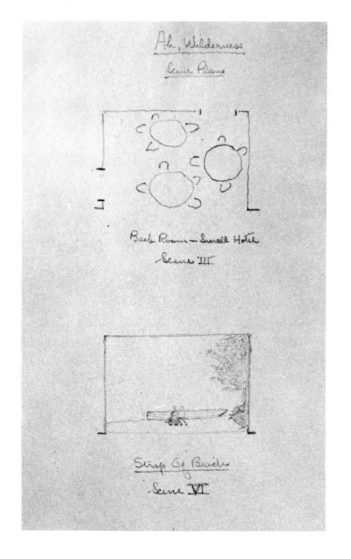

278. William Zorach did this charcoal portrait of his close friend Eugene O'Neill in 1921, the year in which O'Neill won the Pulitzer Prize for *Anna Christie*. That same year three other O'Neill plays came to Broadway: *Diff'rent*, *Gold*, and *The Straw*. 16 × 12". Gift of William Zorach. 35.359.4

279. *The New Moon*, a musical composed by Sigmund Romberg and written by Oscar Hammerstein II, opened on 19 September 1928, for a run of 509 performances. Among its songs were "Lover, Come Back to Me"; "One Kiss"; "Softly, as in a Morning Sunrise"; and "Stouthearted Men." This is one of the sets for the show designed by Donald Oenslager. 20 × 21″. Gift of Donald Oenslager. 50.307.3

▲ 280. *Captain Jinks of the Horse Marines*, one of the many hit plays written by Clyde Fitch (he once had four running simultaneously in New York), opened in 1901. The role of Madame Trentoni was played by Ethel Barrymore, then twenty-one, in her first starring role. This portrait by Sigismund de Ivanowski shows her costumed for that role. Oil on canvas, 68 × 50″. Gift of Miss Barrymore. 53.205

281. John Barrymore's *Hamlet* in 1922 broke Edwin Booth's record with 101 performances. ▲ James Montgomery Flagg painted Barrymore costumed for that famous role. 43 × 53 1/2″. Gift of Mr. Flagg. 46.214.1.

282. The Railroads Building was the largest at the New York World's Fair of 1939. The sculpture is *Europa* by Gleb W. Derujinsky. Photograph by Gottscho-Schleisner. Gift of Gottscho-Schleisner. 50.137.31

283. The "modernistic" style prevailed at the Fair. Despite some grotesqueries (the NCR Building was a giant cash register, RCA a radio tube), many of the buildings in the monumental taste of the thirties were strikingly effective. The Trylon and Perisphere were the trademarks of the Fair, the Trylon a 700-foot-high shaft, the Perisphere a 200-foot steel-framed globe. Photograph by Samuel H. Gottscho. Gift of Gottscho-Schleisner. 50.137.8

284. The symbol of the New York World's Fair of 1964 was the Unisphere, shown surrounded by its fountains. The field in the background is Shea Stadium, built in 1964. The long, low building between the stadium and the Unisphere is the United States Pavilion. Photograph by Joseph Veach Noble. Archive

285. The Stettheimer Doll House was created by Carrie Stettheimer, one of three talented New York sisters noted for their roles in the artistic activity of the 1920s. Florine painted; Ettie wrote novels under the name "Henri Waste"; and Carrie decorated one of the most remarkable doll houses of the century. A carpenter built the outside frame of the house, but Miss Stettheimer did the rest. The interior decoration is a virtual design index of the period, down to the wallpapers, linens, and kitchen utensils. The art gallery, not visible, contains works of artist friends of the Stettheimers. The nursery contains, like many famous doll houses, its own doll house. 29 × 56". Gift of Miss Ettie Stettheimer. 45.125.1

XI: CAPITAL OF THE WORLD

Too new for an empire, too big for its boots,
With cold steel cables where it might have roots,
With everything to offer and nothing to give,
It's a horrid place to visit but a fine place to live.

—PHYLLIS MC GINLEY

A Kind of Love Letter to New York

When the United Nations chose New York City in 1946 as its home and therefore the official capital of the world, it was international recognition by the highest authority of a status already well known. The United States had emerged from World War II as the greatest power in the world, and New York was its greatest city: it was logical that the capital city of the new world organization should be New York. New York had always been the most striving of cities; now the new hopes of mankind for peace and reconciliation were centered on her Island.

The United Nations met first at various places in and around the City: Hunter College, the New York City building at Flushing Meadow Park, site of the World's Fair of 1939–40, and in an unused plant of the Sperry Gyroscope Company at a locality now renamed "Lake Success." These sites were all temporary; the organization was without a permanent home until 1947. Many were the headquarters locations proposed and rejected, until the Rockefeller family, anxious to have the United Nations in the City, solved the problem by a gift of real estate.

Along the East River from 42nd to 48th streets was a site already assembled by the developer William Zeckendorf. This was the old Turtle Bay Farm which had a history of settlement stretching back to the time of the Dutch West India Company. There had been some building in the area before the United Nations, notably the comfortable and successful Tudor City complex (apartments and hotel rooms built on 40th to 43rd streets, Second to First avenues, between 1925 and 1928), but it was not until the six blocks of slaughterhouses along the river were demolished that the area was ready for construction. John D. Rockefeller, Jr., bought the site for $8,500,000 and donated it to the U.N., which began to build there in 1948. The land and buildings are, of course, the property of the U.N., and this is the most international area in the world—with its own post office, police protection, and facilities of every kind for conducting the business of world government.

The United Nations Building was only one relatively small phase of the wave of construction which took place in New York in the immediate postwar years. Midtown and downtown Manhattan were soon covered with new office buildings; each seemed to be larger and more glamorous than its immediate predecessor. A landmark worthy of note was Lever House at 390 Park Avenue between 53rd and 54th streets, which opened in 1952. This office building in a neighborhood hitherto residential used only part of its building lot: the remainder became a plaza with landscaping. This was the immediate ancestor of numerous office structures along Park Avenue between Grand Central Terminal and 59th Street, then downtown and along Second, Third, and Sixth avenues, which have allotted vast open spaces for plazas and concourses at their bases.

286. During 1933–34, after completion of the RCA Building at Rockefeller Center, Samuel H. Gottscho did a series of night photographs from the top of the building which are among the finest ever done of the lights of the City. This view is looking south (or "downtown") and east and includes both the Chrysler (at left) and Empire State (at right) buildings. 19 1/2 × 14 1/2". Gift of Samuel H. Gottscho. 20945

288. The twin towers of the World Trade Center on the Lower West Side are the major change in decades to the skyline of Manhattan. Within a few years of their completion the makings of folklore were already gathering about the towers. The climactic scenes of the remake of the motion picture *King Kong* were acted there before thousands of extras and office workers. A tightrope walker successfully negotiated a wire strung between the buildings. A young mountaineer ascended one with specially designed hooks. Beneath the towers lie the remains of the ship *Tiger*. Gift of The Port of New York Authority.

287. The headquarters of the United Nations were built in Turtle Bay along the East River between 42nd and 48th streets in the years 1947–53 (with later additions). A team of architects (including Le Corbusier) from thirteen countries was responsible for the design. This photograph by Gottscho-Schleisner was taken from the East River. Original print, 14 1/4 × 19 1/4″. Gift of Gottscho-Schleisner.

They have been widely praised by critics; unimpressed New Yorkers can calculate the number of days when the City's climate permits strolling in plazas. Perhaps next to Lever House the most celebrated of the new structures has been the Seagram Building one block down Park Avenue from Lever House, designed by Mies van der Rohe and Philip Johnson and completed in 1958.

The pattern established by Parkchester in housing was followed in the more densely populated parts of the City, the earliest and largest of these multiple unit "villages" being Stuyvesant Town, which was built—on the old Director-General's farm—by the Metropolitan Life Insurance Company in 1947. The plot was bounded by First Avenue, East River Drive, and 14th and 20th streets. This was middle-income housing to be populated in its early years by returning veterans of World War II and their young families—nearly 9,000 of them. Stuyvesant Town was followed immediately uptown by Peter Cooper Village, named for the philanthropist ironmonger of the nineteenth century, and similar complexes were soon being put up all over the City. Tax abatement was offered by the City as an inducement to companies to construct such "villages," and although much desperately needed housing resulted there were plentiful scandals connected with the granting of tax abatement, notably to the "Manhattantown Urban Renewal Project" on the Upper West Side, later "Park West Village."

Many important new public facilities were completed: in 1950, for example, the immense bus terminal built between Eighth and Ninth avenues, 40th to 41st streets (with an entrance to the Lincoln Tunnel) by the Port Authority of New York. The colossal Idlewild Airport (later John F. Kennedy International Airport), originally opened in 1942, was greatly enlarged in 1948 and expanded again and again during the two decades that followed until it covered nearly 5,000 acres.

In 1959, the first ground was broken for the Lincoln Center for the Performing Arts at Lincoln Square between West 62nd and West 66th streets, Columbus to Amsterdam avenues. Various sections of this enormous complex have been opened including Philharmonic (now Avery Fisher) Hall in 1962, the Vivian Beaumont Theater in 1965, the Metropolitan Opera House in 1966, the Juilliard School of Music in 1968, and Alice Tully Hall in 1969.

The population of the City in 1950 was at an all-time high: 7,891,957. Every borough had gained population, and the results were:

Brooklyn	2,738,175
Manhattan	1,960,101
Queens	1,550,849
Bronx	1,451,277
Richmond	191,555

No mayor had ever come into office with brighter hopes than William O'Dwyer. An Irish immigrant, he worked as a policeman, studied law at Fordham, and became active in Democratic politics. A revived Tammany Hall—which had gone through some hard times in the La Guardia era and had actually sold the Hall in 1943—supported him. He was made first a judge, then district attorney of Brooklyn. As a district attorney he was supposedly a "gangbuster," but later in his career unappetizing links with the Mafia and other forces of organized crime were revealed. His first term as mayor was marked by all sorts of strikes, a terrible housing shortage, and many other postwar facts of life over which, the voters believed, he had no control. He was therefore reelected in 1949, again defeating Newbold Morris. A police department scandal known as the "Harry Gross Affair" came to light in 1949. Gross was a bookmaker, a briber of policemen, and a heavy contributor to O'Dwyer's political campaigns. The investigation into the corruption of police and public officials by various criminals, especially gamblers, led closer and closer to City Hall, so close that in 1950 President Truman, a fellow Democrat, appointed O'Dwyer American ambassador to Mexico. When still more scandal came to light, civic groups asked that O'Dwyer be brought back from Mexico to testify. The ambassador at first refused to come back to New York, but in 1951 he testified before the congressional committee on organized crime chaired by Democratic Senator Estes Kefauver of Tennessee. Many lurid facts were brought out about the connection of crime figures with Tammany Hall. O'Dwyer melted under the Kefauver Committee examination the way Jimmy Walker had melted under the Seabury questioning. He later appeared before a grand jury. Although he was never charged with any crime, the reports of the Kefauver Committee and the grand jury were so critical of his behavior that they put an effective end to the political career of New York's one-hundredth mayor.

O'Dwyer was succeeded by New York's first Italian-born mayor, the Sicilian Vincent R. Impellitteri, who served from 1950 to 1953.

The 102nd mayor of New York City was Robert F. Wagner, in office from 1954 to 1965. Wagner, born in Yorkville and educated at Yale, was mild-mannered and conciliatory. He had important political advantages in beginning his administration, one as the son of Senator Robert Wagner, regarded almost as a saint by the members of the labor movement in New York, another as the nominee of the regular party organization and recipient of its still powerful support. He was mayor during a period of difficult, sharply accelerating, and sometimes virtually insoluble problems.

In the late 1950s, every large city in the United States had begun to decline in finances, in the amenities of life, and in prestige, and the decline has continued throughout the following decades. New York, largest and most important city, was of course first and worst. Although immigration from other parts of the world had virtually ceased, the tempo of migration from Puerto Rico and of blacks from the South increased until it became one of the greatest migrations of all time. The Puerto Ricans began to arrive in New York in substantial numbers in the late forties: by the mid-fifties whole areas in New York were Spanish-speaking, especially East Harlem and the Lower East Side in Manhattan, Sunset Park and Williamsburg in Brooklyn, and the South Bronx. The blacks were later in coming but their numbers were much greater; more than a million entered the City during the fifties

and sixties. Crime, violence, and vandalism rose and became commonplace. The City, always noted for its tolerance and the capital city of American liberalism, experienced racial disturbances and serious riots. "Mugging," i.e., street robbery, became identified with New York City all over the world, and the City's notoriety as a difficult place to live in safety constantly increased.

New Yorkers reacted to this influx of new immigrants and to the astounding rise in City crime in a somewhat different manner from their grandfathers. They panicked. In earlier immigrations no considerable number of people had left the City—no matter how much they might have complained. Now the emigration of people from the City became a flood. During the period 1950 to 1970 more than a million white families, overwhelmingly middle-class, left the fear-ridden City. They took with them their taxes, their skills, their support of the arts and cultural institutions, their interest in education and in civic affairs, their desire for peace and law and order, and their cosmopolitan attitudes which had made the middle class of New York unique in America. Their loss was irreparable. Businesses, appalled by the high taxes made necessary by welfare and other demands of the new immigrants, the crime rate, and the lack of reliable personnel, left in huge numbers: many of the greatest corporations of America, founded in New York and the support of its entire mercantile structure, departed for the suburbs of New York or even for other regions. The number of important companies headquartered in New York dropped at an alarming rate especially in the late sixties and early seventies. New York, which had always attracted the young and adventurous from all over America, rapidly declined in public opinion; bad publicity and sheer fear slowed down the traditional entry of the young. Institutions of higher learning were particularly hard hit by the reluctance of students to brave the City.

Nothing was done to halt the exodus of people and businesses. Some things never change in New York history, and one is the affection of politicians for newcomers. Their voices were heard first at City Hall.

289. On 20 December 1938, when Mayor La Guardia, armed with goggles and acetylene torch, attacked a steel girder of the Sixth Avenue "El" at 53rd Street, it was the beginning of the end for New York's most famous transit system. Charles T. Harvey built the first elevated railroad in 1867, and the dream of adequate mass transportation seemed a reality. Over the years, however, it became evident that the elevated lines brought a fearful blight to their avenues. Thus there was much joyous celebration when the demolition of the Sixth Avenue line began. The painting by Maurice Kish depicts the dismantling at Sixth Avenue and 27th Street. Oil on canvas, 25 1/2 × 21″. Gift of Maurice Kish. 73.35

292. With a stability rare in American history, the center of ▶ gravity of New York has never shifted. Heading into its fourth century, the heart of New York still lies where Europeans first set foot. Aerial view of Brooklyn piers and Manhattan by A. Belva, 27 December 1971. archives

290. In addition to legitimate theaters, Times Square has contained numerous movie houses and other amusements. *Shootin' Gallery* on 42nd Street between Broadway and Eighth Avenue was painted in 1945 by James Wilfrid Kerr. Oil on canvas, 27 × 22″. Gift of the artist. 71.78

291. Harlem's most prominent political figure from the forties to the sixties was Adam Clayton Powell, Jr. He was minister of the Abyssinian Baptist Church, which at one time had a congregation numbering over 10,000, and first became a Congressman in 1944. In the 1950s he was indicted for income-tax evasion and censured by Congress, but he was reelected and served eight terms in the House. He died in 1972. Here he is shown as the central figure in a painting by Joseph Delaney entitled *Harlem Parade*. Oil on canvas, 50 × 40″. Gift of Mr. and Mrs. Robert Wallace Gilmore. 73.153.5

At a time of unprecedented general prosperity the welfare rolls grew until more than fifteen percent of the population was being supported by the City's taxpayers; a bureaucracy of unparalleled size and ineptitude ballooned alongside. For the first time in its modern history the City, always associated with the rich and successful, became the home of the poor. Its median income was half that of most of its suburbs. The

City suddenly could no longer maintain itself, and the incomparable physical plant of New York, the work of generations, began to decay. Neglect and ceaseless vandalism rendered many of the City's parks, subway stations, and streets dangerous and unsightly.

During the Wagner administration considerable attempts were made to balkanize the most cosmopolitan city in the world, to split it up into "neighborhoods" and to miniaturize the functions of government. Civil Service, the merit system for which so many Americans of distinction had fought and the road of advancement for lower- and middle-class Americans (especially of the first generation), came under attack. In 1964, riots in Harlem and the Bedford-Stuyvesant section of Brooklyn (which had become largely black) brought many arrests and some deaths. The constant troubles in New York, shown all over the world (since New York was the capital of television, radio, magazines, and newspapers), led to a further decline in the City's prestige. The worst disorders of the civil rights agitation of the sixties in New York occurred during Wagner's term. Among them was the serious attempt to paralyze opening the World's Fair of 1964–65, which kept visitors away for fear of violence by the demonstrators.

The 1964–65 fair cost more than $1,000,000,000 and was very different from its predecessor of 1939–40. This fair, also planned by Robert Moses, was more amusement park than showcase. The first fair, held before television, had served to display new products to the public; by the time of the second fair it was no longer necessary to unveil goods that way. The fair was enjoyable to more than 51,000,000 visitors, but it was plagued with financial difficulties and controversy and never made the impression on the public that the fair of 1939–40 had.

The troubles of the Wagner administration carried over into that of John V. Lindsay which followed. New York–born and Yale-educated like Wagner, Lindsay ran for the mayoral office in 1965 on a Republican–Liberal–Independent Citizen ticket; during his second campaign in 1969, he won on the Liberal ticket. On both occasions his victory was a narrow one.

Urban trials were not of course unique to New York, and in fact they were even more pronounced and critical in many other American cities, but there was more at stake in New York since no other city in the United States came close to its importance in finance, communication, theater, and a hundred other fields. Even after the whole catalog of the City's ills was compiled and rightly lamented, it remained the capital

of the world. Dirges were chanted for the Broadway stage, yet one musical of the sixties—*Fiddler on the Roof*—played more than 3,000 performances, and the attention of theater lovers everywhere remained focused on the latest Broadway attraction, be it *Hair, No, No, Nanette,* or *A Chorus Line.* As long ago as 1926, Floyd Dell, who had been at the center of intellectual ferment in New York during the first quarter of the century, wrote *The Rise and Fall of Greenwich Village* in which he proclaimed the death of the Village as the center of creativity. Yet during the fifties and sixties there developed the whole coffee-house culture, underground movies, "Off-Broadway" (and later "Off-Off-Broadway"), new artists' colonies in the area renamed SoHo, "happenings," and a constant stir in the arts. Long ago opera in New York was considered to be dragging out a society existence; now *two* opera houses give performances a few yards from each other across the Plaza at Lincoln Center. And so in many fields New York remains dominant.

In the decade 1960–70, so difficult for American cities, half of the largest cities in the U.S. lost population, but New York continued to gain: from 7,781,984 in 1960 to 7,867,760 in 1970. It was the *only* large city in the Northeast to gain population.

And still the skyscrapers rise. Many monuments of the City have been pulled down in the great building boom of the postwar years, structures hardly ancient but of respectable age and great dignity like Pennsylvania Station. Preservationists cry out at their destruction, but there is little indication that the average New Yorker is very interested in seeing them preserved. New Yorkers are not sentimental about elderly buildings. The cities of Europe need cathedrals and catacombs; New York doesn't. One hundred and fifty years ago Philip Hone wrote that his beloved City renewed itself every ten years, and so it renews itself today. Tearing down and putting up *is* New York.

In 1960, the Chase Manhattan Bank built a great skyscraper as its headquarters on a newly created plaza bounded by Nassau, William, Liberty, and Pine streets in the most historic part of New York. Innovations of many kinds were incorporated in the structure, including a sunken courtyard, sculpture by Isamu Noguchi, and an amazing array of contemporary art. The 800-foot structure was the signal that great institutions and great financial interests, notably those of the Rockefeller family, were sustaining their faith in the financial district and in the City. Feverish construction began in the area. The center of interest in New York remained in its oldest section: on the very streets where Peter Stuyvesant stumped, where Rip van Dam drove his new carriage, where General Washington and his lady took their evening strolls, where Chancellor Livingston tended his garden, and where Alexander Hamilton went to his law office—new buildings rose on every side. The ancient churchyards of Trinity Church and St. Paul's Chapel were more than ever surrounded by the monoliths of business.

Abraham D. Beame, a Democrat, succeeded John V. Lindsay as mayor in 1974. His one-term administration was marked by the mounting financial problems of the city and its narrowly avoided bankruptcy in 1975. Not for the first time in its history, the City had spent more money than it received from taxes, but this time the loss, besides being colossal in size—in the billions of dollars—was much more difficult to replace due to the erosion of the tax base of the City. At the same time, spending for social services and union demands increased by leaps and bounds, making it impossible for the tax base to support the City government's expenditure. Resort was made to the selling of municipal securities on an unparalleled scale, burdening the City's taxpayers with a debt of more than $13,000,000,000. Finally by late 1974, an overloaded market refused to absorb any more of the City's bond issues. A financial crisis developed which brought New York City's problems to the attention of the world but little help. Although bankruptcy was avoided by various devices, including some federal loans in the summer of 1975, a Municipal Assistance Corporation, immediately nicknamed "Big Mac" after a popular hamburger, was formed to borrow what the City, which had its own nickname, "the Big Apple" (a name with a hazy history), could no longer obtain. For months on end the City government existed on a hand-to-mouth basis. Shortage of money persisted as the City's major governmental problem into the administration of Edward I. Koch, who succeeded Abraham Beame as New York's 105th mayor in 1978.

Some comfort for the financial future of the City was to be had from the continuing flow of foreign companies, especially banks, into the City. In trade and commerce, the second half of the twentieth century will be, as nearly as we can now see, the Age of the Multinational Company. Many of these companies are already quartered in New York City, and the visible symbol of the age is the World Trade Center. Ground was broken for the twin towers of the Center in 1966: construction was completed in 1973. The buildings are 1,350 feet high, and they contain 327 *acres* of offices.

For the New Yorker the skyscrapers are his Pyramids, his St. Peter's, his St. Paul's, his Eiffel Tower. Not that he often thinks of those places. "Outside of New York," a saying goes, "it's all Philadelphia." No one (not even a New Yorker), however, can fail to be impressed by the sight from the Staten Island ferry as it departs Manhattan: the greatest landscape ever.

Three hundred and fifty years ago, Dominie Michaëlius wrote from Manhattan: "this island is the key and principal stronghold of the country." His words are as true today as then. Although the directors of the Dutch West India Company to whom he wrote failed in their attempt to get rich in the New World, no one has ever doubted that they chose the right island.

INDEX